Profit at the
Bottom of
the Ladder

Profit at the Bottom of the Ladder

Creating Value by Investing

in Your Workforce

Jody Heymann

with Magda Barrera

HARVARD BUSINESS PRESS
Boston, Massachusetts

Libray of Congress Cataloging-in-Publication Data

Heymann, Jody, 1959–
    Profit at the bottom of the ladder : creating value by investing in your workforce / Jody Heymann, with Magda Barerra.
       p. cm.
    ISBN 978-1-4221-2311-9 (hbk. : alk. paper)
    1. Personnel management—United States.   2. Employees—United States.
3. Minimum wage—United States.   4. Quality of work life—United States.
5. Industrial management—Social aspects—United States.   I. Barerra, Magda.
II. Title.
    HF5549.2.U5H49 2010
    658.3—dc22

                                                                        2009037771

The paper used in this publication meets the requirements of the American National Standard for Permanence of Paper for Publications and Documents in Libraries and Archives Z39.48-1992.

To people on every rung of the ladder
who still believe the private sector
can help us profit together

Contents

Acknowledgments

No global study can be successfully conducted without an enormous collective effort. *Profit at the Bottom of the Ladder* is no exception. The book is the result of the combined commitment of exceptional companies, a remarkable team of researchers, the belief and substantial support of foundations, and the generous insights of colleagues and students, family and friends.

Each of the companies profiled in *Profit at the Bottom of the Ladder* took an important leap of faith. They allowed my research team to come to factories and warehouses, to conduct interviews without restrictions, and to meet with everyone from line workers to chief executives. They were generous with their time, open and candid about their experiences, and willing for us to hear the perspective of the full range of players in their organization.

This project was made possible by the vision of Helen Neuborne and Wendy Chun-Hoon and the generous support of the Ford Foundation and Annie E. Casey Foundation. Strongly committed to finding ways to improve the conditions faced by low-skilled and low-wage workers, the two foundations wanted to learn what the private sector as well as the public sector could do. As the project became global in scope and deepened in nature, they brought an extraordinary combination of patient understanding of how long a project of this magnitude can take with the sense of urgency that the topic deserves. When we added Canadian companies to the study, support from Allan Northcott, Ralph Strother, and the Max Bell Foundation was indispensable.

Each company we selected went through several phases of research. First, research staff members carried out a field visit, conducting on-site interviews of entry-level employees—from factory operator to warehouse stocker, from baker to concrete mixer—and of middle management and top executives, including CEOs and CFOs for most companies. Second, I conducted field visits to all the companies, which included observation of worksites and follow-up interviews with people at all levels of the company. Third, interview data was rigorously analyzed. Fourth, financial information, annual reports, and other public information about the companies were examined.

I was fortunate to have support from an exceptional team in carrying out the interviews. For just over half of the companies, Stephanie Simmons conducted the first-round interviews and the initial analysis of interview data. A gifted research assistant, Stephanie was extraordinarily skilled at finding companies around the world that have led the way in showing how investing in employees can lead to better profits for employees and companies alike. Her efforts were an invaluable asset in setting in place the case studies and left an indelible mark on this project. Stephanie conducted interviews in the United States, Norway, Ireland, and Australia. The research in South Africa and China could not have been carried out without the outstanding contributions of Eliza Petrow. Her experience working with health issues contributed substantially to our understanding of the South Africa case where the company was grappling with AIDS, and her knowledge of China likewise enriched the Chinese case study. Baijayanta Mukhopadhyay's similarly deep understanding of the Indian context as well as his profound research skills greatly enriched our study in India. Carmen Mandic-Gomez brought a wealth of knowledge of disability issues that contributed to her exceptional work in Peru on the interaction with the bank around disability issues. As part of our Institute's policy fellowships, Adrienne Gibson ensured that this series would include a strong Canadian company as well as companies from every other region in the world.

A team of business students from McGill made important contributions. They researched company earnings, examined companies' social as well as financial profiles, and conducted in-depth background research on health care for low-income workers, training and advancement opportunities for workers with limited formal education, values management across the supply chain, involvement of entry-level workers in decision making, financial incentives for workers at every rung of the ladder, and incentives for companies to embrace corporate social responsibility. The work of these business students—Mauricio Guerrero Cabarcas, Melissa Hui, Jackie Lemaitre, George Milonakis, Sabina Saeed, Sungchul Shin, Carlos Beltran Velazquez, and Grayden Wagner—together with law and political science students Alexandra Lesnikowski and Susanne Greisbach, was indispensable.

In the middle of this massive research endeavor, I was recruited to McGill to found a new university-wide Institute for Health and Social Policy that would span all faculties from Medicine to Management, from Arts and Sciences to Law, from Education to Dentistry. We initiated training programs that in the first three years have taken students to 18 countries and a policy initiative that has examined social and economic policies in 192 countries. Launching this Institute together with colleagues at McGill and around the world has been an immense joy. Inevitably, it also took away from the time I had for writing. Four years into this initiative, it became clear that the amount of time I had for completing the book was far more limited than I had hoped. Magdalena Barrera, an immensely thoughtful and insightful researcher who had been working with me since the Institute's inception, joined the project at the writing phase to work together with me. Throughout the writing, we worked as a true team. For the chapters that had not been written, we outlined, revised, and wrote together. While Magda had not been with the project since its inception or carried out the interviews with me at the companies, she dove deeply into all of the company material, the transcribed interviews of hundreds of employees and managers, and the in-depth data we had on every company. Experienced with the issues at the core of the book but fresh to the companies, she brought new and important questions to the endeavor. The book would not have come out in anywhere near as timely a way nor as well without her.

Getting the ideas on paper is essential but not enough. We were fortunate to have a gifted language editor, Melanie Benard, edit the entire book. Where the prose is clear and the book is readily readable, it owes a great debt to Melanie and to Kristen McNeill, who edited several final chapters. *Profit at the Bottom of the Ladder*, like other books in this vein, seeks to both be accessible to a broad audience and display the rigor academics demand. The research and staff assistance required for double-checking facts, figures, and references is immense. In these endeavors, I am particularly indebted to Parama Sigurdsen and Kristen, who went through the entire book with great care and commitment to ensuring the accuracy of the details.

We are deeply grateful to Kirsten Sandberg, who ushered this project into Harvard Business Press and shepherded its growth, and to Jacque Murphy, who brought it to fruition with such great skill. Ania Wieckowski followed up with care on countless editorial aspects, and Jen Waring, with extraordinary ability and responsiveness, managed the book through production.

This book, like all global work, required a great deal of travel. It also required late nights, early mornings, and long weekends researching, analyzing, and writing. My family's belief in and support for the project made it a joy. Their own questions prompted me to ask new questions in turn. As my older son began to study international organizations and financial institutions, he made me ask why they are not set up in ways to make it easier for companies to "do the right thing." As my younger son thought about studying business himself someday, he queried, "Why don't all companies improve their working conditions? Don't they realize they can make more money that way?"

Profit at the Bottom of the Ladder is dedicated to all students—those in school and those who continue to learn all their lives—who are still asking how we can make businesses work better for those at the bottom of the ladder as well as the top.

JH

Introduction

*Raising Productivity and Profitability by Creating
Better Working Conditions for the Worst Off*

Profit at the bottom of the ladder answers three fundamental questions. First and foremost, the book answers the question C-level executives and other senior managers are asking themselves: Are there additional ways to increase my company's success? The case studies answer young business leaders who are wondering: Can I spend a career profiting in the private sector while bringing benefits to others? At the same time, this research answers the questions raised by labor representatives and all levels of employees: Isn't there a way for the company and its employees to succeed together?

The answers to these three questions are central to the lives of everyone from senior managers in the largest companies to entry-level employees in the smallest firms. CEOs, CFOs, COOs, and other leaders have always had to worry about profitability. The shareholders and board members to whom they report measure success in this nearly singular way. Wall Street has frequently evaluated firms' prospects as rising when leaders cut jobs, wages, and benefits. At the same time, top managers' personal satisfaction has long stemmed from being able to achieve more than profit at the cost of their employees. Moreover, while employees have always cared about their company's competitiveness because it assures the long-term stability of their jobs, they clearly also care about the quality of their working conditions, compensation, and daily lives.

1

While the answers are of fundamental importance in strong economic times, the financial crisis that began in 2008 has crystallized the urgency of being able to answer them. As the meltdown over executive bonuses made clear, corporations faced both an economic crisis and a crisis of confidence. The questions raised by the economic crisis are clear: When will firms be profitable? When will we have economic security? Will the United States, Europe, and other advanced economies fully repair themselves? Will China, India, and other emerging economies rebound or leap ahead? All of these concerns surround economic success. But as demonstrated by the political outcry, demonstrations, and rapidly written legislation, the crisis in confidence has been equally critical and has presented a different set of questions: How "greedy" is Wall Street? Are leaders of the private sector just out to ensure their own personal financial success, and are they willing to risk the financial security of everyone else in the world? Is there any reason to believe that average taxpayers stand to gain by bailing out companies or by ensuring corporate success? All of these questions come down to the fundamental one: Will there be a link between the success experienced by those at the top of the corporate ladder and those on all of the other rungs?

Profit at the Bottom of the Ladder tells the story of companies around the world who have found ways to answer both sets of questions simultaneously. These companies have been profitable for their owners and shareholders not only *while* being profitable for their employees, but *because* they have been profitable for their employees.

Working Conditions That Matter

These firms have been able to do this for a simple reason. How work is structured, how it is rewarded, and how workplaces encourage employee engagement are all central to the profitability of firms and to the quality of the daily lives of working men and women. Employees determine 90 percent of most businesses' profitability.

Often underrecognized is the fact that the most potent impact can come from employees at the bottom of the corporate ladder. In call centers, it is the employees answering the phones who determine the quality, pace, and effectiveness of the company's responses to customers. In maintenance and repair industries, it is the men and women who take the calls and carry out the services who again determine customers' satisfaction, patronage, and loyalty and whether they recommend the company to others. In manufacturing, workers on the factory line leave their fingerprints on the quality of the products and determine the error rate in production. Even in wholesale and retail, success fundamentally relies on the quality of the work carried out in the warehouses and of the interactions between employees and customers.

The caliber of the employees that a company can attract and retain and the quality of their performance are affected by the company's working conditions, including wages, benefits, work schedules, flexibility and leave, support for health, and policies surrounding participation in planning and work design. These policies simultaneously have implications for the company's bottom line in terms of costs and benefits. In evaluating publicly traded companies, Wall Street analysts for years have treated providing decent working conditions as purely a cost, not an investment. CEOs have been pressured to cut compensation, giving little consideration to the long-term consequences of doing so.

Not only is job quality essential to a firm's success, it also plays a fundamental role in determining the quality of the lives of working men and women. Working conditions influence everything from the most pragmatic issues—determining whether a worker loses his job when he has to take time off after a heart attack, if a father loses pay when he stays home to care for a sick child, whether a daughter loses wages when she misses work to care for an aging parent—to the harder to measure, but equally fundamental concerns, such as determining whether employees find their work meaningful and are eager to do their best at their jobs.

While the questions of how much to invest in employees and what kind of investment to make are always essential to companies, they are particularly important now. With intense global competition and declines in consumer spending, firms are particularly concerned about finding ways to cut expenses without losing business. It is natural for companies to wonder whether they can cut costs by lowering wages, decreasing health and other benefits, and limiting support for pensions. As firms restructure in response to economic threats, it is not surprising that employee engagement is sometimes the last thing on their minds. Yet the role of employees is more important than ever in ensuring companies' survival. Companies are dependent on employees to be particularly flexible as firms restructure, to cover for laid-off employees, and to find new ways to cut costs and increase productivity. At the same time, the bursting housing bubble and the dramatic drops in the stock market have made it all the more important to employees to have a secure job with a living wage and adequate benefits. Moreover, even in strong economic periods, people neeed good working conditions and protections such as those that prevent income loss due to illness or the birth of a child.

This book addresses the fundamental question: Is it truly financially beneficial for companies to cut wages and benefits and limit flexibility, or is there a path forward from which companies can profit financially alongside their employees?

Our Research Program

For over a decade and a half, I have led a research program, first at Harvard University and then also at McGill University, examining working conditions around the world. For the first eight years of this program, my team's research focused on understanding how the conditions faced by men and women varied across political, social, and economic contexts. While analyzing the differences across countries, we also examined the differences within countries across classes and sociodemographic groups. In the United States, we studied the experiences of over ten thousand working Americans, including men and women in every state, across all income levels, and in every sector of the economy. These studies included looking at the impact of working conditions on the employees, their families, and their communities. We carried out large national studies; studies that focused on the lowest-wage workers; studies that compared the experiences of workers with limited formal education to those of professionals; studies that included in-depth interviews of multiple family members; and studies in which individuals were contacted daily to inquire about the relationships among the conditions they faced, the work they performed, their daily lives, and their personal health and welfare as well as that of their families.

We then carried out similar studies around the world: we interviewed working adults in the largest city and in a small rural town in Mexico; examined the experiences of immigrant families split across the Mexican-U.S. border; researched working conditions in Botswana, a particularly strong democracy and economy in Africa that has been hit hard by the AIDS pandemic; spoke with workers in Russia about the conditions they faced as the country moved from a centralized to a market economy; carried out research in Vietnam as the Vietnamese economy opened up under

Doi Moi to the international market, and in both Vietnam and Cambodia as these countries walked the long road of economic recovery after the devastation of wars. We learned how working conditions influenced the experiences of Honduran individuals and communities that had survived a major natural disaster, Hurricane Mitch, which destroyed many neighborhoods in the capital, Tegucigalpa. In the end, our studies of working conditions included analyses of surveys of over fifty-five thousand households, and over 2,000 in-depth interviews of employees from entry level to top C-level executives living on all six inhabited continents.

These studies brought to light the many dimensions of disadvantage at work around the world. Those with the least amount of formal education not only received the lowest wages, but their jobs also offered the least flexibility. These workers were the most likely to be fired if they were sick, to lose their meager yet crucial income surrounding the birth or adoption of a child, and to face untenable choices between caring for a sick family member and earning enough money to survive. They were also the least likely to have any autonomy at work, to participate in planning or design, or to have their voices heard within the company. These initial studies delineated the conditions workers faced around the world. Our findings on the impact of poor conditions at work and limited social supports for men and women at the bottom of the ladder have been reported in detail in *Forgotten Families: Ending the Growing Crisis Confronting Children and Working Parents in the Global Economy* as well as a series of articles and reports.[1]

Since 2001, we have increasingly focused on finding and understanding solutions for reducing these disparities, and for five years we have been studying initiatives in the private sector. The findings from the studies of companies in nine countries are detailed in this volume. Findings from our research on public sector solutions and economic competitiveness in 192 nations are reported in *Raising the Global Floor: Dismantling the Myth That We Can't Afford Good Working Conditions for Everyone* as well as in a series of reports and articles.[2]

Research on Business Strategy

While drawing on findings from many studies I have led over the past decade, *Profit at the Bottom of the Ladder* focuses on findings from over five hundred interviews carried out at a dozen companies around the world between 2005 and 2009. In carrying out the research that forms the foundation for this book, we sought out companies that were both finding solutions to the problems working adults faced and succeeding by the financial standards by which all firms are measured. We used a wide range of tools to identify these companies: we solicited the recommendations of company CEOs and other leaders in the business community as well as civic leaders who focused on labor issues and we analyzed a series of published lists of the "Best Companies to Work For" to see how many of them managed to have good working conditions for *all* of their employees, as opposed to only for the professionals or highest-paid employees. We then analyzed the companies that were generated by expert recommendations, awards, and systematic reviews to see if their good working conditions permeated all levels of employees, and we assessed their financial profitability.

Many companies were eliminated from our original list. The majority of the firms that were lauded as being among the "Best Companies to Work For" focused their efforts only on the employees at the high end of their corporate ladder; their policies were either unaffordable or unavailable to their line workers. Among the companies recommended by experts as being particularly innovative, some fell off our list because they were new and had yet to turn a profit, although they showed great promise. After winnowing down a list of hundreds of potential companies, we selected a final group that represented diversity in geography, size, and sector, and that included both publicly traded and privately owned companies. Geographic diversity was one of our main concerns, given that we wanted to assess whether the financial advantages of offering good working conditions and benefits translated throughout a globalized economy, in which companies had to compete with firms around the world. We therefore wished to study companies in diverse geographic locations that managed to ensure good jobs for all their employees. We also wanted to include businesses of every size, since companies of different sizes face very different challenges and constraints in seeking to establish good working conditions. The companies we selected represent small, medium, and large firms employing between 27 and 126,000 men and women. While compiling the list of companies, it became clear that most of the firms featured were privately held. Many publicly held companies do have good working conditions, but they often employ mostly high-wage workers or offer different levels of working conditions and benefits to management employees than to workers at the bottom of the ladder. To ensure that the study included both publicly traded and privately held companies, we made extra efforts to locate publicly held companies that fulfilled our criteria. Finally, we wanted the companies we studied to represent different sectors. We felt that both retail and manufacturing sectors had to be included since they account for so many of the jobs available to workers with lower levels of formal education.

When we approached companies to study them, we asked a lot of each company. We told them that we would need to interview employees at all levels, from the lowest-paid workers to those in top management positions—in most cases the CEOs, CFOs, and COOs. We would need to speak candidly with employees about their experiences. To ensure that workers at the bottom of the pyramid felt comfortable in accurately describing their experiences, we guaranteed confidentiality. The names of these working men and women are not used in the book; only pseudonyms are given. Each of these employees was interviewed in private about his or her experiences, without managers present. In the majority of cases interviews were conducted in the primary language spoken by the employee. When a translator was needed, a translator independent of the firm was employed. Middle managers were similarly guaranteed confidentiality. CEOs, CFOs, and other top managers were advised that their names would be used; because they were clearly identifiable by their position, confidentiality was not possible. Working conditions were observed at each firm.

Managers knew that we would use this information to publish a study and that we would have the final say on the description of their company, since this was the only way that readers could be guaranteed an independent opinion and that we could ensure academic integrity. In spite of these necessary standards, and undoubtedly in large part due to the fact that the companies had faith that their actions would withstand scrutiny, all of the firms we approached agreed to participate, with rare exception. One company had initially agreed to take part, but was then bought out by another company whose reputation for working conditions was far more mixed; the new parent company was worried about participating in a study that might look closely at employees' experiences.

Our site visits and interviews were designed to determine whether these companies' working conditions were as good in practice as they were on paper, as well as what, if any, relationship these conditions bore to the firms' productivity, financial costs, and returns. We carried out at least two site visits at every company we studied. A member of the research team conducted a complete set of initial interviews, visited the work site, and analyzed the data. I then made a follow-up visit to every company, again interviewing everyone from line workers to top management, and assessing sources of potential successes as well as challenges the companies faced and limitations on their accomplishments. In addition to the data gathered through interviews and site visits, we compiled information on companies through publicly available data, financial reports from publicly traded companies, and academic, professional, and media reports on the companies' financial and social performance. We analyzed this information along with transcriptions of every interview conducted and written information provided by the companies. Of the companies that were selected for site visits, all but one demonstrated that they were able to have innovative and strong working conditions at the bottom of the ladder while succeeding economically.

Each of the companies profiled in this book has demonstrated a remarkable accomplishment in at least one of the areas we focus on in each chapter. While a number of companies could have been highlighted in several chapters, we tried to vary the companies selected to enable readers to learn about practices in a range of business sectors and geographic locations. Some of the companies are far stronger in their practices in one area than another; this is natural, and perhaps no less surprising than the fact that top athletes are typically far stronger in one sport than another. The companies are highlighted for their accomplishments in the appropriate chapters, and honest assessments of the limitations of these accomplishments are also included. We don't rate each of the companies across all areas treated in the book and do not mean to suggest that any individual firm is perfect, but rather we examine the impact that good working conditions have had on each company's success and on workers' quality of life.

To these studies we brought the skills of a research team, objective eyes to examine what was working at the company and what wasn't, the time to conduct detailed interviews with a wide range of players, the ability to be seen as independent by CEOs as well as workers, and a commitment to spend the time required to analyze the evidence. Our transdisciplinary professional backgrounds gave us the advantage of neutrality; we weren't seen as representing shareholders, company executives, or employees, as we almost inevitably would have been had we come from a particular position in the business community. This allowed us to elicit full and far less censored stories from factory workers and chief financial officers alike. As researchers, the time we were able to invest in this study over five years also allowed us to examine what worked in the companies and what didn't with a degree of detail that would have been hard for anyone to achieve while simultaneously running a company.

Researchers always begin their studies with hypotheses. When we started this study, we thought we would find companies that had managed to provide good working conditions while succeeding economically, but as was commonly believed, we also assumed that there would be no causal relationship between the two. We knew that researchers had been able to demonstrate the financial gains that companies could achieve by investing in highly skilled workers. But these demonstrations of financial gain relied largely on how much companies stood to gain by not losing employees who are particularly expensive to recruit. We realized that when unemployment was particularly low, companies might also stand to gain by establishing policies and practices that helped them recruit workers into so-called low-skilled jobs. In areas with moderate levels of unemployment, however, it was less clear that companies would experience these same gains. Moreover, the fact that the majority of companies cut benefits and slowed wage growth whenever possible suggested that they thought it was economically advantageous to do so.

Over the course of our five-year study, we went from believing that it was possible for companies to improve their working conditions while being profitable—something we cared about for clear reasons of humanity—to realizing that the majority of the companies we studied had increased their profitability by investing in their employees at the bottom of the ladder. The rhetoric insists that this simply can't be done, claiming that companies can't treat employees as well as they used to if they want to make money; that scheduling flexibility isn't possible in manufacturing; that providing training for employees with limited formal education is not profitable; that employees with special needs are a drain on finances; and that employees at the bottom of the ladder can't significantly contribute to improving the quality of a company's products. The companies we have chosen to focus on in this book have disproven all of these claims.

A note on terminology used in the book seems necessary here. There are many common ways of referring to workers at the lowest level of the corporate ladder. One of the most frequently used terms, *low-skilled workers*, will be used only when it is referenced from the literature or from our interview subjects; our case studies clearly demonstrate that these workers have many important skills, even if they have limited formal education. We also decided against using another common term, *low-wage workers*, to refer to the lowest level workers in a company, since the best companies have made sure that all of their workers receive a living wage, and in some cases also have opportunities to earn substantial wage increases and financial assets. Because of this, we have elected to use employees at *the bottom of the ladder* and *least-advantaged workers* to reflect the situation of the workers featured in this book. We also refer to *least-educated workers*, since having a limited formal education is most often the biggest constraint on people's ability to move up the corporate ladder.

Assessing Causality

Various tools are available to assess causality. Basic scientists can do this by conducting experiments. For example, if chemists want to know what occurs when two chemicals are combined, they mix the chemicals, place them under heat or pressure or another force to combine them, and measure the outcome. If physicists want to know what happens when atoms are smashed, they build an accelerator, run the atoms through it, and measure the outcome. If physicians want to determine a drug's effects on patients, the gold standard is, similarly, to run an experiment in which patients are randomly divided in two groups, one group receiving the real medication and the other receiving an identical-looking placebo. In most cases, we don't have the luxury of using experiments to determine causality in public policy. This also applies to businesses, since CEOs who are responsible for turning a profit are not likely to voluntarily turn their companies over to a scientific venture in which they would be randomly assigned to either implement or abstain from adopting a major policy.

This does not mean, however, that we cannot examine evidence to determine whether it strongly suggests an action leading to a given impact. Instead of using randomized experiments, we examine other criteria that are often used to suggest causality. We can ask the following questions: What action was taken? Was it implemented well? Is there a clear mechanism by which this action could lead to the anticipated results? Did the sequence of events strongly suggest that the action led to the impact? And so on. In short, we can employ the types of questions that scientists and other researchers use outside of the experimental environment—and that indeed all of us use to try to determine causality in our daily lives.

For example, if my neighbor throws a baseball in Boston and there is a death from AIDS in Botswana, I assume there is no causal link between these two events since there is no known mechanism by which throwing the baseball would lead to the death from AIDS, and there is little evidence of a relationship between this small action in Boston and major events in Botswana. Although chaos theory might suggest possible ways in which a butterfly flapping its wings in one location could lead to a hurricane in another, in our everyday lives we assume that there is little if any causality between these distant events. Similarly, if I see my next-door neighbor throw a baseball and my neighbor a block away complains of a broken window, I may be reluctant to assume that there was any relationship between these events; while baseballs can break windows, and while the fact that my next-door neighbor carelessly threw one today might suggest that he could have thrown one carelessly a block away a week ago, we still have no way to delineate this relationship. But, when I watch my next-door neighbor throw a baseball and I see it go through our front window, I am ready to conclude, without conducting a formal experiment, that throwing the baseball led to the window breaking. Of course, the window could spontaneously have broken for some other reason, but this seems highly improbable. Throwing the baseball preceded the window breaking in tight sequence, and there are plenty of mechanisms by which we know that baseballs can break windows. As clear as I would be about causality in that case, a number of the CEOs we interviewed in this study were equally convinced about the causality of their actions and policies leading to higher profitability.

Their degree of conviction arose for a number of reasons. In several cases, the CEOs had taken over companies that had high turnover rates and a poor ability to attract or motivate workers; the CEOs had improved the companies' working conditions, and as soon as they did so, they observed an increased ability to attract and retain employees. As in the case of observing the baseball break the window, the sequence of events was clear and the mechanism was natural. Furthermore, the employees often supported the causality by relaying specific details about how the improved working conditions had led them to apply for a job at the company, to remain there, and to work more efficiently. In other cases, CEOs linked compensation to productivity and watched productivity measurably rise.

Companies Are Not Catastrophe-Proof

In 2009, we are facing the worst economy the world has seen since the Great Depression in the early twentieth century. Some of the world's oldest and most successful companies have already failed in light of this downturn. In this setting, it is natural to wonder if some of the companies profiled in this book will also go under. While we hope they will all survive because we are profoundly impressed by each of them, we recognize there is a real probability that some of them will not weather the storm.

No company is catastrophe-proof. Though investing in working conditions can substantially strengthen a company's profile, no single set of actions can create an impermeable barrier against the inherent risks in different sectors in a global economy, which have recently been dramatically heightened. While we cannot say that all of these companies will remain financially successful, the working conditions at the firms we studied either during economic downturns or when entire sectors were threatened had provided them with crucial tools that markedly increased their chances of survival.

Capitalists, Not Kantians

Some of the top managers we interviewed were as driven by moral principles as any philosopher would be; however, they all saw profit making as one of their top duties. For others, making a profit was their sole focus. They had little time for or interest in engaging in debates about determining the "right thing to do" if it wasn't driven by the balance sheet. We were delighted to be able to include companies that were overwhelmingly driven by profit. In fact, when public questions were raised about the character of one or two of the senior managers in our study, we were asked whether their companies should be dropped from the book. Our goal, however, was the opposite of simply selecting saints. We welcomed including senior executives whose actions were motivated solely by making money. Kant argued that to act morally, one's intentions are important, and that one can't act for personal benefit. In this sense, this book is fundamentally capitalist, not Kantian. The book demonstrates that companies can invest in improving the conditions of the people at the bottom of the corporate ladder purely because they want to be more profitable. We would be delighted to see the world become a better place for the people at the bottom of the ladder while increasing profits for employees and companies alike.

Profit at the Bottom of the Ladder

Changing the lives of the least-advantaged workers while becoming more profitable is exactly what the companies in *Profit at the Bottom of the Ladder* have done. Their approaches, which include raising wages, rewarding productivity with strong earnings and profit-sharing opportunities, providing paid leave and flexibility, providing health care, and many other benefits, are frequently allotted to employees from the middle to the top of the corporate ladder, yet they are truly rare for the lowest-level workers. To take just one example, profit sharing is available to less than 1 percent of those in low-level jobs.

Some of these practices are rarely applied to the lowest-level jobs because they present unique challenges in certain settings. How, for example, does one provide scheduling flexibility in manufacturing jobs without hindering production? Other practices, such as providing good wages, have not been applied because it is assumed that it is impossible for companies to succeed economically if they ensure these fundamentals for all of their employees. The companies described in this book make clear that it is feasible, affordable, and transformative to improve the working conditions of the worst off.

Profit at the Bottom of the Ladder details how a brick manufacturer in the Deep South of the United States and an apparel manufacturer in Los Angeles dramatically increased the wages of their labor force while increasing their productivity. This book shows how profit sharing increased the productivity of a box manufacturer in British Columbia and a cookie manufacturer in Roxbury, Massachusetts. It tells the story of how investments in health care provision at a scrap metal company in AIDS-ridden South Africa and at a cement manufacturer in rural India made these companies more profitable in the long run. It presents the benefits reaped by a roofing manufacturer in Norway that provided training to its employees as it mechanized production, by a bank in Peru that hired autistic and developmentally delayed adults, and by a call center in Ireland that provided advancement opportunities to everyone working the phones. Through these detailed case studies, the book illustrates how and why those at the bottom and the top of these companies report that they profited together.

1

Providing All Employees with More Than a Living Wage

I<small>T HAS BECOME CONVENTIONAL WISDOM</small> that firms can obtain an important competitive advantage by paying the lowest wages they can get away with, thereby reducing their labor costs. This is particularly the case when it comes to so-called low-skilled labor, which is seen as easily and inexpensively replaceable. In contrast, when it comes to high-skilled labor, companies have always used high wages and financial incentives to attract the best talent.

As a result, earnings inequality has tended to increase since the 1970s, rising on average 15 percent between 1970 and 2000 in the Organisation for Economic Cooperation and Development (OECD) member countries.[1] In fact, from 1995 to 2005, earnings inequality widened in all OECD countries except Ireland and Spain. Nowhere is this phenomenon more prevalent than in the United States, which had the highest earnings inequality in 1995 and still had the second highest in 2005.[2] Inequalities that were costly in the best of economic times fueled the credit crisis and placed low- and moderate-income families at particular risk during economic downturns, when they faced falling real income.

But are these rising earnings inequalities really inevitable? Can companies make money while providing decent wages and financial incentives for all employees to improve their performance?

We examined earnings disparities using data on households in diverse countries around the world, including national household surveys and in-depth interviews of urban working men and women. The latter enabled us to delve deeper than the national household survey data and to examine the earnings opportunities of so-called low-skilled workers as well as the daily and long-term threats to their earnings. We carried out these and other studies of more than fifty-five thousand households around the world and looked at the problems confronting the employees at the bottom of the ladder.

We followed up this research with a series of studies looking at companies that stood out because they were highly successful firms providing higher wages than was typical for their sector to their least-advantaged employees. In each company, we examined the corporate approaches to wages for their lowest-level employees, and the costs and benefits of the approaches taken from the perspective of employees at the bottom of the ladder, their supervisors, managers structuring the rewards systems, and the CFOs and CEOs.

In this chapter, we highlight three companies that brought important and divergent experiences to the critical issue of structuring wages and in-centives. Jenkins Brick provided individual workers with incentives above their hourly wage so that those with low levels of formal education could earn far higher salaries than they would otherwise have attained. American Apparel similarly set a modest base hourly wage, but provided teams with financial incentives so that they could increase their earnings by increas-ing their productivity. In contrast, Costco provided strong salary progres-sions so that nearly all employees who remained at the company long term knew they would be able to climb from low to middle income. All three firms saw the higher employee earnings as being in their company's best interest because they increased the company's ability to recruit and retain the top employees for their sector while providing direct and indirect in-centives for greater productivity.

American Apparel: Paying American Wages in Manufacturing

As vice president for operations and president of manufacturing Marty Bailey showed us around the American Apparel factory, he explained how he had converted both the production and the payment systems.[3] American

Apparel stood out from its competitors in the U.S. garment industry, of which very few still produce in the United States, and even fewer provide decent working conditions for their employees. While achieving rapid growth, American Apparel paid the highest wages in the industry and offered a generous range of benefits to its employees. It accomplished this by setting up a team manufacturing system that linked wages to productivity and that drastically increased output.

At a time when most manufacturing companies were moving from the United States to countries with lower labor costs, American Apparel did just the opposite: it relocated its manufacturing from Mexico to Los Angeles. American Apparel began manufacturing in 1997, soon after the 1994 passage of the North American Free Trade Agreement (NAFTA). Like many of its competitors, the company had opted to subcontract its labor-intensive operations to Mexico, where workers were paid lower wages. However, along with the low labor costs came the challenge of influencing working conditions. The company tried to ensure that its factories didn't become sweatshops, but managers felt they had little control over their subcontractors, who might promise to improve working conditions, but often failed to follow through on their commitments. It was difficult to monitor factories in other countries and ensure compliance with standards from a distance. American Apparel eventually concluded that the only way to ensure decent working conditions was to move operations to Los Angeles, where managers could oversee production.

The company's founder, Dov Charney, had gotten started in the garment industry by selling screen-printed T-shirts out of his college dorm room at Tufts University. He dropped out of school after his junior year and worked various jobs in the apparel industry in South Carolina, learning about garment production from the ground up. When jobs dried up in the 1990s as garment manufacturing increasingly shifted overseas, Charney moved to Los Angeles, where he partnered with Sam Lim to found American Apparel. Dov Charney's reputation is mixed; he has been highly praised by some for his innovations, and has been impugned equally strongly by others for alleged sexual harassment. This particular case study is not designed to address the questions about Charney since he is not the protagonist of this story. Our focus is on the less familiar story of Marty Bailey and on how American Apparel managed to dramatically increase its productivity, thus making it profitable to manufacture in the United States.

Having decided to produce in this country, Charney needed to find a way to compete effectively while paying his employees U.S. wages. He recruited Marty Bailey to help him accomplish this goal. Bailey had two decades of experience in the apparel industry; he had worked for Fruit of the Loom for fifteen years, both in the United States and abroad in Mexico, Central America, the Caribbean, and Europe. Most importantly, Bailey was known for taking old, inefficient garment factories and transforming them into renewed, productive entities. He radically changed the structure of manufacturing at American Apparel. Bailey developed and implemented a team approach to making garments in which line workers were rewarded financially if their team excelled.

Setting Up Team Manufacturing and Incentives

Bailey arrived at American Apparel in April of 2002 to find a factory floor resembling that of most older clothing manufacturers. He described his first impression: "You couldn't see a single worker . . . The room was filled with carts of pieces piled high, thousands of pieces waiting for the next step. And we weren't making money on them."[4] There were bundles of half-finished items everywhere. The bundle-manufacturing process at the factory consisted of making clothing in stages. Each group of workers had a specific task: they cut the cloth, sewed a seam, attached buttons, and so on. This approach, focused on individuals, slowed production in several ways. Partially completed clothing items did not even move to the next stage until a large number of items were completed and could be "bundled." Tasks took different lengths of time so large quantities of bundles would pile up between faster and slower stations. Individuals had no incentive to help each other; in fact, they could perceive helping someone else as reducing their own speed. Garments could take weeks to be completed, during which time the company invested in labor costs but made no money. Moreover, when production slowed, it could take the manager weeks to analyze every step of the process and determine the cause of the holdup.

From the outset, Bailey knew that he wanted to introduce a team approach to production, in which a group of eight to twelve machine operators work together to complete an item from start to finish. With this approach, tasks are divided up so that each step takes approximately the same length of time to complete. Instead of being bundled at intermediate steps, partially completed garments go directly from one member of the team to the next until the garment is completed. Items are finished the same day they are started, so there is no incomplete capital sitting on the factory floor. This system makes it easy to assess and improve production since the pace of each team can be monitored and additional help can be distributed as needed.

Right after introducing the team approach at the American Apparel factory, Bailey went back to South Carolina to visit his family, who had not yet moved to LA. He received a call on Friday night informing him of a strike at the factory. By Saturday, he was back in LA talking with the workers, who were clearly concerned about the new team approach; they worried about how it would affect their assignments and wages. After a weekend of intense discussions, however, the workers agreed to give this new method a try. By July of 2002, only a few months later, the factory was producing three times as much—ninety thousand pieces a day instead of thirty thousand—with only a 12 percent increase in the number of workers.

At the time of our visit in 2007, American Apparel prided itself on having the highest-paid workers in the garment industry. Though the company had always been committed to avoiding the sweatshop conditions too often found globally in the apparel industry, American Apparel's wages were not initially higher than the average wages in Los Angeles. Strikingly, earnings increased by over 50 percent after Marty Bailey implemented the team approach. All workers at the company received a minimum hourly wage that was above the minimum wage for California, but their relatively high earnings were linked to incentives. Since they were paid by the piece, they needed to increase their productivity in order to increase their pay. The logistics of the team system made marked increases in productivity possible, and the financial rewards that teams could earn encouraged them to work hard to make these increases happen.

From the company's perspective, compensation increases were earned rather than guaranteed. Bailey explained this important distinction: "I said we had the highest-earning apparel workers in the world. There's a difference. We're not just paying them. We give people an opportunity to be successful. We give them the tools, we give them the equipment, we give them the training, we give them the support, everything . . . but at some point it's up to them . . . It's about . . . wanting people to be successful. So again, we don't just pay them; we give people the opportunity to earn it."[5]

Employees cited the high wages as the main reason they came to work at American Apparel. For work that had a "thirty-second constraint," or on average could be completed in less than thirty seconds, each team member earned 12 cents, and for work that had an open "twenty-second constraint," they each earned 8 cents. Experienced sewers could make as much as $18 an hour, which was an extremely good wage for the garment industry. Even though earnings were based on incentives, many employees also mentioned that the wages were more reliable than they had been at their previous jobs. They emphasized the importance of being able to count on getting paid a certain amount. Even sewers with average skill levels earned around $12 an hour at American Apparel. The company was different from other garment factories, which often raised their production targets as soon as their goals were met. Marta Ruiz, an American Apparel factory worker, told us: "At my other company, you do more, you get more clothes made . . . and they lowered the pay rate."[6] Juan Pena, another worker, stated simply: "The more clothes we made, the less we earned."[7] It is common for garment factories to set nearly impossible targets and offer bonuses if workers manage to reach them. But once these targets are met, workers face a vicious cycle where expectations are raised and wages decrease unless they continuously increase their output.

Like other successful companies we studied, American Apparel believed that it would ultimately benefit from providing opportunities for its workers to increase their earnings. Marty Bailey explained this philosophy, which was based on the belief that employee success was the key to company success:

> You do all you can to help people be as successful as they possibly can be, whatever job they're employed to do. Whether they're a production employee that is going to be paid by how much they produce or a person who sweeps floors at night, you set that person up to be successful. That's the company's job. And if you've done that well, and then the people you've employed are successful, then all you have to do at that point is grab on to the coattails and hang on.[8]

The Productivity Benefits and Practical Challenges of Teamwork

Bailey developed the teamwork approach while working at Fruit of the Loom. He modeled the system on the automobile industry's "just-in-time" approach to production, which had been widely publicized with the success of the Toyota Production System.[9] "Just-in-time" (JIT) has become well recognized as an inventory strategy employed to increase a business's return on investment by decreasing inventory of incomplete products and lowering the associated carrying costs. Central to JIT is the rapid communication of the amount of expended, old stock; this information triggers the procurement of new stock. This saves warehouse space and costs. In short, JIT is about having the right amount of the right material at the right time in the right place, without needing a safety net of superfluous inventory.[10] In JIT production, each step in the production chain produces only the materials required for the next step in the chain, and work flows continuously from one station to the next. By using this method, Toyota avoided the accumulation of partially completed products and greatly reduced its warehousing costs. The Toyota Production System came to be recognized as being more efficient and effective than traditional mass production, as well as having more effective quality control. While JIT was well recognized in the automobile industry, it had not been applied to most clothing factories.

At American Apparel, Bailey similarly set up teams so that a single article of clothing flowed from one member of the team to the next until it was completed. A team of six to ten workers with similar sewing speeds was assembled around a table. Each person sewed one feature on the item and then handed it off to the next team member; when the item was completed, the team supervisor checked it for defects. Some employees played a role on more than one team. Each group of four teams was supported by a worker who focused on quality control, another who focused on mechanics if machinery broke down, and a final person who focused on supplying pre-cut cloth and thread. The factory had a back-up team of twenty-five sewers with different skills who were called upon to replace absent team members.

Teams were given minimum and maximum targets for production, but it was their effort and speed that ultimately determined their earnings. Sewers on the auxiliary teams and those who did specialty work were normally paid a flat hourly rate.

The team approach revolutionized the factory in a variety of ways. Whereas the firm had previously stored an enormous inventory of bundled, partially completed garments worth hundreds of thousands of dollars, garments were now completed and brought to market much faster, and the company therefore made money on them much sooner. T-shirts were sewn in ninety seconds and were shipped out immediately. Stores received their orders much faster once the bundling system was eliminated. Inventory was moved off the floor as soon as it was completed. Bailey wanted to make sure that no time was lost and that production was increased with demand. Only raw materials were stored. The company kept 4 million pounds of cloth in its warehouse—enough for two and a half weeks of production. Bailey emphasized, "[Whereas] others had focused on how rapidly they could get products starting to be made, my focus was on how rapidly we could get products out the door."[11]

Bailey gave us an overview of how team manufacturing had transformed production at American Apparel: "Products are given to the shipping department in four hours versus four months. So you've got products available and ready to ship right now. If you've got issues where you don't have something in stock, you can create it, right now. So you can make vital deliveries to your customers. And . . . average [hourly] earnings for the operators went from about $7.90 to over $12."[12]

In addition to speeding up production, the team approach also improved product quality. Every team was responsible for quality control, and since items were examined on the spot, errors were picked up and corrected immediately. Instead of allowing mistakes to pile up, sewers who were having trouble with a particular type of seam could be identified right away and taught to improve their skills.

This approach also brought about dramatic improvements for the factory workers. Employees reported that their work was easier with the team system, since they no longer spent a lot of time moving partially completed pieces around the factory.

The profits from American Apparel's just-in-time team approach seem so evident that they beg the question: Why haven't more companies implemented a similar system? Though this approach is highly effective, getting it right isn't simple. To turn the idea into a successful operation, teams must be set up in such a way that each worker requires the same amount of time to complete his or her task on an item. Teams must therefore be formed according to skill level, separating extremely skilled workers from average and slower ones. Production steps must also be split according to the length of time they require, and sewing machines must be set up in a way that facilitates the rapid movement of items between stations. Implementing the team approach at American Apparel took considerable patience and commitment. It also required a strong manager like Marty Bailey, who had a clear vision of how to make it a success, and who knew how to both lead and problem solve collaboratively with the line workers so that they could increase their productivity alongside their own earnings and those of the company.

As we walked around the factory in 2007, Bailey pointed out the white-boards hanging over each team's section. Grids were drawn on the white-boards, with rows indicating targets and accomplishments for each hour of production. Team members could see how many garments it was estimated they could complete, how many garments they had actually completed, and how much they had earned each hour.

Teams earned different amounts depending on their skill levels, with the best earning $18 an hour, average teams making over $12 an hour, and slower teams making closer to the $8 hourly minimum wage that the firm guaranteed. Bailey went to great lengths to emphasize that he was as proud of the teams that could produce only fifteen bundles of completed clothes as he was of the group that could produce twenty-three. He mentioned that a number of visitors had asked whether it was fair for people to earn different wages, and his response was: "People are earning [according] to their ability. It's just like education: some people make it through high school, some through college, some beyond. Their earnings are related to that."[13] All teams had the incentive to work harder.

Correctly dividing teams according to workers' skill levels was absolutely necessary since the members of each team were very interdependent. The only way workers could increase their earnings was for their whole team to increase its productivity. Juana Romero, a factory worker, explained how this could be challenging: "Sometimes the team has four or five people who want to work really hard and four or five others who don't. That's the biggest problem."[14] She talked about how teams tried to come up with solutions to balance workers' skill levels by training each other or exchanging tasks in order to help the team collectively work faster. It could clearly be difficult if team members didn't all share the same ambitions.

Marty Bailey was well aware of these challenges. An important part of his job was working with the teams to try to improve their productivity. He was committed to turning average teams into great ones and slow teams into average ones. The new design of the factory floor made it easier to identify the slowest team members: "When it was the line system, I could walk into a factory and there would be a thousand or eleven hundred workers and I'd have no idea where the problem was. It [would] take days to sort out where the constraint was [and] what needed to be fixed. Now with the team system, I can find the bottlenecks in five minutes."[15] The white boards rapidly highlighted which were the slowest teams. Once identified, he could provide them with more training to improve their sewing techniques and their team strategies.

The team approach changed the entire mentality of work at American Apparel. In the old assembly-line approach, workers were paid by the piece based on their function in the production chain. Those who stitched collars might have a different pay rate than those who stitched sleeves. This often led to dissension, to jealousies among workers, and to a lack of collaboration. Workers would be angry that they were earning less money than their neighbors even though they were working on the same number of pieces. The old system also led workers to focus only on how to speed up their own individual work, even if this led to cutting corners in ways that slowed down the factory's overall production speed or damaged quality. With the new team approach, everyone on the team earned the same amount. The only way to earn more was to ensure that more items were completed by the team. This meant that workers would do their best to speed up not only their own work, but also that of their whole team. Moreover, if someone was late for work, the entire team would be penalized, so workers pressured each other to get in on time. In many ways, this social pressure resembles the social codes that contribute to the high rates of compliance in institutions such as the Grameen Bank, where one member's noncompliance has a negative impact on the entire group.[16]

American Apparel's teamwork system meant that workers had incentives to encourage each other to be punctual, stay focused, and work faster and more efficiently. Employees' relationships with their supervisors were also altered; supervisors' recommendations on how to improve work were now seen as helpful tips rather than reprimands. Alicia Guzman, one of the older sewers, described the improvements she had noticed: "The team system works much better than working on your own. You can decide together how to make clothes move through faster, and you decide without pressure from somebody else. You do it so you can earn more."[17]

By tying workers' wages to their output, American Apparel had given employees the incentive to increase their productivity. At the same time, setting up the teamwork system streamlined the sewing process and made it possible for employees to increase the number of garments they produced. Both elements were inextricably linked and resulted in the dramatic increase in productivity that took place after the implementation of the teamwork system. Had American Apparel set financial incentives in place without implementing the teamwork approach, workers wouldn't have been able to benefit as much from them given the production constraints inherent in the individual bundling approach; conversely, had the company restructured manufacturing without adding rewards for productivity, there would not have been sufficient incentives for workers to adapt, work hard in the new structure, and increase their output.

Additional Competitive Advantage of Rapid Adaptability

Throughout the 1990s, garment-sewing jobs were declining all across the United States, including in Los Angeles. By 2000, four out of five of the eighty-one manufacturers surveyed in Los Angeles were outsourcing their manufacturing. Though labor costs were higher in Los Angeles than they had been in Mexico, there were competitive advantages to manufacturing in the United States. Marty Bailey explained how American Apparel viewed the decision not to outsource production: "If you combine efficient labor with good automation in the United States, you can be successful—particularly if you have a direct line of communication to the market, as we do, so you can change rapidly. We can change a hole in the shirt the same day so we don't need to send a lot of clothes to an outlet mall. Outsourcing takes the control of the company out of your hands. If I am outsourcing, there is never a face to the product."[18]

Communication between different departments greatly improved after manufacturing was brought back to the United States, since all units were now located in the same building. Bailey explained how the move had affected operations: "If I need to talk to Jose in production, I go to the second floor, not [to] El Salvador." The entire process of making T-shirts—from design to shipping—now took place in the same building. This meant that turnaround time was reduced and there was no longer a need for a large inventory. The company could respond much faster to customers' changing desires and demands, which was a great advantage in the fashion industry. Products could readily be transformed from an idea on a sketchpad to a product on a shelf in a matter of weeks. On rare occasions, this process could even be completed within four days. From a marketing standpoint, Matthew Swansen explained how this reduced the time between product brainstorming and market testing: "We slim down on the supply and demand idea. I can get a vibe for what's going on—like I could be out last night and think, 'What a cool tie over there . . . this fabric or kind of cut,' and have a sample made today and check it out . . . so then, put it right into the market, basically."[19]

The company has been praised in the media for its efforts to keep manufacturing facilities in America instead of outsourcing production overseas to low-wage countries, and for its labor policies, where workers received subsidized health care benefits and generally made twice the minimum wage.[20] Although American Apparel initially used the tagline "Sweatshop-free," it abandoned this slogan because it felt the phrase relegated the company to a niche market. Instead of targeting only socially conscious consumers who buy sweatshop-free products, the company wanted people to purchase American Apparel clothes based on their style and quality. The tagline became "Vertically integrated manufacturing."

Vertical integration captured the fact that manufacturing, design, and marketing all took place in the same building. Financial incentives fueled the high productivity that enabled American Apparel to manufacture in the United States. Vertical integration allowed the firm to respond to fashion trends more rapidly than outsourcing would have and, as a result, fueled remarkably rapid growth. In 2004, sales were $125 million from the wholesale division and $18 million from retail stores. By the time of our second set of interviews in 2007, sales were $172 million from wholesale and $215 million from retail. The retail division was launched in 2003 with a single store in Los Angeles, and by 2007, the company had 143 stores in eleven different countries.[21]

Jenkins Brick: Managing Through Incentives

Jenkins Brick understood how higher wages could increase productivity just as greater chances for asset accumulation, which will be discussed in chapter 4, could reduce employee turnover. The company's wage structure had two components: a base wage that was competitive with other industries in the area, and a comprehensive system of incentives for increased productivity. These incentives, which provided a sizable addition to the base wage, were what made Jenkins Brick's wages significantly higher than those at comparable companies.

Jenkins Brick made sure to set an attractive base wage that would enable the firm to compete for employees in hiring. In 2005, the director of personnel and safety, Gary Smith, explained how they set their wages:

> Typically, in the fall of every year, I send out a wage comparison . . . I use Boral Bricks in Bessemer, which is probably the most heavily industrialized area we deal with outside of Birmingham. We [also] look

at Henry Brick down in Selma. Both Henry and Bessemer are union-
ized. The union at Henry is very weak, [but it is] fairly strong in
Bessemer. I also look at General Shell. [I] used to look at it in
Huntsville, [but] now they closed the plant down and we started
looking at it in Atlanta. We've tried to add a couple [of] other
manufacturers, [but] we have not been real successful in getting
other folks to share their information with us to date, but we're
working on that. Typically, we'll also look at the bigger [cities too],
which are nonunion . . . Our goal is to stay at the level [of competi-
tors] or above.[22]

Nearly all compensation that exceeded the rate of their competitors
was paid through rewards for productivity. Jenkins Brick set up a wide
range of incentives that could significantly increase wages. Tommy Andreades, the CFO, noted: "Everyone is incentivized—plant managers on
production, safety, and quality, [and] strappers on the number of bricks
moved."[23] He pulled out a series of binders, each several inches thick, that
contained the details of all the incentives. For example, the Mexican immigrants with limited levels of education who moved most of the bricks off
the conveyer belt onto large trolleys could earn over $25 an hour with the
inclusion of the incentives. The end result of this wage structure was that
earnings at Jenkins Brick were substantially higher than at similar businesses. According to Gary Smith, "The other brick businesses that manu-
ally unload had an average rate that is about $5.50 less than our average
rate for all three of our plants."[24]

As we walked through the Jenkins Brick plants and spoke with line
production workers, they raised how important the incentives were to
them. As he rapidly moved hundreds of pounds of bricks between a flatbed
trailer and a conveyor belt, Miguel Mendez spoke about how glad he was
to be working in his position. If he kept up his pace, he could bring home
US$25/hour, a wage that would be practically unheard of at most other
manufacturing sites employing young Mexican immigrants with limited
levels of formal education. Mendez's comments were typical of the workers we spoke with, both as they worked in the production lines and in private as they took their breaks.

It wasn't always easy managing through economic incentives. Andreades
wryly noted: "One of our strengths is that we do not manage by fear. Everything is incentive/compensation driven. And one of our weaknesses is

that we motivate by incentives."[25] He went on to explain how every time management wanted to implement a change, they needed to think about accompanying it with the right incentives. Andreades offered an example: instead of simply telling the sales team to sell tiles instead of bricks, they also needed to modify the incentive structure to reflect this change. To get the incentives right, several issues required careful analysis: What was their strategic economic plan, and what steps did it entail? What indicators could be used to determine whether employees were helping move the plan forward, and how could they provide incentives to make this happen? Just like at American Apparel, though the basic concept of rewarding productivity was well understood, substantial planning and commitment were required to set the right system in place.

Jenkins Brick benefited financially from its incentive structure, and so did its employees. CEO Mike Jenkins smiled as he recounted:

> I call it the automobile survey: when I'd go to our plants in the old days, you'd have these raggedy automobiles with no tags, and all that kind of stuff. But you go to the plants now, there are some really nice cars. But the point is, if we can't provide that kind of workplace and compensation, we need to get out of the business. We'd sell. And certainly if we can't pay competitively and do better, we need to find somebody else who can run the company profitably and do that. Being able to make a profit by taking it out of somebody's hide is just not a good thing to do . . . Maybe it works short term, but not in the long term . . . Now if you get too far away [from what others pay], your competition could be making a product for [much less] money and if you run your costs up and you go out of business, you're not doing your associates a favor by doing that.[26]

With the incentive system in place, employees' increased productivity could easily be measured by the number and quality of bricks they produced and sold.

Costco: Providing Higher Wages as Part of a Corporate Strategy

At a time when the majority of industries in the United States contend that it is impossible to compete in a globalized economy without reducing wages, Costco provides high wages that enable employees with limited formal education to rise into the middle class. While doing so, it has managed to successfully compete with some of the largest retail companies in the world. Costco experienced tremendously rapid growth in the 1990s and continued to do so in the 2000s.

In 2005, when the federal minimum wage was $5.15, wages at Costco in the United States started at $10 an hour for a full-time entry-level cashier, $11 an hour for meat cutters, and $15 an hour for truck drivers. Even two years later, and averaging all levels of experience, national wages had not caught up. In 2007, average hourly wages for cashiers in the United States across all levels of experience were $8.84, for meat cutters $10.45, and for truck drivers $13.86—lower than the starting wages for entry-level employees at Costco.[27] Wage increases at Costco were based on the total number of work hours accumulated by the employee. After four years, a cashier could make around $43,000, more than twice as high as the mean annual wage for grocery store cashiers at $19,430 or department store cashiers at $17,480.[28] Costco's average wage was 42 percent higher than that of its most direct competitor, Wal-Mart's Sam's Club.[29] Director of employee development Vito Romano believed that Costco had been successful in providing its employees with a real living wage: "We have a lot of couples that work for Costco. So you get a married couple, and they're both making [over] $40 000 a year. They're not doing too bad."[30]

The company knew it would need salary differentials between its employees in South Korea and the United Kingdom, and between those in Mexico and the United States. Costco executives were realistic, and they recognized that there was a limit to how high they could raise their wages. Still, CEO Jim Sinegal told us in 2006 that the company aimed to pay "demonstrably better" than its competitors in each country, setting its salaries to be approximately 30 percent higher than local averages.

The Benefits of Providing Higher Wages

Sinegal understood that Costco's success was driven by and dependent on its employees at all levels of the firm—from cashiers and forklift drivers to warehouse managers and senior executives. He contended that Costco's good wages and working conditions led to the higher productivity of its warehouses. At the same time, he acknowledged the business community's skepticism about the link between working conditions and productivity: "It kind of falls on deaf ears when you tell people that . . . taking care of your people is good business. When you hire good people, give them good jobs and good wages and good career opportunities, then eventually good things are going to happen."[31]

The secret to Costco's success lay in the return it received from providing good wages, benefits, and advancement opportunities. CFO Richard Galanti was very concrete about how this worked:

> You pay a living wage that's better than anyone else, provide affordable, quality health care, and you'll be able to hire who you want. If you hire who you want and treat them right, they'll stay longer. If they stay longer and [they] like you, they're going to report on the employee that's stealing out of the back door. They're going to pick up the crushed soda can on their way back in from lunch. They're going to smile when a customer asks a question. And I'm biased, but when you walk into lots of the little neighborhood drugstores or a little shop and you're like, "Hello?" It's not that [the shop's employees are] rude or bad people, it's just, I think it's a different deal. And I think that comes over time by treating [employees] right and having them trust you.[32]

Costco's comparatively high wages and its reputation as a good employer made it easy to attract employees. Vito Romano explained: "We don't spend any money on recruiting. One of the nice things is that we are an employer of choice." Their numbers during a period of low national unemployment illustrated this further: "We receive about eight hundred thousand applications a year for our four hundred buildings; we hire fourteen thousand people or so."[33]

The attention that Costco received from its good working practices meant the company could save significant amounts on marketing and publicity. Costco's 2007 annual report recognized the importance of the company's positive image: "We continually receive comments on the amount of 'publicity' Costco receives . . . whether it's a recent write-up in the Sunday *New York Times*, or a local news reporter commenting on Costco's pharmacy or gas prices being the lowest in town . . . More importantly, we recognize the positive value it brings to our company, particularly given that none of these items are solicited by us. Costco has no public relations department!"[34]

Like most of the companies we studied, Costco was aware that employee turnover was expensive, leading to higher training costs and to losses in operating efficiency due to new employees' lack of experience. It therefore encouraged good employees to stay with the company for as long as possible. Costco's two most important policies to encourage the retention of warehouse employees were offering economic incentives for longevity and providing real advancement opportunities. Employees' salaries increased significantly over their first four years with the company as they gathered new skills and experience. Most employee turnover occurred within the first year of employment, during which time the company weeded out employees who were not well suited to the work. While Costco's good salaries and working conditions made it attractive as an employer, the work was demanding and required a level of commitment that not everyone was ready for. Vito Romano explained:

> At Costco, we experience 39 percent turnover within the first ninety days, for a lot of reasons. Possibly some bad hires—believing in people more than we should have. [And] some of it is a "fit" issue; sometimes they don't fit into the Costco culture, and sometimes we don't fit into their life. With Costco, our fast-paced environment—turning merchandise an average of twelve times a year—and our extremely high service level to our members makes for demanding work. So you can't come to work and go home and not feel tired. Quite frankly, that's not for everyone. [But] past one year, our turnover is less than 6 percent.[35]

"Hiring and training new employees is expensive, so Costco figures their low turnover rate makes up for the higher pay," George Whalin, president of Retail Management Consultants, noted.[36] Past the one-year mark, Costco has one of the lowest turnover rates in the industry. According to a 2004 article, Costco's overall turnover rate was 24 percent a year, which was less than half of Wal-Mart's turnover rate of 50 percent.[37] Beth Hall, a deli manager who had worked at Costco for ten years, discussed the importance of wages in her decision to stay at Costco, stating that she expected to work there long term: "[I'll stay here] forever. You can't earn this kind of money anywhere [else] without a college degree."[38]

CFO Richard Galanti was clear on how Costco was able to offer better wages: "The fact is that we have the ability to afford a higher wage because even if we're paying a $4 to $5 an hour higher average wage than Sam's [Club], we're doing almost twice the sales—70 percent more per square foot."[39] Costco's finances also benefit from its extremely low shrink rate, which refers to the amount of merchandise lost to employee theft.

According to Vito Romano, "The industry average is somewhere between 2 and 4 percent. We're at a less than 0.02 percent."[40] Jim Sinegal concurred that good wages and benefits are the reason that Costco has extremely low rates of theft by employees.[41]

Richard Galanti explained how Costco's beliefs about staff management are fundamentally different from Wal-Mart's:

> Why [don't] other companies . . . [do the same]? I think there's the pressure of Wall Street, the pressure of performing; I think it's embedded in their culture. And no doubt you saw the twenty-seven-pager [from Wal-Mart] that was leaked to the press. I mean, they're claiming a five-year cashier is no more efficient than a one-year cashier. Well, [a long-term employee is more efficient] here. Why? Because our employees care . . . I'm biased, but it's clear to me that [Wal-Mart's] five-year cashier is not going to rush any harder, because she's not getting paid any more. It's not just money. It's the whole feeling around here of being fair, of feeling that you can get ahead if you want to get ahead, of being paid well. Certainly [higher pay] helps, don't get me wrong, but it takes more than just that for you to get that long-term view of "I'll work hard, I'll be that good employee."[42]

As chapter 6 details, Costco employees knew that there were substantial opportunities for career advancement as well.

The combined incentives of wanting to retain their jobs in order to keep the high wages and of wanting to perform well in order to advance markedly strengthened achievement. Employees worked fast and well, increasing both productivity and customer loyalty. As a result, although Costco spent more on wages per employee than Sam's Club, Costco had higher annual sales per square foot ($795 versus $516) and higher annual profits per employee ($13,647 versus $11,039).[43]

Weathering the Storm: The Short-Term Versus the Long-Term View

As a publicly traded firm, Costco operates in a very different economic environment than the privately owned firms we studied. Publicly traded firms are constantly under pressure to make decisions that yield short-term gains, which can make it difficult for them to focus on long-term goals. Regardless of their success, the vast majority of companies go through periods of economic strain. When publicly traded companies encounter economic difficulties, they are pressured to cut workers' wages and benefits. Although there is no inherent link between profits and the reduction of wages and benefits, Wall Street analysts tend to favor companies that use these measures to cut costs. Jim Sinegal described this pressure:

> There's a lot of pressure on organizations . . . 99 percent of the people who are running businesses out there are generally trying to do the right thing. But there are pressures! Do you think we are not pressured on wages? Do you think that Wall Street wouldn't like us to reduce our wages? They'd love it! They'd love us to raise prices! They are interested in making money between now and next Tuesday. Now, I am not saying that with any degree of acrimony. That's the system and I understand it. The system works. But there're a lot of pressures within the system that create that short-term thought process. You know, if you look at it realistically—and, I think, intelligently—you'll recognize that you are not in this business for the short haul.[44]

Senior managers at Costco were aware that the easy way to raise their stock prices was to reduce wages and benefits, but they were also aware that doing so could prove detrimental in the long run. Jay Tihinen, associate vice president of human resources, commented, "Could we prop up our share price by reporting bang-out earnings because we dropped our benefit cost? Sure. But where does 'shrink' come in retail? Employees, if they feel aggrieved and you are not giving them their fair share, you are going to pay for it either in shrink or effort. You are going to pay a price."[45]

Jim Sinegal was in it for the long haul, and he made a clear decision to manage accordingly:

> You know, if you kind of keep yourself focused and moving straight ahead and looking at what you're supposed to be doing, how you're supposed to be running your company, it works . . . I mentioned those things about taking care of your people and taking care of your customers, and we think it's possible for someone to take care of their shareholders, reward their shareholders without thinking about those things, but only on a short-term basis. You can't do it in the long term. You can't have a dissatisfied workforce and expect that your company's going to be a very happy company as it projects itself to its customers.[46]

Jim Sinegal talked about long-term strategy, but more importantly, he practiced what he preached. Having been in business for a long time, he

was well aware that there are times when the economic outlook may be
unfavorable for any number of reasons. He made it clear that the hard part
isn't keeping wages and benefits good when business is steady, but rather
weathering the storm and holding on to your goals when times are tough:

> There are good times and bad times in business . . . and so you've got
> to be prepared to steel yourself for those times and try to run the busi-
> ness as well as you can during those periods of time. But [if you
> always] think, "Oh, there's a hurricane, better cut wages!" What are
> you building there? You're losing the part of your business which is
> the most important. In our company, seventy cents of every dollar that
> we spend—rent, electricity, travel, our facilities, all the things we
> spend money on—is spent on people. [That] pretty much tells you
> this is a "people business." If you're going to fail at that you're going
> to fail at the most important function that you have. You're going to
> fail. Those employees that you have take care of every transaction,
> they handle every customer, buy every piece of merchandise, stock
> every shelf. They do everything that is important . . . So you want to
> make sure that you have people doing it that are doing it as well as you
> think you would do it. You don't do that with people that you're
> bringing [through] a revolving door, in and out of the organization.[47]

While Costco has done well in terms of profits and stock price throughout most of its lifespan, the company experienced a temporary downturn
during a period of rapid growth. CFO Richard Galanti recounted:

> Throughout the eighties and most of the nineties, we could do no
> wrong. I mean, we were Starbucks. We were growing at like 25 per-
> cent a year, selling at some ridiculous multiple peaks. I think one time
> it was forty-five times earnings in the late nineties . . . Our message
> has always been the same: we're going to do things right by the long
> term. It just so happened that the right thing for the long term didn't
> preclude us growing out our business and growing our bottom line
> well too. [During those years], as we matured a little bit, we decided,
> "We're going to ramp up our expansion in new markets [and] we're
> going to continue to grow."
>
> A combination of things happened in 2002–2003: we doubled our
> rate of expansion, almost exclusively in new markets. You know, we
> went from twenty-four states to thirty-seven states, and virtually every

one of those cities in those states we had not been in and Sam's had been in for fifteen years. So yeah, generally those markets were tougher, and we lost money in the first couple of years . . . We said the next year's [growth] will probably be, you know, 10 or 12 [percent], because we're going to be wrapping up expansion in a lot of new markets. Well in fact, instead of being 10 or 12 [percent growth] for two years in a row, it was –4 and +12.[48]

Wall Street responded quickly and negatively to this decline. It had tolerated the higher wages and benefits in the past because the growth had been 25 percent a year, but as soon as Costco faced a downturn, even though it was temporary due to the start-up costs of expansion, Wall Street exerted immense pressure. Deutsche Bank analyst Bill Dreher said in a 2004 *BusinessWeek* article, "At Costco, it's better to be an employee or a customer than a shareholder."[49] Large institutional investors grew impatient as well. Costco's stock price experienced serious hits, dropping 19 percent in one day. Galanti knew that they couldn't sit on these losses. Analyzing the situation, he saw that some of the factors contributing to this downturn were inevitable, such as the costs of starting up in a new, highly competitive market, and some were beyond the company's control, such as the increasing cost of energy. However, other supplementary expenses came into question, such as the rising cost of health care.

For more than a decade, increases in the cost of health insurance had far outstripped inflation in the United States. In 1993, Costco had been asking employees to pay 12 percent of the cost of their health insurance. Despite the marked rise in the cost of health care, the employee dollar contribution hadn't increased, and by 2003, employees were paying less than 5 percent of the cost of their insurance. Galanti summarized the situation: "Of course, Wall Street is saying, 'Give me a break! Fine, be good to your employees, but this is ridiculous!'"[50] But Sinegal recognized that the rapidly rising cost of health care was far more problematic for his employees than it was for the company.

In the end, a compromise was reached: over the course of four years, employee contributions would gradually be increased to 10 percent, which was still less than half of the amount required by most large companies. By this time many small companies were no longer even offering insurance. Readjusted health costs were enough for Wall Street to feel it had seen some response. After another year in the new markets, Costco's earnings began to rise again. The company had weathered the storm with its employee wages and most of its fundamental working conditions intact.

Sinegal was well aware that if he wanted to stay in business, he had to maintain an equilibrium between providing good wages and benefits and succeeding economically. He firmly believed that Costco's good working conditions ultimately made the company more profitable, but he also knew that there were limits to the affordability of wage increases:

> Now if we went crazy and said, 'We're going to start paying our people $35 an hour and we're going to provide health care [free] to everyone [including retirees], pretty soon we're in big trouble. You see what's happening to the auto companies today: who was able to forecast thirty or forty years ago that these retirees, when they got out of the business at fifty-five, were going to live for another thirty-five years and they'd have to provide health care for them? And not only that, but that health care was going to grow at double-digit rates for ten to fifteen years in a row? So there's a limit to what you can do, and you always . . . have that responsibility of taking a look at it and making sure what you're doing is sensible, that you haven't gone nuts. [The] worst thing in the world we could do is go crazy with wages and jeopardize the jobs of 135,000 people in this company. We have that responsibility and we have a responsibility to the shareholders. But having said that, you also have an obligation to those people to provide good livings for them . . . and provide an opportunity for them to buy a home and an opportunity for them to send their kids to school, and you have to take care of their families with health care, and provide good jobs so that if they want to, they can progress and grow with us.[51]

In the end, Wall Street rewarded Costco with a share price that had a higher price-to-earnings ratio than that of most companies. CFO Richard Galanti explained that the stock rebounded as buyers considered the value of the company:

> What we've shown is that we are a for-profit company. We believe in what we're doing to take care of our customers, take care of our employees. Ultimately if we do all of those things—respect our suppliers, respect the law, and all those things—shareholders will be taken care of. They'll be rewarded. Well, that's noble and correct, but most

[people] on Wall Street aren't noble. They want to know what you can do for them today. And what we've shown over the last few years is that we can do both.[52]

Costco became highly valued because its long-term strategy of investing in employees succeeded economically with higher returns per employee and per square foot. Moreover, the corporate social responsibility meant the firm was exposed to less financial risk. Companies like Nike experienced a significant falloff in earnings when they were found to be involved with sweatshops. Seemingly lucrative investments in companies like Enron evaporated due to corruption. Companies like Costco have made it clear that they can have high wages *and* high stock prices because the better working conditions lead to lower recruitment costs, higher retention rates, higher productivity, and greater firm reputation. Jay Tihinen reported with a smile, "I think it's funny. Over the last couple of years we've seen a change: It used to be, 'It's better to be a member or an employee of Costco than to be a shareholder,' but you're seeing suddenly—with the negative press that our competition has gotten . . . that we've gotten such good press for being a good employer. I've seen a total change in the articles about us. Instead of being viewed as a negative, now it's viewed as a positive that we're a good corporate citizen."[53]

Making Wages and Rewards Earn Dividends

It is clear that wages can be a primary tool for improving recruitment and retention and for incentivizing productivity. Wages can also be used as incentives for improving quality and reducing error rates. Given these potential benefits, why is it so common for so-called low-skilled workers to receive wages that are too low for them to live on? The companies in our study clearly demonstrated the strong economic returns that can be reaped by providing decent wages to the least-advantaged workers. Both American Apparel and Jenkins Brick saw substantial increases in their productivity once they had implemented their incentives policies. Costco reaped similar results through a salary scale that made them an employer of choice.

There are, however, real obstacles to structuring wages well so that they can benefit the company and its employees simultaneously. First, in a number of companies, corporate management culture has assumed that positive incentives are more important for high-level employees than for low-level employees. In spite of all the research and practical evidence regarding the effectiveness of positive incentives, these firms have historically developed practices that primarily rely on punitive measures. Moreover, some union and labor organizations as well as managerial associations have opposed differential pay based on productivity.

Second, beyond the institutionalized opposition, structuring wages well is not a straightforward process. As in any setting, for the rewards to be effective, the company needs to have clearly set goals. There must be a detailed understanding on the part of both management and employees of the actions that employees can take to help firms meet their goals. The actions need to be feasible and the metrics for measuring employees' progress need to be appropriate and transparent. The incentives need to be aligned with these metrics as well as with the company's ultimate goals. At Jenkins Brick, the goal for workers like Miguel Mendez was clear: move as many bricks as possible per hour without injury to the worker or damage to the bricks. Yet, as demonstrated by the three volumes of notebooks listing all the company's incentives and as explained by CFO Tommy Andreades, getting the incentives to work for every employee required time as well as a strong understanding of the role of individual employees within the firm.

At American Apparel, one of the most important insights Marty Bailey offered was that the incentives need to ensure not only that individual employees perform well, but also that they encourage collaboration between workers. Teamwork is an essential part of effective production, customer service, sales, and other operations in the majority of market sectors. When incentives are aimed only at individual workers, there is always the potential for individuals to increase their own metrics by cutting corners at the expense of their coworkers, thus decreasing the firm's overall productivity or product quality. It is therefore as critical to effectively structure incentives to foster collaboration across individuals and across divisions in the company as it is to align the metrics for individuals with the company's goals.

Third, the system of rewards and incentives needs to be equitable across employees. Before Bailey improved the American Apparel system, it not only inadvertently provided disincentives for effective teamwork but also led to great dissatisfaction among employees, who saw what they perceived as unfair disparities in the incentives received by those cutting garments, stitching seams, and putting in buttons and zippers.

While many of the elements of effective rewards systems are common up and down the corporate ladder, there are some unique considerations at this level. Adequate living wages must be guaranteed to all employees before developing incentives. The wage floor needs to be adequate for individual workers and be sustainable for the company in the environment in which it is competing.

Finally, when base salaries are raised substantially as they were at Costco, the corporate strategy through which this will raise productivity needs to be clearly thought out. Costco competed on having the lowest prices but also on having the highest-quality experience. By attracting, retaining, and motivating the best employees for the position, Costco was able to create an experience that attracted customers who could buy luxury items as well as essential commodities. This resulted in a high net sales per employee and more than paid for their higher salaries.

In short, translating higher earnings for the lowest-level employees into company profits requires establishing clear, strategic priorities; turning those strategic priorities into actionable steps at all levels of the firm; providing employees with the training and the work environment they need to realistically be able to succeed in reaching these goals; and finding a fair, transparent, and accurate way to measure the success of the incentives. While skill and follow-up are required in addressing these issues, the companies we studied make it abundantly clear that there are substantial economic returns to finding a way to make the wage and work structure more effective. By combining improved work organization with well-thought-out incentives, they increased the productivity of their existing employees two- to threefold. Their subsequent recruitment efforts demanded far fewer advertising and marketing resources. These companies had their choice of the best employees available in their sectors, and this in turn further increased productivity and product quality.

2

Finding Ways to Make Scheduling Flexibility Feasible and Profitable

Despite their proven importance to the health and well-being of workers and their families, work-related benefits such as paid sick leave, paid leave to care for family members, and scheduling flexibility are not always guaranteed, even in rich nations. In 2007, over 40 percent of workers in the United States lacked access to paid sick leave, while less than 10 percent had access to paid leave to care for family members.[1] Although the least-advantaged workers stand to benefit from these conditions the most, they consistently have less access to leave and flexibility than high-income workers. According to data from the U.S. Bureau of Labor Statistics, in 2006 only 45 percent of blue-collar workers had access to paid sick leave, compared to 72 percent of white-collar workers. At the same time, 39 percent of workers with a college education had flexible schedules, compared to 18 percent of workers with less than a high school diploma and 23 percent of workers with a high school education but no college.[2] In Canada, while 89 percent of workers earning $20 an hour or more received nonwage benefits such as sick leave and parental leave, only 42.4 percent of workers earning $12 an hour or less received such benefits.[3] It is often asked whether it is even feasible, let alone affordable, to introduce flexibility in jobs at the bottom of the ladder.

Understanding flexibility and leave has been one of the themes at the core of our North American and global studies over the past fifteen years.

The findings have been strikingly similar across tens of thousands of households and across five continents: low-level employees are far less likely to have any kind of paid sick leave; paid annual leave; ability to set their own work hours; and flexibility to care for their own health or that of their children, or for aging parents. It is often assumed that lack of flexibility is inherent in the type of work these employees perform. For this reason, we were particularly interested in studying flexibility and leave in those jobs where managers often contend they are most difficult to provide: manufacturing jobs. In this chapter, we examine the experiences of factory line workers and managers at all levels in two firms that provided great flexibility at the bottom of the corporate ladder: Autoliv Australia, a manufacturer of automobile safety devices, and Isola, a producer of roofing materials.

Autoliv Australia: Designing Flexibility on the Factory Floor

Autoliv Australia is the Australian branch of the Swedish multinational Autoliv, the world's number one supplier of automobile seat belts and air bags. With a global market share of over 33 percent in 2007, Autoliv had global sales of over US$6 billion, employed nearly forty thousand people, and operated in thirty countries. Autoliv Australia produces safety components for many of the world's major automobile companies, including Ford, Toyota, Hyundai, Mitsubishi, Holden, and Kia. Its annual sales in 2004 were AU$260 million; the company had almost 100 percent of domestic market share, and it exported 40 percent of its business, primarily to South Korea.[4]

Autoliv Australia operated in a country that guaranteed its workers little leave or scheduling flexibility. For example, at the time of our interviews Australia was one of the few countries in the world that did not guarantee paid maternity or parental leave; instead, all families were entitled to a lump sum payment upon the birth or adoption of a child. Providing a child grant to all parents regardless of their employment status can arguably be considered an equitable form of distribution; however, based on the average weekly wage of AU$885 in February 2008, the child check was equivalent to less than six weeks' full-time salary.[5] In contrast, 170 countries around the world provided more than six weeks of paid maternity leave. In a wide range of areas, Autoliv Australia's flexibility and leave policies clearly far exceeded government requirements. They were the product of the company's own initiatives and of their commitment to providing good working conditions.

As general manager of Autoliv Australia, Bob Franklin needed the company to have high levels of quality—fundamental to the safety sector—and productivity—essential to the increasingly competitive automobile industry.[6] To achieve these goals, he knew that he had to find a way to attract and retain successful employees. When Franklin arrived, the firm had unmotivated employees and unnecessary turnover. During our first visit in 2005 he explained:

> What we identified in my early days here [was that] we were an organization that had very good technology both in product and process . . . [but] we looked at things like absenteeism [and] turnover, [personnel problem indicators, and they] were significantly higher than what we would have liked. We said, What can we do to have some impact in those areas? And we came up with . . . our Employer of Choice strategy, which was a way of trying to say, How can we make sure that we can first attract the very best people to our organization? What would make them want to come and work for us rather than go and work for some of the larger brand names that are in this particular area? And then once we've got them, if the nature of our work means that it takes us two or three years to train them to a level where we think we'll really have [an employee working] at a superior level, how do we then make sure that we keep them?[7]

Like many other companies, Autoliv Australia began offering rewards for strong performance. When Franklin began a dialogue with employees at a staff meeting about rewards, he discovered the importance they placed on flexibility and time off:

> When I started off, I said, "Whenever we get a major award or something, let's buy a small gift for our people." And after I'd done that seven or eight times, I ran out of ideas. So in one of my communication sessions with the employees, I said to them, "I'm stuck for an idea for a gift. So if anyone wants to give me an idea, I'll think about it." And one of the women in the front row put her hand up and said, "What about giving us some time off?" And I said to them, "What would you think if I said you could all have Friday afternoon off?" And the cheer that went up . . . was deafening! It was unbelievable, the

response. And I was really intrigued by this. So I walked around and I spent a lot of time on the shop floor talking to people, trying to understand what their issues are. And it became really obvious that [flexibility and leave were] pretty good issue[s] for them.[8]

As workers spoke up, Franklin began to realize that time was their most valued asset. They wanted the option of starting their shifts later and they requested flexible leave policies. Franklin began to develop these policies one at a time, noting afterwards that "it wasn't that difficult once you got started." Over time, Autoliv Australia developed a whole series of options that provided employees with greater scheduling flexibility than other factories.

Franklin and his team based all of their decisions on the fundamental principle of providing equal access to benefits, leave, and flexibility policies to everyone in the company, from workers on the factory line through to top management. Cheryl Woollard, the director of human resources, explained that the firm did not focus on benefits that either could only be made available to a few employees or were only likely to benefit those at the top of the ladder. For example, other companies offered concierge services that made dry cleaning easier to obtain, but this was rarely used by factory workers whose uniforms did not necessitate it and whose budgets could not afford it. When it came to flexible scheduling, Autoliv ensured factory workers had as many options as managers.

Although Autoliv Australia is part of a large multinational, the Australian branch had been granted a significant degree of independence to experiment with new policies.[9] Moreover, the parent company was Swedish and accustomed to providing benefits such as parental and sick leave and so was supportive of Franklin's initiatives. As Franklin explained: "When it comes to some of the big-ticket items like maternity leave, parental leave, carer's leave, and some of those issues, they're no-brainers for the guys in Sweden. Because they kind of say, 'Don't you have that already? Isn't it provided within your society somehow?' And when you say to them, 'No, it's not. It's not funded by the government or by the community, and we think it's something we should look into doing,' you just don't get any sense of questioning."[10]

Uncommon Amounts of Leave and Flexibility for Lowest-Level Employees

Several of the forms of flexibility and leave provided by Autoliv Australia could be found frequently in other workplaces around the world. What made its policies unique was the fact that paid leave was combined with flexibility and that it was provided to the least-advantaged workers in the manufacturing industry, where these benefits are relatively rare, in a country that did not require such guarantees.

Autoliv provided five days of sick leave for workers to care for their own health or the health of their families, and this amount increased to eight days after one year of employment with the company. The firm offered financial incentives for workers not to use their sick leave unnecessarily; at the end of each year of employment, workers were paid for any sick leave they had accrued over 150 hours. The company also paid 50 percent of all accrued sick leave upon termination, with the exception of dismissals for misconduct.

In addition to sick leave, Autoliv offered paid maternity leave to all female employees with at least twelve consecutive months of service. Employees who had worked at Autoliv for one to three years received ten weeks of paid maternity leave, and those who had worked there for over three years got fourteen weeks. As with sick leave, Autoliv Australia considered incentives carefully when constructing this benefit. Workers received the majority of their maternity leave payments at the beginning of the leave, and the remainder after they returned to work. The company structured the payment in this way to decrease the likelihood of women not returning to work after their paid maternity leave. Autoliv Australia also provided five days of paid paternity leave, which could be broken up or used consecutively.

In addition to the four weeks of paid annual leave that all workers in Australia received, Autoliv provided twelve "rostered days off" (RDOs) per year. Employees worked forty hours a week, and for each eight-hour shift, they received a "credit" of twenty-four minutes; these credits accumulated to make up the monthly RDO.

Autoliv was also committed to granting workers greater flexibility and control over their schedules. In 2007, production employees could choose from four different start times for their shifts: 6, 7, 8, and 9 a.m. Franklin explained how Autoliv Australia had been able to provide this type of flexibility:

> We don't offer flexitime where they can arrive whenever they like. But what we do is we surveyed the workforce [and] found out what sort of times they'd like to start, and then we said, OK, there's a group that wants to start early, some as early as six in the morning, because

they've got a husband or someone to look after the kids in the morning but they want to be there at two so they can be there for the kids. We've got another group that would like to start at seven, another group at eight, [and] another group at eight thirty or nine. So we said, well let's break our factory up into departments that work those hours. And then let's find a way that we can move people through cross-training so that they can then apply for jobs in the area that works the hours that suit them. And while a new entrant might not find a job in the right area on day one, what we say to them is that the first opportunity that comes up, they can move into that area. So by and large we're able to provide the kind of flexibility they need without any cost to ourselves. It works really well.[11]

Having flexibility in start times was particularly important for parents, since it allowed them to get their children to school in the morning or to be home when they returned in the afternoon. Sarah Ellis used to start work at 7 a.m., but her asthmatic son had a particularly difficult time in the mornings. She therefore began coming in at 8 a.m. instead so that she could care for her son before he went to school.

It was the combination of paid leave and flexibility that made the biggest difference to employees. When Susan Curran, a production worker and mother of two, told us how she had benefited from Autoliv's maternity leave, she made it clear that the leave's value was greatly enhanced by being able to work part-time hours during her pregnancy and after returning from maternity leave.

RDOs were particularly valued by employees when unexpected personal and family needs arose. When Alicia Clark's washing machine had suddenly broken down and flooded her home two weeks before we spoke, her supervisor had allowed her to take an RDO on short notice. Similarly, when other employees had trouble finding a babysitter, they were permitted to use RDOs on short notice. At no extra cost to the company, this flexibility markedly improved the quality of employees' lives.

Line worker Demet Songun told us how Autoliv's sick leave policy and flexibility had made it possible for her to keep her job despite a serious illness. Songun emigrated from Turkey and began working at Autoliv in 1989. It had taken her nearly ten years to get the job she desired within the company: in 1998, Songun was promoted to team leader. Autoliv had become her home-away-from-home. "I spend more time here than at home.

We are like a family here," she explained.[12] In 2000, Songun was diagnosed with breast cancer. She had surgery, was hospitalized twice, took six months off for chemotherapy, and then six weeks for radiotherapy. Much of Songun's leave was income-protected due to the lengthy amount of sick leave she had accumulated at Autoliv. When she was ready to return to work, she was offered the option of coming back on light duty. She started off working four hours, then worked her way up to six, and finally got back to an eight-hour day. Without Autoliv's leave policies, she would not have been able to keep her job during the treatment for breast cancer. These leave and flexibility policies meant that Autoliv Australia was able to retain employees such as Songun, who might otherwise have left the company when experiencing health problems. While Songun clearly benefited from this continuity of employment, Autoliv Australia also stood to gain from her long-term experience, skills, and commitment.

Esma Erzen's experience similarly showed how long good employees stayed with Autoliv because of the difference the company's policies made in their daily lives as well as in the event of a personal crisis. Erzen had moved back and forth between Australia and Turkey until she reached adulthood. As a young adult, Erzen took a job at Autoliv because she had heard good things about working there, and she had stayed with the company for eleven years because they had been good to her throughout all the transitions in her life. Erzen had two daughters, and she'd been able to take a year off for each birth; fourteen weeks had been paid maternity leave and the rest job-secured unpaid leave. When she returned to work, she was able to work shorter hours. At the time of our interview she was working 9:30 a.m. to 3 p.m. so that she could drop her daughter off and pick her up from school. Erzen had no problem taking five days off when her father-in-law became ill and died. She found her work on the airbag production line to be "very easy . . . [and] basic," but the fact that she rotated positions every hour prevented it from getting boring and enabled her to remain attentive and alert. The year after we interviewed her, she planned to extend her hours to 7 a.m. to 3 p.m. in order to increase her salary; although her $17 an hour wages were comparably high, her family could still benefit from the extra money. Erzen commented on the importance of management's accessibility and involvement with the workers: "The management always comes down and asks how you are."[13] Workers believed that management sincerely cared how they were doing. She summarized: "The conditions at work matter more than [the money] you are making."

Innovative Forms of Leave and Flexibility

Autoliv effectively ensured that all its workers had access to regular forms of flexibility and leave, but the company also went well beyond most other firms by setting up truly innovative and creative forms of leave. In particular, Autoliv Australia had found ways for line workers to take additional annual leave and sabbaticals.

Employees were given the option of taking more annual leave through the 50/52 plan, which entitled them to an extra two weeks off by getting paid 96.15 percent of their salary for fifty-two weeks of the year. Richard McAllister, a maintenance worker, told us how he made use of this plan and what this leave option meant for him: "I'll use it to spend time with my family and work around the house. It's the only place I've ever worked that had the option. I wish I'd had the option when my kids were younger."[14]

Autoliv also helped employees to take sabbaticals. The company gave employees thirteen weeks of paid leave after ten years of continuous service. Employees were given the option of taking their leave as thirteen weeks at regular pay or as double the time (twenty-six weeks) at half pay.

Beyond earning long-service leave, employees could choose to receive 80 percent of their regular salary for four years in exchange for taking one year off. Another option allowed them to spread five years' salary over six years. Cheryl Woollard disagreed with other companies' contention that this kind of extended leave was too disruptive: "What kind of succession planning are you doing if someone gives you three years' notice that they're going to take a year off and you can't replace them?"[15]

Stories and anecdotes from Autoliv workers exemplify how they have benefited from these leave policies at different points in their lives. Alicia Clark, a production operator, had been working at Autoliv making seatbelts for Toyota vehicles for nearly seven years. She had started working at Autoliv as soon as her son was in school full time. Her son was now thirteen, and her twenty-year-old daughter had already given her a grandson. When asked what the best thing was about working at Autoliv, Clark didn't hesitate: "It's flexible. They understand when you have family needs or personal problems."[16] Clark had taken advantage of some of the different kinds of flexibility that were unique to Autoliv. The year before we spoke with her, she had used the 50/52 plan; she and her husband had never taken a honeymoon, and they decided to go to Malaysia and Singapore to celebrate their twentieth anniversary. She was considering using the 50/52 again the following year. In regard to the slight reduction in pay it entailed, Clark explained that "if you have two hours of overtime, you earn it back . . . [and] if not, it doesn't make much difference."[19] Overtime was frequently available on the Toyota seatbelt line. Clark's satisfaction was only one example of Autoliv workers' appreciation for the company's flexibility, which had made a great difference in their lives, and as a result had led them to want to stay at the company long term.

The Challenges and Advantages of Implementing Paid Leave and Flexibility

Setting up flexibility policies means overcoming preconceived notions about scheduling limitations in manufacturing. Many companies contend that flexibility and leave policies are not viable in this industry due to the nature of the work. Though Autoliv's management disagreed, they did confront some challenges when implementing these policies.

Seamus Power, general manager in manufacturing, explained that the key to making this work was having employees be flexible in terms of the factory lines they worked. The necessary restructuring "is free [except for training]. It just takes a bit of time to organize it. And there's a massive pay-off."[18] In order to implement the flexibility policies without disrupting production, employees had to be trained for work in different assembly lines. Since each auto company's products have a unique production process, it can take several months to get employees trained to work on several lines.

Additionally, as midlevel manager Marcella Romano explained, managers had faced a steep learning curve as they figured out how to switch staff around to cover for absences.[19] Despite the challenges associated with initiating these policies, Autoliv management felt they were worthwhile considering how much the company stood to gain in terms of lower turnover and a more motivated and productive workforce. Leny Plonsker, employee relations manager, summarized Autoliv's philosophy:

> Other companies see HR as an expense, [but] it's not . . . If you put money into your assets, your machinery, buildings, and all that, you have to invest in people. But people are not the same as machinery. It's very important. Without the people, there would be no production. And then if people are leaving, what does that come to? Cost— because you're gonna be retraining people. [But] other companies don't see that side. They see HR as having no value. But you actually

have to cost and evaluate a situation so you can say, "This is how much it will cost us to implement, for example, training. How much will it cost us if we don't implement it?"[20]

Autoliv saw a huge reduction in employee turnover after it implemented the new policies, with turnover rates dropping from 15 to 20 percent down to approximately 3 percent. Between 1998 and 2000, the turnover rate dropped to an unprecedented 0.4 percent. In 2005, it was back up to 3.6 percent, still a very low rate for the industry. The company also had many "boomerang" employees, a term they used to describe workers who had left the company to earn a better salary elsewhere, but had then returned to Autoliv once they realized that other workplaces did not offer the same benefits. Ashley Roberts, a production worker, told us how she had left Autoliv for another job but had returned after only a month.

The bottom line was that Autoliv's flexibility policies were inexpensive in relation to the benefits the company reaped by being able to retain qualified, experienced workers. Franklin explained:

> From a business-case point of view, so far we've spent nothing on these programs at all. It's taken a little bit of time and effort in terms of management, but in terms of dollar outlay, it hasn't cost us anything, or virtually nothing. And yet the benefit in taking our turnover in people from 15 percent to virtually zero is enormous . . . Let's say nine hundred people [are] here at the moment. Even if you said a hundred of those people were getting replaced every year, our estimates are that it costs us at least six months' salary over the first two years to bring those people up to the level of the person they're replacing. So one hundred people by . . . let's say $25,000 AUD [Australian dollars] for six months—that's a lot of money that we'd be spending on simply replacing and then retraining new employees. So the bottom-line benefit to the company was enormous. And I don't know how you get that for no money in any other way. It's a simple business case. An answer to a problem that we've all got. Just by providing some flexibility, you'll get an enormous result . . . One hundred people by $25,000 AUD a year is $2.5 million AUD a year in savings that we get from not having to replace these people.[21]

Autoliv's low turnover rates clearly reflected employees' satisfaction with the company, as did the results of the firm's regular surveys of the workforce. In December of 2004, 85 percent of employees agreed with the statement, "Overall, I am satisfied with Autoliv Australia as an employer"; 84 percent said, "I enjoy working here"; and 81 percent said, "I would recommend Autoliv to my family and friends."[22]

High levels of employee satisfaction made recruitment, as well as retention, easier. Moreover, although the cross-training and organizational changes were an initial challenge, they ultimately helped to increase productivity during inevitable absences due to illness. Cross-training also made production much more efficient since employees could cover for each other if someone had to leave early, and they could easily make up for time they had missed during the week. Finally, cross-training made it easier for the company to keep up with customers' changing demands since employees could be switched to different assembly lines according to production needs.

Although Bob Franklin saw these policies as straightforward, his peers saw them as wishful thinking. Franklin described his conversations with colleagues in the industry:

> I'm fairly active in our industry association here in Australia . . . and going back two or three years ago I used to get beaten up because of the sort of precedents we were setting in the industry. And they said, "Bob, how can you offer maternity? Do you realize now we'll all have to offer it? How can you do that? Have you thought about the costs associated with that?" And I said, "No, funny, I haven't. I really just thought about the benefits, because the cost is inconsequential to me." . . . There's an increasing number of people who are starting to realize that [providing leave and flexibility to attract and retain employees is] such an important part of [a successful] business mix that I think they're starting to reconsider it, even if they haven't gotten to the point of being brave enough to kick it off.[23]

Benefits in an Adverse Economic Climate

Autoliv Australia had implemented leave and flexibility benefits as incentives to reduce turnover rates and improve recruitment and retention, thereby lowering costs and increasing productivity and the quality of production. Its policies proved to be effective not only during a positive economic climate, but also when the company faced worsening economic conditions.

Autoliv Australia's future was deeply tied to that of the Australian automotive industry. As long as Australian car companies sourced locally, Autoliv Australia had almost 100 percent market share. The company faced some critical economic challenges, however, when firms began making sourcing decisions on a global scale and moving production overseas in order to lower costs.

As a result of being a model employer, for years Autoliv had successfully competed locally by achieving high levels of quality in an industry concerned with safety and error rates. Then came what Franklin described as the "rude shock" of losing GM, a company that had previously been a major loyal customer. Instead of basing sourcing decisions on its long-term relationships with suppliers or on the quality of their products, GM gave Autoliv an ultimatum: "You need to supply for x price," or else the company would source in another country.[24] Since Autoliv Australia couldn't meet the price demanded, GM decided to source from South Africa and China, where labor costs were lower.

While other manufacturers tried to hide their losses from their workers for fear of a strike, Franklin told everyone at the plant as soon as he found out they had lost the GM contract in February of 2004. Approximately six hundred line workers had to be laid off at Autoliv over the span of two years, and given the culture and the openness of the workplace, the loss was felt by everyone within the organization. Demet Songun spoke to us about how she and other production line workers felt about the layoffs, and about their concerns regarding the company's financial viability: "It did hurt. I [shed] a few tears as I thought to myself, 'Are we going to pull this off or be shut down?' . . . When someone has been here fifteen years—and I have been here seventeen—you think about it. When they downsized Ford, it makes you think. That affects us, as we do business for them. Bob is good about communicating. He told us a couple of years ago what was going on. It helps us prepare ourselves, but [we] still don't feel it fully till it hits. It's losing loved ones."[25]

Autoliv set up programs to help laid-off employees find new jobs by providing them with vocational training and access to help from a placement firm. Laid-off workers also received severance pay proportional to their length of service. Bob Franklin explained the situation:

We're already talking to people right now about how we can help with the transition. We work with a company here that does all of our recruitment for us, and they themselves recognize the skills that the people within this organization have . . . As well as that, for the past couple years—as we've known this was inevitable—we have been trying to provide more vocational training, more opportunities, and more skills for the people in the organization so they can prepare themselves. And we'll do more over the next year to make sure that they're in a good position to be going forward.[26]

Suddenly facing the pressures associated with offshoring in the global-ized economy, Autoliv Australia had to reexamine its business strategy. The company had to decide whether to keep manufacturing in Australia, and if it chose to do so, whether to keep its wage, benefits, and flexibility policies. Other Australian industry leaders were putting pressure on Franklin to offer fewer benefits since they were also being pressured by purchasers to cut costs. These companies wanted to take a unified stance by lowering their employee benefits, and they urged Franklin to do the same. He recalled: "People beat me up. They demanded, 'How can we afford to provide these conditions?' My answer to them was that if we don't, we are dead."[27] Auto-liv's response was characteristic of its reputation as a company; it decided that providing good benefits was not negotiable. Franklin explained: "[Get-ting rid of these benefits] would be like throwing the baby out with the bathwater. We recognize that these things have given us enormous benefit. As soon as we lose the value of that by trying to be mean and stingy . . . we'll lose any competitive advantage we've got, and I think it would be suicide."[28]

While fighting an external battle with competitors, Franklin was also fighting an internal battle with headquarters about whether or not they should move all of their plants offshore. The company inevitably had to reexamine its strategy. The most labor-intensive manufacturing, such as the production of seat belt retractors, was moved to low-cost countries, but other work, such as airbag production, remained in Australia, at least for the time being. Airbag materials were expensive, and labor costs made up only 2 to 3 percent of production costs. There was less incentive to move this production offshore since it would risk increasing production errors due to the lack of experience in a new factory, decreasing the com-pany's ability to deliver on time, and increasing transportation expenses, all without substantially reducing total production costs.

Survival in the new economic climate required flexibility; workers who remained at Autoliv often needed to alter their roles as the company tried to compete by changing and reducing its production lines. As the nature of their jobs evolved, workers faced the challenge of having to be more productive in their new positions. They told us how they had had to learn new tasks and adapt to new jobs. One worker explained how the company had brought in a new trainer to facilitate this transition. The adaptation was not easy, but employees' loyalty to the company made them willing to put in the extra effort. Sandra Taylor admitted that the adjustment had been difficult. Prior to the retrenchment, she had been a team leader, but she was now back to being a regular team member. She had ultimately decided to stay at Autoliv because she liked the people and the company's working conditions. She was still paid the same salary she had received as a team leader, but her wages would not increase until other line workers' earnings caught up.

In the end, Autoliv's policies helped ease the adaption process. Jasna Knezac, a production worker, explained that although people were worried about layoffs, they felt that they had been dealt with openly and honestly. The company had been able to adapt in large part because the workers supported the changes. Franklin was struck by how much the employees helped the company make it through this difficult time. In fact, Autoliv's quality performance improved from 2006 to 2007; the return rates on its parts decreased from 10 to 0.2 returns per million due to workers' commitment and to the quality of their work. Employees simply "didn't want to let the company down." In their exit interviews, Franklin explained, those who had been laid off frequently stated that "if a job opens up, they want to come back."[29]

Nearly three years after this downturn, Autoliv began winning business back from GM because Autoliv had higher quality and performance ratings than its competitors—essential factors in manufacturing safety devices. The technical support aspect of its business, which required more training, increased. Autoliv Australia's managers ultimately felt that they had advantages over their low-cost competitors, which justified keeping some of their production in Australia. They had an educated and well-trained workforce and a very high overall quality of production. In the long run, Franklin felt that these advantages would compensate for the higher labor costs:

> [Our advantages are] the quality [of our work] and our ability to be agile, our ability to introduce change quickly, our ability to respond to the customer's needs in a much better way, the quality of our people

on the shop floor . . . We've grown this business five times, but we basically haven't increased the management staff at all. So what we've done is simply relied on the skills of the people on the shop floor to run the business . . . They're extremely capable people. What we're finding when we go to places like China . . . is you have to put in an enormous amount of cost in terms of management overhead. My view is when people start to experience the problems with producing in low-cost countries, they'll find that it doesn't bring the sorts of returns that they're hoping for. I think we're going to have to ride out a pretty rough four to five years, but there'll be a place for us.[30]

To weather the storm, Autoliv would clearly need to undergo some restructuring. Cheryl Woollard shared her thoughts on the future of the company:

> The company will change. There'll be a different emphasis. But we see ourselves like . . . a technical support center of excellence for Asia-Pacific, so a training ground, a teaching ground, almost like a "best-practice center." A lot of the things that we do in manufacturing—like the way that we treat employees and that employees are developed here—is seen as a benchmark. So I do a lot of coaching of the other HR practitioners in the area, [and] our technical people do a lot of support for the regional auto testing . . . You have to reinvent yourself. You have to have the technology value-add or the intellectual value-add. So what happens is that usually in low-labor-cost countries, the cost of capital is high. So things that require capital and high technology like our test centers, our airbag manufacturing, they make sense to have here—at least in the next five years, and probably ongoing in the future. The things that are mainly dependent on labor . . . will go offshore. So we will be a smaller company, but incredibly profitable, because you actually make more money on airbags than you do on seatbelts.[31]

While the company's future remained uncertain at the time of our interviews in 2005 and 2006, one thing was clear: Autoliv Australia had fared better than other branches of the multinational and than other high-wage companies facing similar challenges. Autoliv's U.K. branch had already closed down because it had been unable to restructure.

Far from suffering financially as a result of its policies, Autoliv reaped marked gains from its employee benefits and policies, including having lower turnover rates when the economy was strong, workers who were willing to adapt and were knowledgeable of different positions when globalization threatened production and required restructuring, and consistently high levels of productivity and quality control.

Isola: Meeting and Exceeding National Requirements

While Autoliv Australia needed to develop most of its own leave and flexibility policies since it operates in a country with few governmental requirements, other companies, such as Isola in Norway, operate in countries that have more governmental requirements, such as legislated guarantees for paid leave and flexibility to meet personal health needs and the needs of family members. It is equally important to understand the practical and financial implications of these legislated requirements.

Manufacturing roofing supplies in Norway, Isola had to produce and remain competitive while complying with some of the highest wages and most generous benefits standards in the world. Founded in 1940, Isola produced a range of products, including metal and asphalt roof shingles and steel and PVC gutters. The company expanded in the 1980s and 1990s, and in 2009, it had a total of six factories in Norway in addition to factories in Hungary and the Czech Republic. Isola sold its products in Sweden, the United Kingdom, the United States, Canada, Spain, Hungary, Belgium, Denmark, Finland, Poland, and the Czech Republic.

National laws guarantee every Norwegian worker at least five weeks of paid annual leave, and workers over the age of sixty-two are guaranteed six weeks. Workers are guaranteed up to one year of sick leave to meet personal health needs in addition to ten to thirty days a year to care for family members' health. Parents are entitled to a range of benefits: new parents can receive up to twelve months of paid leave at a wage replacement rate of 80 percent or full pay for forty-two weeks, and mothers may leave for breastfeeding.[32] From a business perspective, what does this mean for the work and personal lives of the employees, for the quality and quantity of their work, and for the efficiency and productivity of the firms they work for?

Flexibility and Leave: What Isola Provides

We first met with Isola CEO Erik Withbro in 2006, the day of his return from a three-week vacation, which he had mostly spent on the beach with his children and grandchildren. The company hadn't needed the CEO's assistance during those three weeks given that the entire factory was closed. By law, all companies in Norway had to provide a two-week summer vacation between June 1 and September 1. Even though summer is the high season for construction, construction-related companies, including Isola, had to comply as well. The company had the option of staggering the holidays of individual workers and running the factory at a lower production level, but Isola felt it was more efficient to simply close the whole factory down at one time.

Though many of Isola's leave policies were guaranteed by law to all workers in Norway, the company went beyond legal requirements in a number of ways. For example, although Norwegian employees over the age of sixty-two are legally guaranteed six weeks' vacation, Isola added a seventh week for these employees. Isola also added one extra week to the guaranteed two weeks of summer vacation for all workers—all Isola factories shut down for three weeks in July.

Isola employees repeatedly remarked that the company stands out from other employers by making it easy for workers to use their leave and by trying to accommodate their scheduling needs whenever possible. Terje Udeng, the plant manager at Eidanger, explained Isola's attitude toward employees: "If they need to . . . go to their parents' because they are sick or something, we always make that happen . . . The operators also know that if they work an extra shift, sometimes they don't put it in for pay, they can build up a time bank. An hour bank." Undeng went on to describe how workers would use that time bank for additional family or personal leave. When someone takes time off, he explained, "another one fill[s] in. So . . . in a way we help each other to make it happen."[33]

Implementing and going beyond Norway's flexibility and leave policies required Isola to cross-train employees so that leave did not lead to disruptions in production. As it did for Autoliv, the cross-training not only made leave and flexibility feasible at Isola, but it also benefited the firm financially because it strengthened the plant team's ability to continue to meet production deadlines when workers were sick. Moreover, cross-training strengthened teamwork on the plant floor by increasing employees' understanding of the challenges and constraints faced by their peers operating different segments of the production line.

Making Use of Flexibility and Leave: Employees' Experience

Having flexibility and leave proved to be just as important to the workers we spoke with in Norway as it was to those in Australia. While visiting Isola, we met with many workers who told us what a difference it had made in their lives to be able to take leave. This was true both for the forms of leave guaranteed by the government and for those implemented by the company. Johan Fosberg, a team leader with two children, had worked at Isola for twenty-five years. He spoke of his experience as a working parent: "I was a single parent and Isola helped me—I had only day shifts. I didn't have to work nights or afternoons."[34] Fosberg clearly felt that having this option had made a difference in his ability to care for his children. He added, "It was important to me that I could come in at 6 a.m. and take care of the kids after school. They weren't alone after school." Isola's flexibility also enabled him to take short-term leave to care for his children when they got sick: "I never had any problems with leaving work for sick kids. One of my friends [at work] has two small kids, and he never has a problem staying home either." Fosberg explained what the company's flexibility in accommodating employees' needs means for working parents more broadly: "Isola is a good place for people with families. We try to cover for each other when someone is having a family situation . . . and Isola tries to make the work-family balance better. You can get time off to meet with the school or a family partner. We all try to support each other."

Sigrid Lund was a truck driver who had been at Isola for twenty-five years. She had started at Isola when she was eighteen years old, expecting to be there for only three months, but she never left. "I haven't really tried anything but Isola, but compared to my friends' [experiences], it's nice [here]. It's open and there's lots of communication."[35] Lund explained how Isola had accommodated her health needs by allowing her to move to a regular day schedule when her doctor said she couldn't work other shifts anymore. Although not required by law, Isola was also flexible when she needed to change her work hours to care for her young son. Lund said, "They let me move from 7–3 to 8–4 so that I could take him to kinder-garten. They understood and supported me."

Flexibility also meant being able to accumulate hours to take time off when needed. Martin Ervik was a mechanic who had been at Isola for twenty-nine years and had two children aged seven and twelve. He had initially decided to work at Isola because of its good wages and working conditions, which he still regarded as important draws. Ervik explained: "They're very flexible here. There's a time account—if you work some overtime, you can take hours out as time off. Right now I'm using this time to pick my kid up after summer camp. You can also work the hours later to make up for lost time. A timestamp machine keeps track of the hours you work."[36] He had also been able to take leave when his wife was hospitalized: "I stayed home for five days, but I could have stayed home for ten days if I'd needed to."

Isola's Productivity and Profitability

Central to Isola's competitive strategy were two elements: producing a high-quality product that was both needed on the market and better than what was being produced elsewhere, and using teamwork and machinery to produce it more economically. (Note: Mechanization at Isola and its effect on employees will be discussed further in chapter 5).

Isola produced high-quality shingles and other roofing materials, a necessary product in Norway's harsh climate. Isola president Erik Withbro told us: "So long as Norway needs higher-quality products, we can compete. We invest a lot in modern technology and automate the process more."[37] There were several components to Isola's strategy of providing higher-quality products. First, Isola produced shingles that were easier for construction workers to use since they had better self adhesive; other roofing tiles took a long time to seal. In Norwegian weather you cannot easily wait long enough for lower-quality shingles to seal. Second, the contents of the tiles themselves were of higher quality. Because Isola used more bitumen and less filler in its asphalt, its shingles locked more effectively around nails and were more waterproof. Third, Isola took a "systems" approach. For example, the company recognized that a quality roof required ventilation that matched the shingles as well as a matching roof edge that fit snugly into the gutters; it therefore produced all three components and sold them together.

Creating high-quality products required a highly experienced workforce. While certain levels of turnover can be productive from the perspective of both the employee and the employer, turnover is costly when it benefits neither the career of the employee nor the skills and experience available to the firm. Whether developed by a firm or by the country in which it operates, paid leave and flexibility policies can prevent unproductive and needless turnover. Providing leave and flexibility means that workers don't have to leave their jobs as a result of sickness or care-giving

responsibilities, and that companies don't experience increased recruitment and training costs due to unwanted departures. For example, if a
man or a woman has two children during a period of high work-related
productivity and needs to switch jobs upon the arrival of each child, the
firm experiences a needless loss of expertise among its workforce. Similarly, it is costly to *both* company and employee if, simply because of scheduling difficulties, working parents of school-aged children are unable to
continue to work in a service center or factory for which they have developed many job-relevant skills. Clearly, both individuals and firms can benefit from turnover that is driven by reasons directly related to work
exigencies. Employees can find work that is better suited to their interests,
and firms can find employees whose skills better match their needs. This
generally occurs when there had been a poor fit between a position and
the employee's skills and interests to begin with, or when there are
changes in the employee's or the firm's goals.

Isola's flexibility and leave policies have led to greater employee loyalty
and retention. These policies were highly valued by Isola employees, who
repeatedly told us that the company had made it easier for them to care for
their families. Many of the company's policies are mandated by government regulations, but their implementation was enhanced by Isola's strong
belief in the importance of flexibility. Other policies were initiated by the
company, such as considering workers' needs when assigning shifts and
schedules. Together, these policies facilitated recruitment and retention for
Isola. Most of the workers we talked with had been there for a long time
and had every intention of remaining at the company.

Retention was important to Isola in several ways. First, its whole business was based on quality. Employees who had spent more time at the firm
had a greater understanding of and a deeper commitment to the desired
standards of quality. As CEO Erik Withbro explained: "Our employees,
they are so used to producing high quality, the cost of producing lower
quality is nearly the same because they cannot produce a lower-quality
[product] . . . they don't want to put it on the market."[38]

In many ways, Isola's long-term strategy was similar to that of Norway
as a whole: it reaped the benefits of its policies by having a more highly
trained and experienced workforce that efficiently produced high-quality
products.

Second, retention was extremely important to Isola due to safety. The
newest employees had some of the highest accident rates because they

were unfamiliar with the production process and safety procedures. All industrial accidents brought substantial financial risks to the firm, and the skills developed by experienced Isola employees were crucial to maintaining low accident rates and high performance. Third, leave and flexibility policies benefited the company by reducing the problems associated with presenteeism. While for years there have been concerns about the costs of absenteeism, more recent studies have demonstrated that having workers show up sick and spread diseases to their peers can have a substantial negative impact on production.[39] Leave and flexibility policies help prevent this problem by ensuring that workers who are present are healthy, alert, and capable of performing their jobs.

Broader Experience of Companies in Norway

Although Isola was clearly succeeding as a company, it would be reasonable to ask how most Norwegian firms were faring at remaining economically competitive with good guarantees of flexibility and leave as well as high minimum wages, among other social protections. Across competitiveness and employment indicators, Norway's private sector showed strong signs of success—Norwegian businesses were more successful at producing jobs, and the country was more successful at attracting business than most nations. A common criticism leveled at countries with high social protections and labor guarantees is that these measures are conducive to unemployment and to a less competitive economy. Yet over the past ten years, world business leaders have repeatedly ranked Norway among the top fifteen nations in terms of economic competitiveness, according to the World Economic Forum's Global Competitiveness Report.[40] The country's social policies do not appear to have had a negative impact on employment. Unemployment rates declined from 5.8 percent in 1990 to 4.4 percent in 2004, and then to 2.6 percent in 2008.[41]

Norwegian employers and employees alike benefited from having one of the healthiest, best-educated labor forces as a result of their good labor conditions and strong social supports. Norway ranked second in the United Nations Development Programme's Human Development Index and third in overall health achievement.[42] It also had one of the highest life expectancies in the world (79.8 years) and one of the lowest infant mortality rates (3/1000).[43]

Norway's economic and social success was not random or accidental, nor was it simply the result of the country's oil reserves; there are many resource-rich countries that have achieved nowhere near the same level of social and human development. Rather, it was the product of strategic economic policy, investments in good labor conditions that expanded their workforce, and investments in education and training, which raised workers' skill levels.

Extending Flexibility and Leave to the Least-Advantaged Workers

Whether offered as part of company policy or guaranteed by government regulations, there is no doubt that flexibility and leave make an enormous difference to the lives of working women and men around the world. The ability to take time off to meet family health needs or to deal with unforeseen emergencies without suffering financial penalties can transform families' lives as well.[44] As Autoliv Australia employees explained to their general manager, flexibility and leave can be among the most valuable benefits a company can offer.

It is frequently assumed that providing scheduling flexibility is beyond the capacity of companies employing workers in manufacturing because of work disruptions involved, and that paid leave is too costly relative to wages for those employing the least-advantaged workers. However, the companies profiled in this chapter show that flexibility and leave policies are viable across job positions and economic sectors, and that companies reap substantial rewards in productivity and quality gains from their implementation.

Isola and Autoliv Australia were unique because of their innovative approaches to making leave and flexibility available to the least-advantaged workers, who do not often have access to them. The benefits these companies experienced as a result confirm what research has demonstrated in settings where flexibility and leave have already been implemented: when workplaces are more supportive in terms of flexibility and leave, employees have higher levels of job satisfaction, which has a positive impact on retention and commitment. Flexible working time can lead to greater motivation, better customer relations, and improved productivity as a result of fewer mistakes resulting from fatigue.[45] Overall, the majority of companies that implement these policies are as profitable, if not more so, than employers without them.[46] In the United Kingdom, the Department of Business, Enterprise and Regulatory Reform estimated that extending existing flexible working programs to employees with older children, at an estimated cost of £69 million, would benefit employers £91 annually: £64 million from increased productivity, £21 million from reduced recruitment costs due to lower turnover rates, and £6 million from lower absence costs.[47]

Isola operates in a context in which companies are required by law to provide several forms of leave, and it is not the only company thriving in a country with high standards; many of the nations ranked among the most competitive in the world have a floor of decent standards for all workers.[48] Autoliv Australia showed that even in countries where there are few regulations establishing paid leave and flexibility, it is possible for companies to profit from providing these benefits. When employees can return to their jobs after life events such as having a baby or dealing with a long-term illness, the company benefits from the knowledge, experience, and commitment that the worker brings back to the job. These benefits were experienced by both Isola and Autoliv Australia, and have been documented among other companies as well. Having access to paid leave has been shown to increase the likelihood that women will return to their job after having a child.[49] A study examining the responsiveness of American companies to their employees' family needs found that 42 percent of the companies that provided some form of wage replacement during maternity leave experienced a positive return on their investment, while an additional 42 percent found the program to be cost-neutral.[50] In short, companies benefit from family leave policies by being able to retain experienced workers rather than having to replace them.

Autoliv Australia and Isola both made time available to their workers to address health needs. Supporting workers' health needs has economic benefits for firms. When workers come to work sick, they endanger productivity in several ways. First, sick employees may infect coworkers, leading to the spread of infectious illnesses such as influenza in the workplace.[51] Second, employees are unable to work at their usual capacity if their health is compromised; this impairs both their own productivity and that of their coworkers. Third, employees delaying their health care can lead to longer and more severe illnesses and absences.[52] Considerable research has been done on the connection between a number of illnesses and the lost productivity that can result either from sick employees' absence from work (absenteeism) or their presence at work when ill (presenteeism).[53] For the ten mental and physical illnesses that require the highest expenditures by employers in the United States, presenteeism has been found to account for 61 percent of the total costs to employers. Additionally, the productivity losses resulting from employees who came to work when they were ill were costlier to employers than the lost productivity caused by absence and medical benefits combined.[54]

Autoliv Australia's innovative leave programs, including the 50/52 vacation option, were a creative way of ensuring that workers were able to take time off when they needed it. Isola shut down its factory for three weeks in July to ensure that its workers were able to take vacation. Both firms felt that their leave policies contributed to reduced turnover, higher motivation and commitment, and ultimately higher productivity. These companies' experience that providing employees with sufficient time off work was beneficial to productivity is unsurprising, considering the findings of a number of studies that show a negative relationship between excessive working hours and productivity.[55]

Managers and companies may be worried that certain policies will be abused. One of the inevitable challenges in implementing leave and flexibility policies is ensuring that they are available to employees who need them, yet reserved for the purposes for which they were designed. There is little risk that employees will pretend to have a new child to take unwarranted parental leave, and policies such as the 50/52 vacation option cannot be abused by their very nature. But policies such as sick leave can be potentially misused. The companies explored in this chapter found viable solutions to this problem. Autoliv Australia put financial incentives in place to encourage employees not to use sick days unnecessarily. Isola's teamwork method of production created a culture in which one team member's performance affected the performance of the entire team and therefore discouraged absenteeism. At the same time, senior management at both Autoliv and Isola ensured that their company cultures facilitated the use of leave when necessary. The next chapter highlights additional steps companies can take to promote employee health and reduce the need for absences for illness and injury.

3

Increasing Productivity and Reliability by Investing in Health Care

E MPLOYERS HAVE BEEN CALLED the "new gatekeepers" of health care and health in recognition of the crucial importance of working conditions.[1] At the same time, there has been a growing realization that just as work is a major determinant of health, so does workers' health play a key role in the quality and productivity of their work. An increasing amount of research evidence shows that companies can reap economic benefits from investing in the health of their workers. Despite this evidence, there are important challenges to creating and maintaining a successful relationship between work and health, such as determining how to share and control the cost of medical care.

Over the past decade and a half, we have brought together top researchers from around the world to examine the relationship between working conditions and health. We have carried out collaborative studies to examine the impact of working conditions on the health of individuals, families, and communities. Findings from these studies of how working conditions affect health globally are summarized in *Global Inequalities at Work: Work's Impact on the Health of Individuals, Families, and Societies* and elsewhere.[2] Since 2001, we have been studying both public and private sector initiatives aimed at improving the impact of working conditions on the health of employees and the family members in their care. In this particular initiative, we examined what companies around the world were doing to improve the health of all their employees, including those who occupy the lowest rungs of the corporate ladder.

We visited health clinics, observed safety measures in factories, examined steps taken to increase ergonomics, and reviewed policies designed to promote healthy work environments. We interviewed CEOs, human resources managers, company health personnel, and line workers on these topics. The companies we studied adopted a wide range of approaches to improve the health of their workers, from building comprehensive health clinics at the work site to providing insurance to increase access to community-based health care, and from addressing physical risks in the workplace to improving the ways in which the social environment influenced workers' health.

In this chapter, we present the experiences of two companies working in very different environments. SA Metal separates and sells scrap metal in South Africa, a country that has been hit particularly hard by one of the world's worst health crises: the AIDS pandemic. American Apparel manufactures clothing in the United States, a country that has one of the highest health care expenditures per capita in the world while having one of the highest rates of uninsured citizens among affluent nations.

SA Metal: Health Care Amid the AIDS Pandemic

South Africa Metal (SA Metal) is one of the largest metal recyclers in the country, collecting and processing all forms of ferrous (iron) and nonferrous (copper, zinc, aluminum) scrap metals. The company was founded in 1919 by Wolfe Barnett and is now run by his grandsons, joint managing directors Clifford and Graham Barnett.[3]

SA Metal takes in scrap metal collected from factories, brokers, and individuals. The distance the scrap is transported depends on its value. Since ferrous metals have less value, the company doesn't go more than a few hundred miles to collect them; they are mainly sold locally or melted down at their mill and exported as steel. Nonferrous metals, including copper, nickel, and aluminum alloys, have greater value, and they are brought in from as far away as Angola; since there is little local demand for these metals, they are separated into their component parts and turned into processed scrap, such as copper tubes and bars that are exported internationally.

Competition in the industry is significant, including RECLAM, Collect-a-Can, and Mittal, as well as smaller scrap dealers and local foundries that compete for available scrap. SA Metal is headquartered in Epping, greater Cape Town, and has expanded its operations to other sites, including Salt River, Bofors Circle, and Johannesburg. In 2007, the vast majority (nearly nine tenths) of the firm's racially diverse employees had limited formal education.

Like all companies, SA Metal is affected by economic changes in the global market. For example, in 2007, the demand for SA Metal's products was high, particularly in China and Japan; however, the cost of shipping its products overseas had increased. Bulk shipping, which used to be very inexpensive at $20 per ton to Taiwan, was on the rise with the commodity boom in China and the accompanying increase in demand for bulk carriers. Falling water levels in the Rhine River had led to a decline in Europe of nuclear power, which requires water as a coolant, and to an increased demand for coal. These factors led to increased costs for bulk shipping worldwide. At $50 per ton, shipping in containers was two and a half times as costly. Nonetheless, business at SA Metal remained successful. Although there are not many uses for scrap metal in its raw form, SA Metal made money by separating it into its component parts, processing it, and shipping the processed goods.

CEO's Vision: Caring for Workers' Health as a Competitive Strategy

Clifford Barnett comanaged SA Metal with his brother Graham. During our visits to the company in 2005 and 2006, his pride in the quality of their product was readily evident as he guided us through the scrap metal yard. To have a successful business, they needed to be able to retain workers who were productive and whose experience led to high-quality work separating valuable metal from worthless scrap. Clifford Barnett affirmed: "Your most important asset in your business [is] your people."[4] Instead of seeing health care for employees as a luxury or a bonus, SA Metal considered it an important investment. Barnett compared providing health care and training for employees to maintaining spare parts for machinery along with the skills to repair them, since both greatly contributed to production.

Having determined that the health of its employees was central to its operations, the company was prepared to invest in the health of its workforce by providing the services that best suited workers' needs. SA Metal began by opening an on-site clinic for employees. When it became clear that HIV/AIDS was affecting a significant portion of its workers, the company decided to invest in providing on-site HIV/AIDS treatment.

The fact that Clifford Barnett lived near the company and worked side by side with the employees deepened his commitment to providing a healthy work environment. In reference to the cleanliness of the factory yard, he said, "It is very simple: I live here too, [so] I want the air to be clean."[5]

Health Care Provided by SA Metal

South Africa has one of the largest income disparities in the world, with over 50 percent of the population living below the poverty line. In a context where millions lack adequate access to water, sanitation, and basic health resources, SA Metal offered a variety of health services to its employees and their families.

FREE ON-SITE CLINIC

While many moderate- and high-risk workplaces have on-site occupational health clinics, SA Metal's free clinic went two steps further in protecting employee health: first, recognizing that many employees did not have access to quality care for basic health problems, the clinic offered primary care in addition to occupational health; second, recognizing that HIV was the greatest threat to the health of many working-age adults in South Africa, the clinic began offering HIV-specific care.

The free on-site clinic began in 1996 as a small operation. Dr. Harold Amaler, head of the clinic, described the early days: "When I started here, the clinic was just a little factory clinic in a small room downstairs and was manned by a nurse four days a week. We had just basic meds. I came in just one day per week. I identified a much broader need for health interventions than was being offered. It grew organically from there."[6] By the time of our visit in 2006, the clinic had multiple rooms, medical equipment for primary care exams and more, lung-function equipment, an audiometer, and a small dispensary where, according to Dr. Amaler, the "drug formulary is more comprehensive than many GPs'." The staff had increased accordingly, and the clinic now had two part-time primary health care doctors, two full-time nurses, one occupational health care doctor, one trained counselor, and one administrator. The clinic was open Monday to Friday and was available to all employees at all SA Metal work sites, including part-time workers, fixed-term contractors, and casual employees.

The limited access to water and sanitation in the townships where many of the employees lived had led to a high prevalence of health problems, and inadequate preventive measures had further compounded them for the entire population, leading to lengthy lines at the public clinics. Head of human resources Renata Opperman explained the context in which SA Metal operated its clinic: "The public health care system is overwhelmed and there is a shortage of staff. So, you have spent the whole day [waiting to see a health care provider], you are sick, and then you are told, 'Sorry, I can't see you, we have taken in enough patients,' and you have to go [back] the next day."[7] Given this strain on the public system, SA Metal's on-site clinic provided the least-advantaged workers with more ready access to health care. For SA Metal, this meant that employees did not need to be absent from work for as long.

SA Metal employees greatly appreciated having access to the clinic. As Thandiwe Nqanqase, a boiler maker, explained: "I use the free clinic. A private doctor charges about 120 rand for a consultation fee, plus medications. So it is nice to have the clinic here."[8] Workers also mentioned that the free clinic saved them from having to wait for the publicly provided health services. Alan Botha, a monthly employee working as a driver, told us: "It is convenient because it is right there. You can just pop in."[9] The clinic was frequented regularly by employees; it recorded 2,277 visits between January and July of 2006.

ADDRESSING HIV/AIDS: TESTING AND TREATMENT

As a company operating in South Africa, SA Metal has had to deal with the impact of the HIV/AIDS epidemic. With a national prevalence rate of 21.5 percent, South Africa has more people living with HIV/AIDS than any other country in the world, most of whom are concentrated in the working-age population (fifteen to forty-nine years old).[10]

As the impact of the HIV/AIDS epidemic became more widespread in the late 1990s, SA Metal began to recognize the need to implement broader health interventions. The small clinic it had set up in 1996 was not equipped to deal with the new health issues that were arising with the increasing number of employees living with HIV/AIDS. Having already reaped significant economic benefits from providing primary health care services, SA Metal began to prepare itself to address this new challenge. Dr. Amaler described the logic behind the company's decision to offer HIV/AIDS treatment:

> Here at SA Metal, in the late nineties, we realized that we were seeing more and more HIV-positive people and that there was only one cost-effective way to deal with it. This was to create an in-house

service, since there was no government rollout of ARVs [antiretrovirals] yet. Private costs for drugs are really high. We decided to develop a structured program. We costed it out. We knew that if we did not provide ARVs in-house, that people would seek [them] elsewhere. They would either pay or go to the government, but this takes a lot of time, and the company incurs lots of costs such as prolonged downtime. This was the broad principle driving the health care program here: it saves money. It is an internal fallacy that managing HIV in-house is more expensive than not managing it. We have to ask ourselves: can you afford *not* to do it?[11]

In April of 2000, SA Metal expanded its medical services to include a broad range of HIV/AIDS treatment services, including voluntary testing and counseling, treatment for sexually transmitted infections, prophylaxis for opportunistic infections, free ARVs, and monitoring of treatment. Despite initial concerns about the costs associated with these services, it became clear that investing in health services was ultimately a better option than spending money to hire and retrain substitute workers when employees were absent for HIV-related reasons.

Initially, SA Metal acquired ARVs from a variety of sources, including participation in clinical trials, Doctors Without Borders clinics, and private funding. Since 2003, it has been able to purchase ARVs at preferential prices through programs such as the Glaxo Smith Kline Access Programme. As a result, in 2006, SA Metal spent approximately 88 rand (US$12.50) per employee on ARVs, which constituted only a small percentage of the total health care expenditure. As Barnett put it, "The powerful number is how little it costs if you do it properly."[12] He was particularly proud of the fact that none of the employees on ARVs had died; before the treatment program was implemented, several employees had died from suspected AIDS-related causes.

In 2006, the clinic was managing twenty-eight HIV-positive patients at the weekly chronic illness clinic, which treated a total of 104 patients suffering from various chronic conditions such as hypertension, asthma, and diabetes. Employees were under no pressure to reveal the conditions for which they were being treated to their supervisors or colleagues; confidentiality was an important issue given the ongoing serious stigma and discrimination against people living with HIV/AIDS.

HIV/AIDS PREVENTION EDUCATION

In addition to providing HIV/AIDS testing, care, and treatment, SA Metal set up a prevention education program. All employees at SA Metal were required to participate in the HIV Peer Educator Programme, which held classes once a week for eight weeks. Employees who did not attend at least six of the eight classes were required to take the course over again. Among the diverse topics covered in these classes were transmission, testing, treatment, positive living, support, and company policies regarding HIV/AIDS. Education as a prevention strategy was seen as an extremely important component of the company's efforts to address HIV/AIDS. In the company's HIV/AIDS policy document, Dr. Amaler stated that the education program "is possibly the single most critical element . . . Knowledge is power, and people must be empowered to take personal responsibility for turning the pandemic around."[13] Because SA Metal wanted all employees to participate, classes were offered during the workday and employees were paid their regular wages to attend. Though this was costly, it was seen as a good investment and as a way to have an important impact on the workforce and on the community at large. Clifford Barnett explained: "At the end of the day, [our workers] have more knowledge. They educate those with whom they interact, not only in the workplace, but also outside of the workplace."[14]

Indeed, Nombeko Butshingi, a cleaning employee, told us, "I am also an HIV peer educator and . . . I even give classes outside of SA Metal, at the church."[15] While SA Metal ultimately stood to gain by reducing infection rates among its employees, the community benefited as well from the decreased infection rates that resulted from prevention education.

Education was particularly important since, despite SA Metal's efforts to protect confidentiality, the stigma against people living with HIV/AIDS had a serious detrimental effect on the number of workers who used the HIV/AIDS services. Barnett explained: "Statistically we believe that about 15 percent of our workforce is HIV-positive, and that will translate into about 120 people. With all of our efforts—with celebrating AIDS Days and peer educators and education on all levels—I think that we have only been able to identify under forty people who are coming [to the clinic for care]. That is potentially [only] one third of the people who are HIV-positive."[16]

MENTAL HEALTH SERVICES

While alcohol abuse and depression exist in all settings, the history of oppression and deprivation in South Africa has exacerbated their prevalence and impact on the township populations. The HIV/AIDS crisis has also increased the need for social and emotional support to deal with family illness and death. In response to this distress, SA Metal set up mental health services to give employees the opportunity to attend counseling sessions. Renata Opperman explained the economic rationale for providing these services: "Sometimes you just need to talk to someone. If a guy is healthy, it is a [benefit] for him and for us. [Otherwise] both sides lose at the end of the day." She reiterated the mantra from the human resources department: "A healthy employee is a productive employee."[17]

SA Metal's mental health services were offered through SANCA, an organization that provides mental health and substance abuse counseling services. Opperman recounted how the company had expanded its services: "SANCA just used to come here for half a day per week, but last year I picked up on a lot of emotional and psychological issues outside of our clinic's frame of reference, so we asked them to come for a full day. It is like our health care: we started small and now we have the clinic open five days a week for a full workday." To attend a counseling session, employees simply notified their manager of their appointment at the clinic, and they were automatically given the paid hour off to attend the session. There was no set limit on the number of sessions an employee could attend, and the duration of the treatment was left to the discretion of SANCA and the employee being treated.

Economic Gains for the Company

Although SA Metal operated in a context of high unemployment in which it was easy to hire new workers, the company still believed that there were substantial economic returns to investing in their current employees' health. Barnett recognized the valuable skills of his so-called low-skilled workers, acknowledging that they were costly to replace. As he showed us around the factory, he described the process of transforming junk metal into marketable products. As he did so, he stopped at every workstation to examine the quality of his employees' work. He sampled every pile of junk metal to ensure that its components were being accurately separated, and if he found a mistake, he always brought it to the attention of the worker responsible. These mistakes were expensive for the company since they reduced the quality of its products and thus the prices it could charge for them. Workers became more efficient and made fewer mistakes as they accumulated experience in separating scrap metal.

The company spent a total of 792,706 rand (US$122,900) on health care in 2005, including the salaries of medical staff. After internal restructuring in 2006, it spent a total of 665,577 rand (US$93,479), the equivalent of 1,142 rand (US$160.39) per employee.[18] In the month of June, the on-site clinic received 331 visits for acute illnesses, 80 for chronic illnesses, 12 for mental health services, 28 for workplace injuries, 5 for medical exit exams, 4 for medical preemployment exams, and 13 for routine medical checkups. If these appointments had been conducted off-site, the company would have lost a substantial number of productive work hours due to travel time. Dr. Amaler explained that whereas it cost the company 750 to 1,000 rand (US$105 to US$140) a day when a truck driver and a truck were out of commission, HIV/AIDS treatment never cost more than 25 rand (US$3.50) a day. The return on investment had been considerable; the company experienced reduced absenteeism and turnover in spite of the ongoing HIV/AIDS epidemic. In Barnett's words: "With an HIV program, I get a hell of a lot more productive hours out of people. People sick at work make businesses less and less efficient. It's an endemic problem. It's not just people living longer; it's people having more meaningful work lives."[19]

Timely product delivery was essential to SA Metal's ability to keep clients as well as to avoid paying large additional fees or fines for delayed shipments. The bottom line was that "downtime," whether due to equipment or to personnel, was costly. Providing on-site medical care had been extremely effective in reducing the number of work hours lost for health reasons. Barnett explained: "You don't have to be a genius to figure it out: if you don't provide it on-site, your staff will be absent from work, and it will be very expensive to go and find health care of whatever quality."[20]

Improving Access to Existing Health Care Resources

SA Metal established a health care program that suited its socioeconomic reality. The challenges it faced, such as the high rate of HIV/AIDS and the lack of infrastructure, were particular to its environment and made on-site health care the best option. Companies have developed diverse approaches to caring for their employees' health based on the needs they must address and the constraints they face.

In some communities, services must be developed in order to adequately meet people's health needs; in other settings, such as the United States, services are available but largely inaccessible to the uninsured. Workers earning lower wages are particularly likely to lack health coverage as part of their employment benefits. Figures from the Bureau of Labor Statistics for 2008 showed that 91 percent of workers earning in the top decile of the population had access to medical benefits, compared to only 25 percent of workers earning in the bottom decile.[21] In 2008, overall 46.3 million people in the United States lacked health insurance, and the percentage of people who had access to health insurance through employment had been decreasing.[22] Whereas 70 percent of the population had employment-based health insurance in 1987, only 62 percent did in 2007.[23]

Health insurance was one of the areas in which American Apparel stood out from its competitors. The company's health insurance plan covered preventive care, hospitalization, and prescription drugs. Twelve hundred employees participated in the plan, paying $8 a week ($32 per month) for individual Blue Cross HMO medical insurance coverage. American Apparel paid approximately $150 to $170 per employee per month. Vision and dental coverage were also available to employees for $13.32 and $42.32 per month, respectively. Although family coverage was available, few employees chose to participate due to its higher costs.

The health insurance plan was offered to all American Apparel employees, but human resources staff explained that it had been challenging to get employees to choose to pay for health insurance rather than take home a higher paycheck, in part due to the company's high proportion of immigrant workers. Kristina Moreno, director of human resources, explained: "People come from their national country of origin [where] there is a national health plan. They are not used to contributing any monthly premium, and so it was a challenge to get people to sign up and to look at it as preventative care."[24] The company conducted educational campaigns to inform workers about the importance of health insurance and the way the health care system operates in the United States.

American Apparel had also placed increasing emphasis on occupational health in an effort to reduce the rate of workplace injuries. Due to the nature of work in the apparel industry, minor lacerations and strains were the most common injuries. The company employed a safety coordinator as well as an occupational health specialist. Every employee saw a massage therapist approximately every two weeks in an effort to help reduce repetitive strain injuries. "The insurance company that we just signed up with was very impressed. People want to insure us because we have low injury rates," said Moreno. Lupe Caro, American Apparel's safety coordinator, explained how he emphasized changing employees' behavior and attitudes toward safety measures. People were sometimes reluctant to wear the protective gear the company provided, saying things like, "I look funny when I wear gloves." The company needed to help employees understand the importance of wearing masks and gloves and of using safety devices. "Positive change trickles down through managers and employees," he explained.[25]

In addition to safety measures, American Apparel implemented programs aimed at overall health promotion. Daily exercise breaks were part of the company's health and safety program. During the break, all employees got up from their stations and stretched and stepped in place. By making these exercise breaks a group activity, the company ensured that employees did not feel they were slowing down their team's production by participating. The company also offered low-impact exercise classes three times a day, three days a week. Efforts were made to ensure that the cafeteria had healthier options and increased quantities of fruits and vegetables. The director of human resources in 2007, Kristina Ledesma-Davies, explained that the exercise classes and improved diets had clear benefits for the company, since workers were more energized and productive. In the long run, they expected the health promotion programs to lead to a reduction in the use of health care services, which would enable them to negotiate better rates with the health care company.[26]

At the time of our second visit in 2007, American Apparel was planning to open an on-site clinic that would provide free health services to employees and their families. This was seen as a good investment since it would improve employees' health while reducing the amount of time they needed to seek external health care services. The medical clinic was opened in October of 2007 in partnership with Health Care Partners.

Impact of Other Working Conditions on Health

Working conditions are a leading factor in determining health outcomes for the majority of the population. The World Health Organization

(WHO) has estimated that 37 percent of lower-back pain, 16 percent of hearing loss, 13 percent of chronic obstructive pulmonary disease, 11 percent of asthma, and 8 percent of injuries are work related.[27] One quarter of workers in developed countries and three quarters in developing countries are exposed to potentially harmful physical conditions and chemical and biological risks.[28] Research also shows that employees at the bottom of the ladder are more likely to face inadequate working conditions, including physical strain, low job control, greater noise and air pollution, and hazardous shift work among many others.[29]

Just as physical health problems resulting from working conditions are costly to both employees and companies, so too do risks to mental health exact tolls on employees and companies alike. Research has linked workplace stress to a variety of illnesses, including cardiovascular disease, hypertension, diabetes, depression, anxiety, carpal tunnel syndrome, and tendinitis.[30] At the same time, excessive work-related stress has been found to lead to deteriorations in performance and to job dissatisfaction, accidents, unsafe working practices, higher likelihood of turnover, and high absenteeism.[31] Conversely, research has shown that efforts to improve the psychological welfare of employees can reduce absenteeism and improve job performance.[32]

In addition to affecting the health of individual workers, working conditions have a significant impact on the health and well-being of workers' families. In a world where an increasing number of parents are in the workforce, working conditions are a central factor in determining whether parents are able to provide the support their children need to lead healthy lives. For example, mothers can contribute to children's health by breast-feeding, which leads to a mortality rate 1.5 to 5 times lower than for children who aren't breast fed, in developing and industrialized countries alike.[33] The breast-fed infants have lower rates of gastrointestinal infections, respiratory tract infections, otitis media, meningitis, and other infections.[34] Working conditions and benefits, including paid maternity leave and breast-feeding breaks, frequently determine whether and how long working mothers breast-feed. Similarly, studies have shown that barriers to parents taking time off from work have an impact on whether their children are vaccinated.[35] A third example is the fact that children recover more rapidly from illnesses and injuries when their parents are involved in their care,[36] yet parents' ability to care for their sick children is strongly affected by working conditions such as the availability of paid sick leave.[37]

As demonstrated by Autoliv and Isola, when companies offer leave and scheduling flexibility to care for family as well as personal health needs, companies also benefit in their ability to recruit and retain experienced employees, as well as earn the commitment and engagement of these employees.

Companies Profit from Investing in Health

Illness can be costly for companies by decreasing productivity and increasing unanticipated absences. In the companies we studied, not surprisingly, employees greatly valued their companies' provision of therapeutic health care services and appreciated the difference these services had made in their lives. The senior managers clearly contended that the financial benefits of focusing on health were substantially greater than the costs since employees were more productive, more likely to remain at the company for longer, and less likely to be absent. Even in the context of a health crisis such as the HIV/AIDS epidemic in South Africa, turnover and absenteeism were reduced.

Our case studies highlight the return on investment (ROI) to companies of ensuring that employees have access to clinical care; the evidence is at least as great as returns on health promotion programs that target employees' well-being through measures such as exercise, improved nutrition, smoking cessation, and stress management. A study of a comprehensive health promotion program at a large industrial company reported that the use of disability days among blue-collar workers participating in the program had declined by 14 percent over two years.[38] Studies of company health improvement programs have shown that participation resulted in 3 to 16 percent reductions in absenteeism rates and showed ROI of US$2 to US$6.40 for each dollar invested.[39] An analysis of twenty-four studies showed positive returns in all the studies that analyzed cost effectiveness.[40] Research on Workplace Health Promotion programs concluded that these initiatives "not only lower health care costs, but also decrease absenteeism and improve performance and productivity. Other benefits include improved ability to attract and retain key personnel, greater employee allegiance, and improved public image of the company."[41]

Given the important impact that working conditions can have on employees' health and that employees' health can have on financial returns, there is great potential for both companies and employees to benefit from corporate health initiatives. As these case studies have shown, companies around the world can adopt a variety of approaches to health care, adapting their health programs to suit their social and economic environments and their employees' needs. Some businesses, such as SA Metal and ACC India (whose experience is described in detail in chapter 8), faced a substantial lack of infrastructure in the areas where they operated, which created a need for on-site health care. Others, such as American Apparel in the United States, operated in areas where health resources were present but unaffordable, which created a need to facilitate access to existing health care services.

Both the companies' experiences and the statistics demonstrate that employers stand to benefit from investing in the health of employees. The question remains: What should be the responsibility of employers and what should be the responsibility of the public sector?

Some aspects of health promotion can only be addressed well by companies themselves. To provide just one example, companies that place a strong emphasis on ergonomics, providing regular exercise breaks and work equipment that is conducive to healthier working routines, play an important role in preserving the health of their employees. American Apparel addressed ergonomic issues on-site by providing exercise breaks and massage therapy. Novo Nordisk also took this approach: at its factory in Tianjin, China, all employees took exercise breaks twice a day to stretch and do aerobic exercises. The company's equipment was ergonomically designed to ensure that employees took the necessary steps to avoid repetitive stress injuries. For example, one machine required the worker's hands to be in a "resting" position in order to continue working. This meant that workers had to manufacture products in ways that avoided injuries. Novo Nordisk's policies were especially noteworthy since they were aimed at factory workers, a demographic that frequently suffers from inadequate working conditions. Furthermore, the company's efforts to promote safe and healthy working practices were well above legal requirements and surpassed the common practices among most of its competitors in the region. Novo Nordisk addressed physical and structural risks within the workplace. Whether or not there are national policies mandating that they do so, companies also need to address the health impacts of workplace demands, opportunities, paid leave, flexibility, and other factors inherent in the work experience.

Other aspects of employee health promotion can be carried out either by employers or by national governments. Providing health insurance is an important example of this. The CEOs we spoke with recognized that their companies would be better off if their national governments more fully supported health care. Even large companies that had the infrastructure to set up on-site programs felt that the government had a key role to play in ensuring access to health care. Clifford Barnett at SA Metal and Sumit Bannerjee at ACC, which similarly developed health clinics where the country had none, saw their companies' actions as "filling the gap" until their national governments provided the services needed in these regions.

While the benefits of caring for employees' health are clear, the costs are considerable. Providing on-site health care necessitates investment in infrastructure and personnel. In regions that lack health care infrastructure or where the existing infrastructure is overwhelmed, it may be in a company's best interest to provide the necessary health services. In some cases, this will mean providing basic health care services through an on-site clinic. In other cases, there are specific health problems to address, such as the high prevalence of HIV/AIDS in some regions, particularly sub-Saharan Africa. Providing workers with on-site access to testing and treatment as well as education and prevention programs may be a beneficial investment. The costs associated with setting up an on-site clinic will be lower in poorer countries that are more likely to lack adequate infrastructure. If workers do not have to travel off-site and endure long waits to access health care services, their absences from work will be shorter. If workers have access to health care services, they will also be healthier and less likely to be absent or to quit for health reasons. Though we have studied large companies like ACC and midsize companies like SA Metal that have demonstrated the feasibility, this investment may be difficult for the smallest companies.

In the only industrialized country that lacks public medical care, the United States, the costs are greatest. A significant percentage of the population lacks access to health care because they cannot afford private insurance. Providing workers with affordable health insurance is a significant investment for companies, but it can yield returns in terms of increased productivity and retention. In some cases, even if the infrastructure already exists, companies may find it beneficial to set up on-site clinics. American Apparel believed that its on-site clinic would not only benefit its employees by providing free health care, but would also benefit the company by reducing employees' health-related absences.

The balance between the critical role that companies need to play in ensuring the health of their employees and the essential role of the public sector will be discussed further in the final chapter of this book. Finding the right place to draw that line is as important to the health of companies as it is to the health of employees. Regardless of the role of national governments, it is clear that companies have a strong financial interest in investing in the health of their employees. Moreover, all of the managers featured in this chapter had another fundamental element in common in their approaches to health care: they saw the health of their employees as vital to their success. In the absence of comprehensive government programs, they believed that taking care of employees' everyday health was an essential investment, not an unnecessary expense.

4

Building Assets to Ensure
That the Lowest-Level
Employees Are Not
Left Behind

T HE PRESS HAS PAID attention to the rapidly rising inequalities in
income between the rich and the poor. Although it has received less
attention, the gap in wealth—which encompasses all assets, including
home ownership, stocks, bonds, and pension plans—is actually far greater
and is increasing more rapidly than the gap in income. The wealthiest 2
percent of adults own more than 50 percent of all global wealth, with the
richest 1 percent owning 40 percent of global assets; in staggering contrast, the bottom 50 percent own barely 1 percent. North American
households account for 34 percent of global assets, while 30 percent is enjoyed by Europe, and 24 percent by the rich Asia-Pacific countries.
African households are the poorest, owning only 1 percent of assets. Latin
American and Caribbean households are not far ahead of them, with a
share of only 4 percent. Although China and India comprise 75 percent
of the global population, they own only 3 percent and 1 percent of assets,
respectively.[1]

While large inequalities in income exist all over the world, they are
particularly grievous in the United States. In 2001, the richest 1 percent of
the U.S. population accounted for 20 percent of total income, while the
poorest 40 percent received only 10 percent. Inequalities in wealth were

even more pronounced—the top 1 percent of the population held 33.4 percent of wealth, while the bottom 40 percent held only 0.3 percent. Over the course of the 1990s, the top 1 percent saw their average wealth increase by 63 percent, while the middle quintile gained 24 percent. In contrast, the average wealth of the poorest 40 percent of the population actually declined by 44 percent.[2] The enormous gap in assets has contributed to the gap in home ownership in the United States and the country's vulnerability to the subprime mortgage crisis of 2008.

In a study on wealth distribution in twenty countries, the share of assets owned by the richest 20 percent of the population ranged from 39.3 percent in Japan to 71.3 percent in Switzerland.[3] The share of the assets owned by the richest 1 percent ranged from 10.4 percent in Ireland to 34.8 percent in Switzerland. Meanwhile, the poorest 30 percent held 5.8 percent of assets in China but only 0.3 percent of assets in Germany. The share of assets held by the bottom 50 percent ranged from 14.4 percent in China to 2.8 percent in the United States.

The enormous gap in assets has serious implications. Currently, in the global economy, a lack of savings and financial assets leaves hundreds of millions of people without resources to fall back on when they face personal crises such as serious illness or job loss. The risks are equally profound when low-asset employees and their families endure economic downturns.

Should companies help address asset deficits? There is compelling evidence that companies stand to gain when they share their profits with employees. A British study of ninety-three randomly selected manufacturing companies showed that profit-sharing firms were more productive than their non-profit-sharing counterparts; profit sharing increased productivity by 6 percent over a three-year period.[4] Allowing workers to participate in their companies financially acted as an incentive for them to work harder and more efficiently, thus increasing productivity.[5] In Japan, a study of very large firms (more than ten thousand employees) found that the adoption of profit-sharing programs increased productivity by 9 percent.[6] Similarly, a study using data from a survey of five hundred U.S. public companies to examine the relationship between productivity and profit sharing found that the adoption of a profit-sharing plan was associated with a 4 to 5 percent increase in productivity.[7] This effect was also found for employees of Canadian financial institutions,[8] workers in U.S. chemical industries,[9] and employees in U.S. firms in general.[10] Companies stood to gain through improved employee recruitment and retention as well as higher productivity. Empirical studies in the United States have evidenced these advantages. U.S. companies that participated in profit-sharing schemes from 1988 to 1994 were found to have lower turnover and greater productivity.[11] Finally, a review of different studies on the relationship between profit sharing and productivity concluded that although a range of different techniques was used in the studies, nearly all showed that profit sharing led to increased productivity.[12]

Having interviewed representative samples of workers in cities and towns in the Americas, Africa, and Asia as part of our study on global working families, we were aware of the rarity of asset-building opportunities for men and women with limited levels of formal education. Beyond pensions, none of the workers we interviewed in each setting spoke about any profit-sharing or asset-building opportunities. Many of these workers barely earned sufficient income to survive on and received no protections in the form of paid sick leave or parental leave, creating periods during which they were likely to be without income. National data from several countries upholds our global research findings on employed men and women.

While many companies have established asset-building initiatives for their high-skilled and high-income workers, very few companies have done so for their lower-level employees. The disparities are marked even between low- and moderate-income employees. In Canada, for example, 17.7 percent of workers earning C$20 an hour or more participated in stock-purchase plans, in comparison to only 3.2 percent of workers earning C$12 an hour or less.[13] Is this omission of asset-building policies for the least-advantaged workers inevitable? It is often argued that to attract highly skilled workers, companies have to offer extras such as stock options in addition to higher salaries. But is there less economic incentive to offer asset-building programs to employees at the bottom of the corporate ladder?

We examined this issue in our recent five-year study of businesses in nine countries. In each of the companies we visited, we examined the extent of their asset-building opportunities as well as their wages and other forms of compensation. This chapter looks in detail at two of these companies; they were selected because of the ways in which they were able to translate profit sharing into increased productivity and profitability. Jenkins Brick implemented a common form of asset building—retirement savings plans—uncommonly well, and also set up a more unusual form of asset building for its least-advantaged workers—profit sharing. While both forms of asset building were also available at Dancing Deer Baking Company, the emphasis was shifted to profit sharing. The extent to which asset building had an impact on performance was examined from the perspective of both line workers and senior management.

Jenkins Brick: Traditional and Uncommon Approaches to Asset Building

Mike Jenkins V's level of personal investment in his family's company was evident in all aspects of his work.[14] Son of the current CEO and next in line to take over the business upon his father's retirement, Jenkins V showed us around the Jenkins Brick factory in Montgomery, Alabama. Following his father's example, he was spending time working on the factory floor in order to gain a better understanding of the company's daily operations, of the working lives of its employees, and of what it would take to achieve success. He had grown up around the factory and knew it as well as his own backyard. He strode through the plant with ease, past 1000-degree kilns and flatbeds that each carried sixteen thousand bricks.

Establishing Asset-Building Programs

Three Mike Jenkins preceded the current CEO. In the late 1800s in Wetumpka, Alabama, Mike Jenkins I developed a passion for apiaries. Endeavoring to build some newly designed beehives, he decided to make the bricks himself using the clay that was readily available on his property. Chance intervened when a fire burned his town to the ground, and he became the closest thing to a brick manufacturer in the area. By the time he had made enough bricks to rebuild the town, he had changed the focus of his production from honey to brick manufacturing.

His great-grandson, Mike Jenkins IV, unpretentiously described his own journey to become CEO of the company in 1974 and to take over ownership in 1985: "I think 1974 is when I really took operating control of the company . . . I was thirty-two and I didn't have a clue . . . I always wanted to do what my grandfather did, and when I was in junior high I worked out here. And in high school and college . . . I had a job [here in the summers]. When I . . . got out of the army I worked here a year as a salesman. Then I went to graduate school and got a masters in ceramic engineering."[15]

Jenkins IV had two goals when he took over the company: the first was to make the company economically successful again, and the second was to make working at the company advantageous for both management and line employees.

> In '85, we consolidated the ownership [and] bought the other share-holders out. And really from that point forward we were able to begin [working] on two issues: one of course was that we wanted to create the type of economic environment that would allow us to attract top-flight folks for our work, and to be able to [grow], . . . we had to do a lot better than what we were doing. And the other was a matter of equity. It didn't feel right . . . it felt lousy to see the old fellas who'd been here forever leave and have [nothing but] social security and literally not have health care.[16]

He was embarrassed to run into elderly people in the community who had worked their whole lives at the factory and yet were nearly destitute because they had so few resources for their retirement. Jenkins IV also saw that equity went hand in hand with economic growth, and that by providing employees with better benefits, the company would attract and retain better, more productive employees:

> I think we've matured to the point where we realize that if you work hard at recruiting the right people and you compensate them very well, it's one of the best investments you can make. So you can be entirely mercantile about it, or you can be philosophical. Philosophical meaning [that] it's the right thing to do, mercantile meaning [that if] you invest in "quality" people, you get "quality" output. And I believe it.[17]

Mike Jenkins IV established two distinct asset-building programs: the first was retirement savings in the form of a pension plan, and the second was profit sharing. Both of these benefits were available to all employees. Jenkins Brick provided these benefits in the context of an industry that was very susceptible to downturns in the economic cycle; when the economy was strong, families and companies did more building and brick was in high demand, but during recessions, building markedly declined, as did the demand for brick.

A Clear Vision: The Link Between Investment and Growth

Jenkins Brick is a medium-sized company in a competitive industry. It produces approximately 190 million bricks a year, and at the time of our first visit in March 2005, it employed 523 people. Its labor force was ethnically diverse: one in seven workers were Latino, the majority of whom were immigrants from Mexico, and one in five were African American.

Jenkins IV wanted to do well economically *and* do well by his employees, and he understood the link between these two goals. The quality of the company's products was essential to its ability to succeed in an increasingly competitive market. If the bricks were better in shape and structure, if their delivery was speedier and more reliable, then he would be able to sell more. Jenkins recognized that the company's ability to attract and retain the best workers was deeply influenced by the return it offered its employees. Better employees could produce better bricks and run the production more efficiently.

Jenkins IV wasn't the only one to recognize the link between the economic success of the company and that of its employees. Wyatt Shorter from the board of directors was also concerned with their ability to retain the best employees:

> [Management has] a solid appreciation of what it costs to train someone. I don't think we've ever had a directors meeting where we haven't discussed turnover.[18]

It was in the company's best interest to help employees build assets, since employees were more likely to stay out the year if they knew it would guarantee them a bonus. Similarly, employees would be motivated to work harder if they saw a return on their efforts by earning bonuses that increased in relation to their productivity. Finally, turnover would decline even more if employees knew that the longer they stayed with the company, the more savings they would accumulate for their retirement.

The 401(k) Pension and Profit-Sharing Plans

All Jenkins Brick employees have the option of participating in the pension plan, and their investments are matched by the company; the company contributes 50 cents to the plan for every dollar contributed by the worker, up to 6 percent of their wages. This money is invested in a tax-deferred 401(k) plan. The company is committed to making this plan accessible to everyone—not just to executives, but to forklift operators and plant workers as well.

Although the firm's costs increased with each additional associate who took out a retirement plan, the company wanted participation to be as widespread as possible. It held quarterly pension-education sessions for employees, explaining how the plan worked and how much money they could save. Tommy Andreades, executive vice president and chief financial officer, explained how the company tried to encourage employees to participate in the pension plan in a way that ensured that they accumulated assets for retirement:

> We just recently changed some things to try to motivate associates to start participating more [effectively]. We ha[d] a loan feature in our plan [so] that you could borrow any of the money that was in the plan, whether it came from profit sharing or your contributions to the match. We changed that now so the only money you can borrow from the plan, going forward on new loans, is money that you put in yourself. We're not allowing [employees] to borrow money that the company put in for them. We also just recently lowered the waiting period to get in. It used to be that some people, depending on when they were hired, had to wait up to eighteen months to get into the plan. Now they can get in every quarter.[19]

The same plan covered the company's CFO, a factory worker who had been with the company for less than two years, and a forklift driver with an eleventh-grade education who had been working there for seventeen years. Victor Fuentes, the forklift driver, earned enough money to keep investing in his 401(k) while his wife stayed home to raise their four children. Midlevel employees invested as well, including Melissa Coleman, who had been working in sales at the Birmingham yard for two years.

By March of 2005, 60 percent of Jenkins Brick employees had invested in the 401(k) program. In 2006, the company made another change to its regulations for plan participation, implementing an automatic enrollment program. Going forward, instead of having to actively enroll in the program once they became eligible, employees would automatically be enrolled. To be excluded, they would have to actively withdraw their participation. As of August 2007, the 401(k) participation rate was 95 percent.

The pension plan was not the company's only asset-building initiative. Jenkins Brick also established a defined contribution profit-sharing program for all of its employees. The company decided how much to put into the profit-sharing accounts on a yearly basis. Employees were fully vested in the program once they had been with the company for six years, at which time they could either take their money with them if they left or keep saving until their retirement. The six-year waiting period to vest encouraged longer employee retention, which in turn benefited the company economically.

Profit-sharing outcomes vary yearly since they are dependent on the company's performance. Prior to 2007, profit sharing had averaged approximately 5 percent of wages and salaries for the past five years, for a total of $1,095,000 in 2006. The company reported that its profit sharing was generally two to three times higher than the national average. Even more noteworthy was the fact that the profit-sharing program affected the lives of every employee; it was neither a stock-option plan limited to professionals nor a reward system solely for top management.

Jenkins Brick managed to contribute to asset building through these programs while keeping its benefit costs at 23 percent of total compensation. It was not outspending other companies, staying very close to the U.S. average of 25 percent. Its programs concentrated on long-term investments, and the firm leveled the playing field by providing the same benefits to line workers and executives. Moreover, these plans were weighted toward asset building; of the $4.5 million the company spent on benefits each year, $1.2 million was committed to employee retirement funds.

Linking Asset-Building Programs to Improved Performance

In establishing the pension and profit-sharing programs, Jenkins IV was concerned with equity and with making employment at Jenkins Brick financially advantageous for every worker. He was equally concerned with the company's financial success, for the sake of his family and his employees. Without improving the company's finances, it was clear that Jenkins IV could not ensure stable jobs for his employees, let alone provide them with good working conditions. The firm was not on solid financial footing when he took over in 1985; its productivity and earnings were paling. Brick manufacturing is difficult and labor-intensive work. The company had been having difficulty hiring workers, and the employees were not very productive, requiring two people to complete the work of one.

Jenkins IV turned the company around by creating the financial incentives that enabled him to hire better employees, motivate them to perform well, and retain them. Higher wages attracted better employees, and wages linked to productivity boosted performance, as discussed in chapter 1. Profit sharing allowed employees to reap the benefits of everyone's increased productivity. Both programs for asset accumulation encouraged retention since workers had to stay with Jenkins Brick for six years in order to fully vest in the profit-sharing program, and their pension savings increased the longer they remained with the company.

As a result, Jenkins Brick saw a marked decline in employee turnover. CEO Jenkins took this matter seriously: "We found that turnover can be a proxy for how well we're doing as leaders."[20] He noted that their investment in employees had helped them to cut their turnover rates in half— from a high of 41 percent down to close to 20 percent. The remaining turnover was largely attributable to immigrant workers who returned to their countries of origin, bringing with them the savings they had accumulated at the company.

The turnover rate in 2005 was 25 percent overall (19 percent from resignation and 6 percent from termination). This was not only lower than other brick manufacturers, but it was also lower than other factories in the region—furniture laminating factories faced a 38 to 39 percent turnover rate and chicken-processing plants faced a turnover rate of 75 to 80 percent. Turnover at Jenkins Brick further decreased over the following two years, and the company saw this as a significant achievement. Its turnover in manufacturing through May of 2007 was 17 percent, and the company estimated that the rate for the entire business was about the same.

The company reaped substantial financial gains from the low turnover, since it lowered accident rates as well as recruitment and training costs. Jenkins summarized: "Turnover is directly related to safety . . . People with less than one year [of experience here] in general have a higher incidence of accidents than people who [have been here for more than one year]. And of course it's very expensive to recruit and to train."[21] Providing benefits that encouraged workers to stay with the company was therefore as much a matter of economics as it was of principle.

Attracting the best employees had been one of the managers' goals when they implemented their new policies. As they had hoped, their new policies had facilitated employee recruitment. Jenkins Brick's financial rewards and asset-building programs led employees to recommend the company to their family members and friends. Because its workforce was partly made up of immigrant workers, there was often movement as workers returned to their native countries. However, because these jobs were highly valued, immigrant laborers often recruited people to fill their positions before they left. Anita Barrera, the controller, explained: "The reason they leave is to go back to Mexico. It's not to leave and go to another job in Montgomery. They leave to go home, and usually they've got people lined up [to replace them]: family members, friends, or whatever, who say 'So-and-so's leaving,' and we're like, 'What? We haven't heard that yet.' "[22]

As is the case at most companies, at Jenkins Brick, many departments and employees influenced the quality of the company's products and overall performance. The laborers who worked at the kilns and on the factory floor determined the quality and quantity of bricks produced, and the sales team influenced consumers' experiences in the store. At Jenkins Brick, everyone received economic benefits from the pension and profit-sharing plans, and everyone was therefore equally invested in the company's success and in the quality of its products. Improvements in efficiency and productivity resulted from employees' increased motivation to maximize the firm's profits by increasing their own productivity, as well as that of their peers.[23] Jenkins Brick's board believed that investing in their employees was also central to maintaining the quality of their products. Wyatt Shorter shared his own philosophy as well as that of the board: "This is something I've noticed over the years. A company that makes a high-quality [product] generally treats its employees well because they know the employees have such a huge influence over what the product is."[24]

Product quality was particularly important to Jenkins Brick because the company's competitive strategy entailed filling a niche in the market by providing some of the highest-quality bricks and service available, and charging a higher price for them. Its quality bricks were easily identified by their color, texture, and durability. The firm sought to fully and promptly meet its clients' needs; its high-quality service affected the prices it could charge for its products.

Jenkins Brick's Competition and Strategic Vision

Jenkins Brick had little competition from international shipments, but substantial competition from international firms. While high shipping costs had prevented the brick industry from facing significant competition from production in distant countries such as China and India, international firms had invested heavily in the industry in the United States. Jenkins IV described the dominance of international firms in the market:

Now the brick industry itself is, I think, about 80 to 85 percent . . .
owned by offshore people. The largest is Boral, who is the largest
brick manufacturer. And I think they produce something like a billion
or 600 million bricks a year. Compare that to us: this year we'll produce something like 190 million. There's a huge gap between the top
four [manufacturers in the United States]; we're probably somewhere
around tenth in size as a manufacturer in the country, and probably
second or third maybe in distribution. So the Australians with Boral
are number one; number two would be the Austrians [with] Wiener-
berger; and three is Acme Brick, Warren Buffett's outfit. Four would
be Hanson, which is English. From there you drop down to a handful
of folks like us, who . . . are really American-owned.[25]

In addition to competing based on quality, Jenkins sought to diversify in
ways that might protect his firm from changes in customer preferences and
some of the worst impacts of the building cycle. In an industry that is very
susceptible to economic downturns, Jenkins Brick has differed from most
companies in its approach to diversification and self-protection against economic fluctuations. The company manufactures and sells its own bricks, but
what is unusual is that it distributes bricks from its competitors as well.
Moreover, Jenkins Brick sales agents are not given any incentives that would
lead them to sell more of their own company's bricks. As a result, distribution only performed poorly when no bricks from any manufacturer were
selling. At the same time, the manufacturing arm does not rely solely on its
own sales team to sell its products; Jenkins Brick products are also distributed by other vendors across the country. As a result, if construction was occurring anywhere in the country, the firm had an opportunity to sell bricks.

The distribution arm of the business has grown and the company has
maintained good relationships with its competitors, who trust Jenkins
Brick to sell their products fairly. In the end, the relationships it has fos-
tered have given the firm access to far larger and more diverse markets,
and this has ensured a consistent demand for its products. When a particular market experienced a downturn at a given time, there was likely to be
activity in one of the other markets it had tapped into. Moreover, the wide
range of products carried in the showrooms continued to attract new
customers.

Jenkins Brick's belief that investing in its employees brings financial
returns is representative of its overall long-term vision, which has been

reflected in other company initiatives as well, such as its investment in environmentally clean energy. Jenkins Brick was one of the first companies to recognize the potential of using landfill gas to meet its energy needs. Landfill gas accounts for about 60 percent of the fuel used by the new $56 million plant near Birmingham. The company sees its investment in environmentally sound technology as having both national and economic value. Experts have contended that similar projects generate savings of between 20 and 50 percent of the cost of natural gas. According to Mike Jenkins V, "It benefits us and it benefits the world."[26]

There is little doubt that as a privately owned company, Jenkins Brick had greater flexibility to pursue paths that managers thought would be financially beneficial for their investors and senior executives as well as their employees. Although they had to convince senior management and the board of the value of their plans, they did not have to convince stock analysts. Tommy Andreades recalled:

> I came from public accounting and was in a public company for ten
> years. And what's very much enjoyable about being private is that we
> can sit around and think about what's best for the company as opposed
> to what our shareholders are going to think about our decision and
> the short-term benefits of it. Personally, we take some pops. We're
> building a new plant. Everyone who's on bottom-line incentive—
> there's four of us—we're going backwards for two or three years.
> And that's fine. We know that it's the right thing for the company
> and what the rewards will be down the road if we do a good job of it.
> So we don't have to worry about what our shareholders think about
> it. And we make good decisions more times than not.[27]

Of course, Jenkins Brick was not immune to the general economic climate. The downturn in the housing market brought about a new set of challenges and resulted in cutbacks in production. However, as the following chapters will show, companies with lower turnover rates and greater employee loyalty are better at weathering economic downturns.

Dancing Deer: Profit Sharing as a Way for Small Firms to Increase Compensation and Productivity

From the outside, the company's main building looked much like the other two-story warehouses in its relatively poor Boston neighborhood.

Inside, however, it was completely different. The building's ground floor housed the clean and well-lit bakery, and the second floor was where all the sales and management staff workstations were located, from entry-level administrative staff to the CEO. There were no walls or partitions between the desks.

The company's CEO, Trish Karter, had experience working at other firms and she knew that she wanted something different for her company. She was convinced that she could make a larger profit by treating her employees better.

The Challenge of Operating Within the Constraints of a Small Business

Though the company was born out of chance encounters, its long-term success stems from business acumen and commitment. CEO Trish Karter left college one semester short of completing her BA in order to help her father with his recycling business. She later received an MBA from Yale and gained business experience working in Coca-Cola's marketing department, in satellite television, in commercial real estate development, and in consulting. She explained the path to Dancing Deer Baking Company's opening:

> Actually, I [had been] a businessperson in the entrepreneurial world, and then [I] quit and I was painting pictures . . . We had a house-painter whose wife, [Suzanne], was a baker and she came to us for business advice. She was carrying her pots and pans to a rented kitchen facility at night. So the genesis of it was really a hobby invest-ment; we put $20,000 into setting her up in an old pizza parlor on the corner of Grove and Washington in West Roxbury. Originally the concept was to put all-natural baked goods in coffeehouses because the coffee craze was coming east from California; you could buy these incredible brews of coffee but there wasn't anything good to eat with them. Everyone who [tasted one of Suzanne's baked goods] said, "Wow, it's wonderful! I'll buy that!" And in about a year and a half she was overwhelmed with business. She could barely hold herself up. She was doing great things and everybody loved it, but she was exhausted. I volunteered to go in for a few months and hire some people and put some systems in place and clear off the foot-and-a-half tall stack of unprocessed CODs on her desk . . . That was ten

years ago. And we had fun together. I never left . . . One thing led to another, and we made a great partnership . . . We knew we wanted to have a brand from it. The business was building in a strategic direction . . . and we brought in an old friend of mine with talent to help us create an identity for the company. You know, just spadeful by spadeful, we built it up.[28]

But the development of Dancing Deer had by no means been a fairy tale free of personal and professional challenges. As Trish Karter explained, "In . . . 2000, we nearly blew it up because my ex-husband and I got a divorce. That year . . . was kind of a near-death experience for many of us. But at the end of it all, I ended up staying and buying [Suzanne and my ex-husband] out."

Dancing Deer's founders shared a vision of how to make the company profitable for the management by making it profitable for the employees. They were committed to creating a quality workplace for all of their employees, based on the principle that "if bakers like what they do, it shows in the food." As Karter described:

We all wanted to have the company be better than what . . . we saw around us, and that meant better in every way, including personnel policies. And we believed in everybody having a piece of the value that's created. Everyone that participates in creating value should have some upside. It shouldn't be just about collecting a paycheck. We also wanted everyone to be knowledgeable about what we were doing because we believed that the more people understood the business, the better thinking we'd get on how to improve and grow the business.[29]

As a small business, Dancing Deer had always faced challenges in providing well for its employees. Starting wages were low ($7.25 per hour for packers and $7.50–$8.00 per hour for bakers), but they were higher than the minimum wage and equal to or higher than food production jobs elsewhere. Nonetheless, these wages were low for an individual to live on in an expensive city like Boston, and they were lower still for a family. From the company's standpoint, they were also low when it came to employee retention. It all boiled down to economics: because the baked goods they produced were already being sold at the top end of the market, the company executives worried that they would go out of business if they raised prices further to allow for higher wages. They felt their best long-term prospects for survival lay in increasing their productivity, their sales, and their share of the market. Karter explained how they dealt with these constraints:

> I would love to be able to tell you that everyone who walks through the door gets $12 an hour, but we can't do that. In the world we live in, with a huge component of our product being the manual labor that goes into it, and being challenged and very pressured competitively, we're at the top end of the market in terms of pricing. What we have to do in order to make it all work is to manage our numbers so [that] as we raise wages, it's in lockstep with raising efficiencies and getting smarter about running the business.[30]

They were looking forward to the time when their fixed costs would go down and their production would go up, leaving more room for wage increases without increasing the prices of their products. But what could they do in the meantime? Small businesses often find it harder to offer benefits such as health insurance coverage in countries like the United States, since large companies are able to negotiate better deals with insurance providers. Yet this does not mean that small companies are incapable of providing benefits. While recognizing its limitations as a small business, Dancing Deer sought to provide all of its employees with good working conditions and asset-building opportunities.

In start-up companies, executives often take the calculated risk of receiving stock options in exchange for lower salaries, based on the belief that they will make more money in the long run that way. CEOs and top management can afford to defer their income gains, since their earnings and assets are still more than sufficient to live on and tide them over. But hardly any companies have offered stock options to their line workers. Companies have assumed that line workers won't understand or value these options. Moreover, low-income workers clearly can't afford to defer their income in the same way as managers.

In 1996, Dancing Deer defied tradition and put stock options in place for everyone, from bakery and factory floor workers to senior management. The company ensured that it paid its line workers wages that were at least as high as those paid for similar jobs elsewhere. Unlike management, line workers were not asked to accept lower salaries in exchange for stock options; that would have been utterly unrealistic since there was no way they could have lived adequately on reduced salaries. It was also unnecessary for them to do so, since the company was able to price its goods in line with similar products from other companies.

Management believed that providing stock options would be good for employees since it would allow them to grow assets and share in the company's financial success. The company would benefit from employees' increased sense of ownership. The stock-option program provided a way to distribute the benefits of everyone's hard work while ensuring that employees felt the importance of increasing the company's productivity.

Providing Stock Options

It is extremely rare for a small business to provide stock options to its lowest-level employees. According to the U.S. Bureau of Labor Statistics, only 1 percent of employees in small businesses receive stock options as part of their employment package, and those who do are overwhelmingly professionals.[31]

At Dancing Deer, all employees enter the stock-option program when they are hired. There is a four-year vesting period, and at the end of each year an additional 25 percent of stock is vested. The amount of stock that employees are entitled to is determined according to five employee categories, starting with nonsupervisory workers, who are entitled to a thousand shares. The second incarnation of the plan began August 15, 2006, at which time the company closed the original plan and paid those with stock options, with amounts ranging from $1,000 to $10,000. How much are Dancing Deer stock options worth? Karter did the calculations: "Stock options are tied to the sales of the company. Employees get one thousand to ten thousand shares. There are 3 million shares outstanding. The goal is to get one year's annual wages out of the market transition (in approximately four years) . . . Eventually there will be a merger or a strategic acquisition. If Dancing Deer [gets] to $100 million in five years, even with only a thousand shares, it's a lot of money."[32]

This was their vision, but were they able to make it happen? Like many rapidly growing companies, Dancing Deer periodically needed to seek venture capital to enable and stimulate growth; in exchange for venture capital, investors received stock options. Dancing Deer had to raise capital when it moved out of its facilities in the old pizza shop into the commercial production facility in Roxbury. Every time the company had to raise more capital for growth, it ran the risk of a decline in the value of employee stock options unless its productivity and sales outpaced the dilution of the stocks. Thankfully, company growth was rapid, and it was significant enough for employees to notice it. Between 2005 and 2006, sales increased by 74 percent and stock options increased in value by 40 percent.

Even if the company's value grew to only half of Trish Karter's aspired $100 million—either because the company itself did not grow rapidly or because of the downturn in the overall economy—and even if this more limited growth required bringing in more capital, employees' assets would still be significant. Keith Rousseau, the controller, calculated: "So if . . . [we were up to] $50 million, and I'm assuming 4 million shares . . . that might get you to $10 an option, which would leave you about eight or nine grand for a thousand [options] for a four- or five-year period."[33]

Dancing Deer was aware of the stereotypes about so-called low-skilled employees not understanding the stock options, but their experience contradicted these generalizations. Management developed clear tools for explaining stock options to employees who had never owned stock and who did not know anyone who had ever received options. The employee handbook explained what the payout would be for stock options after the $40 million valuation point and it gave a straightforward explanation of the link between employees' efforts and the worth of the stock options: "These options are a valuable part of your earnings and are an incentive for you to use your best efforts, every day. We believe this program is one of the key reasons why we are a healthy and growing company. We also believe it's the right thing to do . . . The increased value is tied directly to the increased sales level of the company. Since each of you impacts our ability to grow, we think you each should share [in the] upside."[34]

Employees were clearly aware of the stock-options program and of its potential to benefit them. Keith Rousseau described how the stock options became much more concrete for all the employees when they saw other employees cash in their options. He gave the example of Carlos Cardoza, a monolingual Spanish-speaking employee who had been with the company for ten years. Cardoza was about to return to Colombia to care for his elderly mother. His options had vested and he would be turning them in before he left in exchange for a check. Rousseau described the situation: "He doesn't speak English well, but he certainly understands that . . . when he started, they were packing cookies in a little pizza shop, and he knows [the company's growth] is worth something . . . I think people understand that they have ownership."[35]

Trish Karter further elaborated on employees' sense of ownership:

I would say the minority of [employees understand] the technical functionality of the shares. But how many of them get the sense, understand that they've got some piece of it, and that they're all valued, that it's not just a meritocracy, but there's an egalitarian sense that there is no unimportant work? [They all understand that] whether you're a dishwasher or you're running the marketing of the company, your job is important and you have a say. It might not be a huge say, economically, but your voice is just as loud.[36]

Crucially, these stock options did not replace retirement benefits. In companies where all of line workers' pensions have been invested in the company's own stock, employees face far too great a risk if the company fails. The stock options at Dancing Deer gave employees a chance to earn from the company's profits while still receiving wages consistent with the industry and pension benefits to live on once they retired.

TRANSLATING ASSET BUILDING INTO RETURNS FOR THE COMPANY

Dancing Deer had two main motivations for implementing the stock-options program, one of which was a sense of fairness. Management believed that employees should receive some share of the growth resulting from their hard work. The other motivation was economic, based on the notion that enabling employees to have a stake in the company would result in higher earnings.

INCREASING PRODUCTIVITY

When employees were hired, they were told that they would be getting stock options and they would therefore have a stake in the company. But this alone was not enough for ownership to translate into economic performance. In practical terms, translating partial employee ownership into increased productivity required two crucial steps.

First, all employees had to be made aware of how the company was faring against its target outcome measures. Rousseau described how they accomplished this by holding a series of meetings with employees:

We have a flash group which [consists of] pretty much all the senior management. We went through [this with them] last Tuesday and then what we're going to do is have two or three different meetings [with all the employees] . . . We'll bring everyone up, show them the sales, show them the expenses, show them the profits; explain to them what looks good compared to last year and what looks good compared to our budget, and what doesn't look good compared to last year, what doesn't look good compared to our budget; [show them] our strengths and weaknesses; and try to explain the best we can—without giving them an accounting course—how we're doing. And that seems to be one of the things that people really enjoy hearing . . . Since I've been here we've certainly had great quarters of sales and great quarters of earnings and we've had poor quarters of sales and poor quarters of earnings. And people take it to heart if things aren't going right, or if things are going great. It's the same as with a sports team . . . Everyone feels very [involved] . . . There's a good deal of ownership.[37]

The second step was more complicated. It required ensuring that the whole staff—from production to sales—participated in improving outcomes and understood the reciprocal relationship between their performance and the quantity of sales. Rousseau explained:

You're just not going to continue to grow your sales at a 30 to 50 percent growth rate if you don't have a good product, if you don't have good customer service, if you're putting the . . . cookies in the wrong boxes . . . Because a lot of times . . . there's a mentality with the operations folks that they don't have any control over the sales, and there's the perception that we're always trying to fight. [They say,] "How can I affect how much sales you bring in?" And the sales guys have the also misguided perception that they have no control over operating margins or that kind of stuff. Where in fact, it's a continued conversation. The operations team very much has an effect on sales based off of the product and the experience that the customer's going to get. If operations is just mixing up boxes and giving out stale cookies, that's going to hinder the sales [team's] ability to sell. And the flip side, if the sales guys are continually creating these low-margin items that are difficult to manufacture, they're gonna impact the manufacturing operations and margins. So trying to have one common theme throughout . . . How do you increase your sales? It's [by having] better sales, better operations, better customer experience. I think that's what we've proven. It's one of the major contributors to why we've grown so fast . . . Really having a great customer experience, really pushing to have the highest quality, [the] best product out there.[38]

Encouraging involvement and input from workers at all levels of the company was essential to the success of employee ownership. Management had to be willing to listen to the production staff. Trish Karter made frequent visits to the bakery, during which she listened to employees' suggestions. Employees at all levels felt that their input was valued and influential. Marta Sánchez, a mother of two, had been with the company for six years. Originally from El Salvador, she had worked at a restaurant in a neighboring town before coming to Dancing Deer to pack cookies. She summarized the company's openness to suggestions: "Good ideas are appreciated."[39] This was not the case for many workers at the bottom of the ladder in other companies. Keith Rousseau explained how the company benefited from employees' suggestions:

> One of the things that we love doing and that Trish loves talking about is being able to ask any of the employees: "What is working about this particular line or this particular process? What can be improved?" And we've had a bunch of things come up. We had one [situation] recently where one of the packing supervisors was playing around with one of our machines and packed cookies differently and brought it upstairs and said, "You know, this is a lot faster than the way we're doing it and it looks kind of cool." And of course one of the sales guys gobbled it up and said, "You know, we're looking for new packaging for one of our other customers. This would be perfect." And so there's a good chance that [it] . . . might show up as one of our new product lines. So we're continuously trying to . . . get feedback from everyone in the organization. One of Trish's great mottos is that some of the best ideas come from the people that you typically wouldn't ask first-off. So that's one of the reasons we've grown so quickly and the processes have increasingly gotten better.[40]

Receiving quality input from employees was an essential ingredient in ensuring that Dancing Deer's investments in its employees at all levels led to improved performance and profits.

LOWERING TURNOVER AND RECRUITMENT COSTS, AND OTHER ECONOMIC BENEFITS

Two of Dancing Deer's rewards for its efforts to provide good working conditions have been its low turnover rate compared to other companies in the industry, and its ease of recruitment. Like at Jenkins Brick, management was aware of the fact that the length of an employee's stay with the company had an impact on productivity. They also knew that they had to outdo their competitors, for whom turnover was a big issue. When we spoke with Lissa McBurney, the production manager, she noted that only one baking employee had left in three and a half years. Apart from the temporary employees they hired only for high seasons, only two packers left per year out of a staff of twenty-two.[41] Of those who left, very few did so due to dissatisfaction with their jobs; most left to pursue better opportunities, such as starting their own businesses.

The company's low turnover rate was achieved through the financial incentives offered to employees and the overall commitment to good working conditions. Keith Rousseau explained:

> I think the folks that really understand where Dancing Deer is going and really have a good understanding of what the potential upside is [are] more inclined to stay and wait it out, you know, and hope for this big payout . . . Being able to keep people here [also] tends to be something that's a result of people being happy, people feeling like they're respected, and the ability to have equal communication throughout the company.[42]

In addition to fostering low turnover, Dancing Deer's reputation as a good place to work has made it easy for them to attract good employees. Karter delineated how they had gathered a large pool of applicants to choose from:

> What we have going for us . . . We have a great pool of people that want to work here. We put an ad on Craigslist or Monster . . . or we put a word out to the network—just my network of people in the business—and we're swamped with [applicants]. And we [hear] the same thing, largely, which is: "I love your company. I don't exactly have the qualifications you're looking for, but I'd really love to

figure out a way to work with you." And so you have options [of whom to hire].[43]

Outside observers commented on the impact. Referring to her conversations with a management consultant, production manager Lissa McBurney said: "He is . . . amazed at how well our people perform . . . That people want to do well. In working with him over the past six months I've realized [how much the investments do] pay off for us economically."[44]

Most companies offer asset-building programs only to their highest-level workers, in spite of the greater financial risks an absence of assets presents for their lowest-level employees. The companies profiled in this chapter clearly demonstrate that there are both ready means and strong benefits to companies offering asset-building opportunities to all employees. Dancing Deer's stock-option program was formulated in such a way as to provide incentives for employees to remain with the company, which in turn contributed to a reduction in turnover rates. The company had lower recruitment and retraining costs, as well as higher productivity from highly motivated employees. Jenkins Brick chose to contribute to employees' asset building by establishing a pension plan and a profit-sharing scheme. Like Dancing Deer, Jenkins Brick had benefited from these programs by experiencing reduced turnover, since employees' gains increased with the duration of their stay with the company.

Both companies offered programs that greatly benefited their workers by providing them with rare asset-building opportunities, and both companies also gained from these programs. Profit sharing and stock options linked employees' productivity to the companies' financial returns, since employees' assets increased alongside the company's improvements in performance. As a direct result, both companies experienced gains in employee productivity and product quality.

Beyond reaping the direct economic benefits, these companies also had the advantage of having a harder-working, more engaged, and lower-turnover workforce. Dancing Deer's overall commitment to providing good working conditions has brought them reputational advantages.[45] Trish Karter saw Dancing Deer's reputation as an important asset to the business: "Our social activism builds consumer loyalty and attracts highly motivated employees."[46]

Challenges of an Asset-Building Approach

Despite profit sharing's demonstrated ability to improve productivity among professionals when it is structured correctly, three perceived obstacles have kept many companies from expanding profit-sharing programs to workers at the bottom of the corporate ladder: first, the misconception that profit sharing does not motivate everyone across the economic spectrum; second, the concern that many of the usual ways to profit share are too complex to be readily understood by line workers; and third, the concern that it is difficult to find the right incentives.

We hope this chapter and the experiences demonstrated by Jenkins Brick, Dancing Deer, and others have convincingly laid to rest the misconception that economic incentives function so differently across the corporate spectrum that they are not transferable to employees at the bottom of the ladder. Clearly, there are differences across income levels. Everyone needs to earn enough to survive, and employees earning lower salaries cannot be expected to defer compensation in exchange for profit sharing. That being said, the knowledge that they will share in the company's profits motivates line workers just as it does vice presidents.

Dancing Deer demonstrated the feasibility of implementing complex forms of profit sharing such as stock options by making them both comprehensible and tangible to employees with limited formal education. The company developed materials that explained their stock options, guided workers through concrete examples, and talked in clear terms about what the money would mean for them. Jenkins Brick as well as Great Little Box (a company that will be discussed in chapter 7) are examples of companies that have found straightforward ways to share profits on either an annual or a monthly basis without requiring workers to understand the concept of stock options. Setting such programs in place requires one of two things: either using a transparent mechanism or developing materials that translate complex mechanisms into straightforward explanations of their impacts on individuals.

Perhaps the most complex—but still solvable—dilemma is how to get incentives on profit sharing right. Clearly consideration needs to be given in any particular setting to the advantages and disadvantages of profit sharing done on a monthly basis as it has been at the Great Little Box Company, so that workers can receive immediate rewards for progress;

on an annual basis to encourage intermediate-term thinking as done at Jenkins Brick; and longer-term vesting, be it through profit-sharing plans such as the one at Jenkins Brick or the stock options offered at Dancing Deer, which reward longevity in the company but provide far less immediate returns. Most successful companies in our research found a way to structure asset building so that workers both experienced immediate rewards—either in the form of immediate payment or of up-to-date notification of asset accumulation—and had long-term incentives to stay with their firms, either because vesting required them to do so or because they wanted to stay long enough to reap the investments that the company had made as a whole.

5

Offering Training Where It Is Valued Most

COMPANIES CAN REAP TREMENDOUS benefits by offering training to their employees, most directly by improving their workers' job-related skills and productivity.[1] Because training opportunities are valued by current and prospective employees, they can also facilitate employee recruitment and retention. Research has found that firms that offer training opportunities attract more competent workers who are also more likely to stay with the firm.[2] Despite these clear advantages, few companies offer training opportunities to all of their employees.

Although training and skill building give adults access to advancement opportunities at work and provide them with skills that increase their value and potential on the job market, access to training is limited for the lowest-level workers. In fact, the overwhelming majority of training opportunities worldwide are offered to those who already have an advantage. While countries and companies vary in the amount of training they offer, almost all demonstrate a steep gradient, with workers who have the least amount of formal education having access to the fewest opportunities for further training. According to a survey on adult education and training in Canada, participation in employer-supported training varied widely by skill level, with workers in professional or managerial occupations having the highest rates of participation (35 percent), followed by white-collar workers in clerical, sales, and service positions (20 percent) and blue-collar workers (16 percent).[3] Participation in job-related training also increased with workers' level of educational attainment: over half (52 percent) of workers with a university degree participated in training, while only 18 percent of workers with a high school education or less did so. While participation rates increased substantially between 1997 and 2002 for workers with higher levels of education, the increases were negligible for workers with a high school education or less. Research in France showed that while 56 percent of engineers and 42 percent of supervisors had access to training, the same was true for only 12 percent of "unskilled" workers.[4] The U.S. Bureau of Labor Statistics' *Survey of Employer-Provided Training* found that 60 percent of workers with a high school education or less had access to employer-provided training, compared to 90 percent of employees with a college degree.[5]

As part of our study of companies in nine countries, which included interviews with more than two thousand working adults, their supervisors, and company executives, we spoke with individuals at each firm about the training opportunities available to the lowest-level employees. We examined what their training programs were designed to do in theory and how they were implemented in practice. We interviewed C-level executives and senior management about their goals in designing the training and their perceptions of its impact; we spoke with the least-advantaged workers about their experiences with the training; and we talked to middle managers, who often played a particularly critical role in determining whether the training was implemented in the manner in which it had been designed and whether or not all employees had practical access to it. We also analyzed the evidence that the training had markedly influenced both the lives of the least-advantaged workers and the productivity of the firm.

The skill sets acquired during training can be essential for employees to perform entry-level jobs, can improve the quality of their work, can be necessary for advancement within the company, and can be beneficial to the employee in seeking jobs elsewhere. This chapter focuses on training that is important for employees to be able to perform well at their current jobs.

The companies featured in this chapter were chosen because their experiences demonstrate the varied forms training can take in small, midsize, and larger firms in a range of manufacturing, service, and sales settings. Each highlights different important aspects of successful training. The experiences at Isola underscore the critical role that training can play in ensuring that workers with limited formal education can continue working at a firm after mechanization and computerization take place.

Novo Nordisk illustrates training in a large, multinational context. Dancing Deer demonstrates the feasibility of providing training in the smallest of firms. Finally, the case study of Banco de Crédito del Peru and the Ann Sullivan Center is included because their experience with autistic and severely developmentally delayed adults highlights the role that training can play in creating employment opportunities for individuals who might otherwise not be able to work.

Career tracks for the lowest-level employees will be addressed in the next chapter. We look at career tracks separately for several reasons. First, they are the rarest of all decent working conditions available to workers at the bottom of the corporate ladder. Second, while career advancement often requires training, training in and of itself is not sufficient to create career tracks; top management also needs to believe in the importance of career tracks for everyone, and hire and promote accordingly. Third, while providing excellent training opportunities to lowest-level employees can support career tracks, training can be crucial even in the absence of career tracks. It can increase employees' productivity by making them more efficient, which also increases all wages and assets that are linked to productivity. Mechanization and computerization of a wide range of tasks are increasingly occurring in manufacturing and service sectors alike. Individuals often require training to be able to use this new equipment in order to obtain entry-level positions or to retain low-level jobs.

Isola: Training Employees to Keep Up with Change

Producing in Norway with high wages and benefits, Isola managing director Erik Withbro was aware that his company needed employees to be more productive in order to remain competitive with lower-wage countries in Europe.[6] An essential component of the strategy that enabled them to do so was the automation of production and the introduction of a team system that required less middle management. The new machines could produce more with fewer employees, but more advanced skills were required to operate the high-tech equipment. Similarly, the new, flatter structure in operations, which gave teams more decision-making power, also demanded that they have more skills. Although Isola had the option of hiring new workers who had the necessary skills to operate the new machines and to collaborate as a semiautonomous team, instead it chose to keep its existing pool of workers and upgrade their skills through training.

The company set up a variety of training programs that were made available to all workers.

Factory Mechanization

Located in two vast warehouses next to corporate headquarters in Porsgrunn, one of the Isola plants produces shingles and other roofing materials. When we visited the factory in 2007, there were hardly any workers in sight. One employee was driving a forklift and a few others were washing machines and working at computers, but the plant was virtually empty. This vacancy was deceiving since one might easily assume that the factory was not in operation. In fact, the machines were working at full speed, placing asphalt on shingles, cutting them into preselected shapes and sizes, and covering roofing materials with steel. Robotic forklifts were moving heavy materials from one section of the plant to another. Virtually the entire production process had been automated; all of the equipment was being run by computers.

The mechanization of the plant had drastically reduced the number of employees required to do the work. While 145 workers were needed in 1988, by August of 2007 this number was down to 28, and Withbro knew that the workforce could be further reduced to 23 or 24 employees while still increasing production. What was striking was that Isola had not needed to lay off employees. Its workforce was naturally reduced as many of the workers reached the age of retirement. Furthermore, although there were fewer workers at each plant, the company's steady growth had allowed it to open more factories, which created new job openings. In the end, the firm had avoided mass layoffs by becoming more efficient, thereby enabling expansion. Most employees found the remaining jobs to be more varied and interesting, as well as less physically demanding.

Mikkel Nanseth had a mechanics background but had required additional training to adapt to the new machinery; he had taken classes at the factory to become a machine operator. Isola offered a free six-month training course that took place twice a week in the afternoons. Workers at the plant rotated between the morning shift (6 a.m. to 2 p.m.) and the afternoon/evening shift (2 p.m. to 10 p.m.). When they were on the early shift, they stayed a few hours late to attend class, and when they were on the afternoon/evening shift, they were permitted to leave work early twice a week to attend the training sessions. Nanseth told us how he felt about the classes: "It's not so much fun taking the class at this age, but it's worth it.

The class is free and you get a new profession."[7] After taking a certification test, he would also get a raise once he knew how to operate the new machinery. Nanseth made it clear that he took the class "not so much for the money," since the raise wasn't substantial, but rather because of the new opportunities it would open up for him. He told us what it was like to work in the mechanized factory: "I like the work better now that it's more mechanized. The factory is more open; you can see the whole process. You have to be involved in more things and it makes the day go [by] faster."

Teamwork Production

In addition to mechanization, Isola decided to implement a new structure for production and set in place a team-based work method, which will be explained in more detail in chapter 7. The teamwork method meant that production was restructured so that groups of six or seven workers formed a team with a team leader selected by management. Workers were given significantly more decision-making power and autonomy. This meant that for a team to be successful, Isola needed workers to have the training that would enable them to make far more production decisions independently.

Isola offered a variety of training opportunities that allowed workers to gain the necessary skills to operate in the newly mechanized workplace and to take on the greater responsibilities brought on by the teamwork approach. Kristian Nilsen, one of the workers we interviewed, exemplified both the skills and the attitude Isola was looking for. He was happy to perform many varied tasks and went around the plant looking for ways of improving production. He had ideas about safety that he wanted to share after an accident involving an older worker. On rare occasions when products were returned by purchasers, he wanted to examine the returned products himself so that he could determine how to fix the problem and do a better job the next time. He had taken a course that provided production management training and certification. Although he had limited formal education, the company profited from his abundant experience with machinery.

Improving Basic Skills

It was not easy for some of the workers to adapt to the mechanization of the factory and to its new production structure. Employees had different reactions to the need to undergo more training. Some were enthusiastic, recognizing the advantages of having new skills, while others were resistant, having difficulty admitting that they first needed to acquire basic literacy skills. The training was daunting for those who had never worked with computers before and even more so for those who lacked basic skills such as reading and writing. While literacy skills had not been required for manual labor, they were essential in the mechanized factory. Isola offered special classes to help workers improve their basic reading and writing skills.

The production manager and one of the main union leaders at the Porsgrunn plant had publicly admitted that they had difficulty reading and had attended the classes at the factory. These leaders' participation in the basic skills classes was the key to the program's success, as it made other workers more willing to get involved. Erik Withbro told us: "People who have hidden these problems for so long, I admire them for going to the course and [letting] everyone . . . see they have a problem."[8] Those who attended the courses succeeded in acquiring these basic skills and went on to succeed at the technical training courses needed to adapt to the new machinery.

Workers at the plant in Platoon were more reticent to take part, preferring to try to hide their inability to read and write. Those who refused to participate in the literacy classes continued to face difficulties with the machine-specific training and often ended up taking an early retirement.

Advanced Courses

Isola also offered several more-advanced training options, for which participating employees were paid wages. Upon completing the advanced Technical Education class, employees could take the Skilled Worker test. If they passed both the theoretical and the practical components, they got a raise. In addition, team leader training courses took place one week a month for five months. Morten Stiansen, a production worker with a primary school education, had been with the company for twenty-one years. He had just finished an Isola training course to receive a Fagbrev (certificate of specialization). The course had taken place two evenings a week, and Stiansen had attended the class during his afternoon shift. He had passed the theory test and would get a raise if he passed the upcoming practical test.

While workers showed different levels of enthusiasm for training, they all agreed that the opportunities were available to anyone who wished to take advantage of them. As one worker explained: "The company is supportive of people, encouraging [them] to take [part in] education."[9] A sales employee who had been at Isola for thirty-two years told us how the company had paid for several of her external courses in addition to offering internal training. "Employees can take whatever education they want to. I've taken business and upper secondary courses [and] a lot of sales courses. In general, you can just apply [for an external course if Isola does not offer the class] and the company will let you do it."[10]

Training in a Wide Range of Companies: From Local Firms to Multinationals

Nearly all the top companies we studied not only valued the skills that people at the bottom of the ladder already had, but also built on them. Regardless of firm size, sector, and geography, they found a way to profit from providing the least-advantaged workers with training opportunities, both general and job-specific.

Dancing Deer: Building Human Capital

In addition to setting up programs to help its employees build financial assets, Dancing Deer strongly invested in human capital. The company went beyond providing job-specific training by offering training that would help employees both while they worked at Dancing Deer and when they sought jobs outside of the company. Their on-the-job training covered basic workplace skills such as answering the phone and dealing with interpersonal issues at work. In addition, the in-house training included English as a Second Language (ESL), and employees could apply for reimbursement of up to $500 a year for external education courses. This form of human capital building is rarely available to employees at the bottom of the ladder.

Most production employees at Dancing Deer are immigrants with fairly limited English skills and little or no work experience in the United States. During our visit in 2005, production manager Lissa McBurney described her staff: "They come from Cape Verde, [from] all over Central America and . . . South America; a few [are] Chinese [or] Vietnamese, and [there is] one native-born American. We have a few staff [members] who are Cape Verdean but were born or came to this country as small children and are more Americanized, but the vast majority of people have come to the country recently or have been in the country for a while but speak very little English . . . There are some people who don't read or write in their native tongue, and they don't read or write in English either, so it's a fairly low skill level."[11]

Research has shown that poor English skills are associated with higher rates of unemployment and lower wages for immigrants. Data from the National Adult Literacy Survey (NALS) showed that immigrants in the United States who had the lowest level of English language proficiency (Level 1) had an unemployment rate of 13 percent, and only 68 percent were in the workforce; immigrants with proficiency levels of 4 or 5 had next to no unemployment and had a 95 percent workforce participation rate. The study also showed an association between English proficiency and immigrants' wages.[12] Recognizing the importance of English skills, Dancing Deer held ESL classes during shift time and paid wages for attendance. The company received some state funding for this training, which it used to pay the teachers. In the summer of 2004, thirty-three employees—nearly the entire baking and packing staff—participated in the eight-week in-house ESL courses offered at two different levels.

Most companies offer only job-specific training because they worry that workers will leave once they have acquired new skills. The management at Dancing Deer felt that this risk was counterbalanced by the benefits of having a higher-skilled workforce. When asked about the cost/benefit ratio of providing the training and ESL classes, CEO Trish Karter explained that the expense was more than paid back by improving communication between employees, which in turn increased the efficiency of operations at all levels. In addition, Karter felt that the ESL classes strengthened employees' loyalty to and investment in the company.

> You know, it's practical . . . [Employees think]: "Well, wow! This company's going to pay me to sit in that classroom for two hours to improve my English skills, and I've only been in this country for a year or two . . . and I just started to work here? Really?" You cannot substitute a positive outlook for anything. You just either have it or you don't. People who don't have that good feeling about what they're doing and the place where they're doing it, you can push them real hard in a sweatshop but it's never going to be as good as what you're going to get when it's a voluntary effort.[13]

Karter knew that Dancing Deer would benefit from its employees' increased skills for the duration of their stay with the company.

The firm was also supportive of employees who moved on. According to Dancing Deer controller Keith Rousseau, immigrants sometimes used these jobs as a way to gain the language and business skills they needed to launch their own small enterprises. Karter offered an example of how departures could be an occasion for both pride and sadness:

> Attalina . . . had been [in the communist government] in Albania, and got a green card. And three weeks later she was knocking on the door of Dancing Deer with a friend who [acted as] the translator. We were busy that day and I was literally packing cookies and needed help so I said, "You know, come on in." And over the years she learned to speak English. She brought her husband in; he ran the night shift [and] gained food-handling skills. Both of their English skills improved dramatically. They learned a lot about running a small business. He actually bought his own pizza parlor and has been running that ever since. [He] makes a very decent living. Is it because of Dancing Deer? Partly, yes. There are skills he learned here. And then Attalina, she eventually ran the whole packing area, making really good wages, and finally this summer she had an opportunity to work in an organization that does . . . student loans, [where she could] actually use her economics skills. And it was a better job in terms of work hours. She has children [and] she wanted to be able to be with them more. [The new job] was more predictable, the commute was easier, [and they offered] higher wages than we could afford to pay at that point for someone running the packing crew. It was one of the saddest and happiest days of my life to see her go on, having come through here with nothing. She knocked on the door with nothing but she learned so much [here] about management and business and English.[14]

Overall, contrary to common fears, investing in human capital did not lead to increased turnover for Dancing Deer. The company had extremely low turnover since the training was done in the context of a good work environment with other asset-building programs that provided employees with an incentive to stay.

Novo Nordisk: Training in a Global Context

Novo Nordisk, a multinational Danish pharmaceutical company with over twenty-six thousand employees worldwide, is a world leader in diabetes care.[15] Its production facility in Tianjin, China, provides an example of how multinational companies producing in countries with lower labor standards can provide employees with working conditions comparable to those in any of their locations around the world. Novo Nordisk's emphasis on training opportunities was part of its overall focus on employee well-being, which included paying attention to workers' health. There were numerous opportunities for promotion within the company, and managers saw training as a way to maintain employee motivation. In a 2006 interview, Christian Larsen, senior manager of economy and logistics, explained the importance of providing employees with opportunities to acquire new skills: "People development is essential. If [employees] do not develop, they lose energy and motivation and they will talk [to their coworkers] and make other people lose energy."[16]

Novo Nordisk Tianjin had developed training in three areas: on-the-job training, external training, and English language courses. Liu Lin, an operator in insulin packaging, pointed out that with training, "Whether you are a leader, a manager, an operator, or whomever, your opportunities are equal. It depends on your own capabilities. Everyone has the opportunity to be promoted."[17]

On-the-job training consisted of informal training by managers on the factory floor. Zhong Xi Liang, a machine operator, gave us an example: "Each month, technicians will collect all the problems they have met this month and they will explain to us how they fixed them. All the workers will try to do this on their own after the lesson."[18] On-the-job training not only made workers more efficient, it also enabled them to gain skills that could lead to advancement. Gao Fang, an operator in the insulin department, explained: "When I first started to work here, I was only an operator. I have since had a lot more training and then became a team leader. I am very optimistic about the future and it depends on my own ability. If I can meet the skill requirements, then I think I can move up."[19]

Some employees traveled to Denmark for external training lasting from several days to several months. Workers were selected for this training based on whether the additional skills were necessary for their jobs and whether their language skills were good enough to understand the courses, which were offered in English. By the time of our first visit in 2006, a total of twenty-six employees had gone to Denmark for external training, and some engineers and technicians had gone multiple times.

Novo Nordisk had invested substantial resources in providing its employees with English courses; this was seen as a necessary investment since the company conducted the majority of its business in English. The company felt that if employees improved their English skills, they would be better able to understand the training materials and to express their questions and ideas, and this would ultimately lead to better overall performance. All employees could participate in the English courses once they had passed the initial six-month probation period. The company paid for the classes, which were held at the plant and in Tianjin, where most of the operators lived. Machine operators received two-hour English lessons after work, and managers received five-hour lessons. It was clear from our interviews with the factory workers that the opportunity to learn English was seen as a huge advantage of working at Novo Nordisk, since they felt that it improved their chances of advancing both within and outside of the company. Zhong Xi Liang remarked, "I really like English because . . . it is becoming a more and more useful tool internationally and it will be good for my future to develop it."[20] English skills raised employees' human capital and increased their employability on the labor market. As Gao Fang explained, "I think that learning English is really important as a tool, not only in China, but it is also the trend of the world. Everyone seems to know at least some English. I am pretty happy to receive this kind of training as it is not only useful here, but if I leave here and go somewhere else it will be hugely useful as well."[21]

Banco de Crédito del Peru and the Ann Sullivan Center: Training for All

The Banco de Crédito del Peru's (BCP) supported employment program for people with disabilities stands out from the training programs we have discussed thus far, which were primarily conducted from within and had clearly set goals of improving performance. The training at BCP was initiated by an outside organization and the long-term benefits of the program turned out to be substantially different from what the company had originally anticipated. The employees targeted by the training program were also different. While the training at Isola, Dancing Deer, and Novo Nordisk was aimed at current company employees, the BCP program targeted people who would not normally be considered potential employees of the bank.

The Ann Sullivan Center (Centro Ann Sullivan del Peru, or CASP) trained people with developmental disabilities to work at BCP, providing them with the necessary skills to become productive employees at the company. Employees who participated in the supported employment program received the same salary and benefits as their nondisabled counterparts, worked in integrated settings, and received ongoing support and skills training.

People with a wide range of disabilities have more limited access to employment opportunities, and their unemployment rates are on average 40 to 60 percent higher than those of the general population.[22] Legislation protecting the rights of people with disabilities is often not sufficient to equalize their participation in the labor market. Although the United States has some of the most comprehensive legislation protecting the rights of people with disabilities, studies have found that nondisabled adults aged twenty-one to sixty-four had an employment rate of 82 percent, compared to 41 percent for those with a mental disability and 32 percent for those with a functional limitation.[23] The situation is even more severe in developing countries. In Peru, although the law protects people with disabilities' right to work and gives companies tax deductions for the salaries of their disabled employees, there is no specified funding for support personnel, technical support, or structural adaptations. According to the Institute for Social Security in Peru, less than 1 percent of individuals with severe disabilities were employed in 2004.

The Ann Sullivan Center is a world-renowned facility in Lima, Peru, that provides early intervention services, education, vocational training, and support for newborns to forty-six-year-olds with developmental disabilities ranging from autism to Down syndrome. It also provides extensive training and support for their families. Founded in 1979 by Dr. Liliana Mayo, CASP began modestly with Mayo teaching eight children in her parents' garage. In 2007, the center was operating on a budget of approximately US$670,000 per year and supported approximately 450 students with mental retardation, autism, and emotional and behavioral difficulties. CASP does not receive government funding and is entirely supported through donations from private enterprises and grants from primarily European foundations. Most of its funding is spent on providing training in basic living and communication skills and support for parents.

CASP's supported employment program was founded on the principle that "everyone can have a real job based on their abilities."[24] According to

Enrique Burgos, director of supported employment, students are trained to work with precision, speed, independence, and persistence in order to maximize their chances of success on the job. All supported employees are initially supervised by a job coach who assists them in learning about the job and adapting to the work environment. As supported employees' job-specific and social skills improve, they often learn to work without a job coach, but CASP continues to provide support as needed. When supported employees begin a new job, CASP conducts orientation sessions for their coworkers, and the center remains available afterward to retrain, help manage challenging behaviors or aspects of job performance, and provide any necessary consultations. As of March 2006, CASP had placed seventy-eight of its students in twenty-five businesses across Peru, including a major grocery chain, petroleum and mining companies, and financial services firms.

In 2003, CASP approached the Banco de Crédito del Peru regarding participation in its supported employment program. Headquartered in Lima, the bank has 217 branches throughout the country and employs eight thousand workers. CASP already had a long-standing relationship with the bank, which had handled its accounts for over two decades and had provided support for various CASP fund-raising activities. BCP carefully analyzed the program before agreeing to collaborate. Its human resources department had concerns about whether the CASP graduates would be able to work well in teams in a financial institution. Numerous consultations took place over several months, and Maria Teresa Merino, BCP's director of selection and training, visited two companies that had already implemented supported employment programs. These visits helped convince her that CASP graduates could successfully be integrated into BCP:

> I had the opportunity to visit two companies where they had employees with disabilities, and I was really amazed at how these young people could perform. That helped me decide to support the program. There aren't too many companies [hiring employees with developmental disabilities], but the ones that are doing it are doing it well. This motivates you, doesn't it? I think companies are afraid that . . . young people with disabilities may not be able to succeed in becoming a part of the work team. [The companies] simply don't see it . . . There is not a model [for supported employment programs].[25]

In January of 2004, eight CASP graduates were placed in different departments at BCP, and four more graduates were placed in 2005. Their positions were carefully selected to match their skills, and BCP identified managers who were predisposed to incorporate supported employees into their teams.

The supported employees had a wide range of skills and consequently performed diverse tasks, such as filing confidential legal documents; picking up, preparing, and delivering mail; processing credit card applications; and entering data. Adequately matching supported employees' skills to the bank's needs has been critical in ensuring the program's success.

The program has had a large impact on the lives of the supported employees. Integrated into the community, the jobs were a source of great fulfillment, as was the opportunity to set and meet goals, to earn their own salaries, and to contribute to their households. Moreover, the extra income significantly improved the economic conditions of those from poor families, such as Ernesto Flores, who told us that his salary paid for electricity and water and helped to buy food for his family.

During the first years that they participated in the program, supported employees benefited from increased professional development. Many of them took on additional responsibilities and more complex tasks, and four of them began working independently without a coach. Supported employees also benefited from the opportunity to develop relationships with their coworkers, which substantially improved their communication skills. As Enrique Burgos explained, these are the areas where CASP graduates experience the greatest difficulty: "I can say with certainty that the [employees with developmental disabilities] do learn to perform their assigned tasks, [but] these are not their major difficulties . . . Those [difficulties] lie in areas of behavior, social interaction. and communication."[26]

Management executives at the bank clearly saw the program as a great success. It received significant positive media coverage, which provided free publicity and a public relations boost for BCP.[27] Employees at the bank, including those who'd had direct contact with the supported employees as well as those who hadn't, expressed positive feelings about the sense of social responsibility demonstrated by the program. They were proud that they worked at the only bank in Peru with such a program.

The greatest benefits of the program, however, were not necessarily those they had originally expected. BCP's participation in the supported employment program initially began as an act of charity stemming from a sense of moral obligation and an established commitment to community service. There were few expectations that the bank would benefit economically in any substantial way. As CEO Raimundo Morales explained: "What I was thinking is that we were giving help with few expectations . . . It was not that we were thinking that the program would fail, but we wanted [the supported employees] to feel appreciated, and so we felt we were doing an act of charity or generosity."[28]

Two years later, the bank viewed the main benefit of the program quite differently. People spoke about the positive impact it had had on employee morale and on the work environment as a whole. According to Raimundo Morales: "What I perceive, and what surprised me the most, is that [employees] around the [supported employees] are . . . much better off than they were before, including [being] more satisfied professionally with themselves . . . That generates a better work environment at the bank . . . It makes the whole organization feel and perform better, and for me that is the payback."[29]

One of the strengths of many supported employees is their ability to carry out tasks that are necessary but monotonous and repetitive without losing their motivation or enthusiasm. Several workers at the bank commented on how the supported employees set an example with their commendable work ethic and positive attitudes. A human resources manager explained:

> I think that there are two aspects to their contribution: [It has] definitely served to help people individually break their old paradigms with respect to whether people with [developmental] disabilities can or can't perform ordinary jobs. It has helped people . . . realize that these young people are capable of doing excellent work. [It has also] served to motivate people because when they run into a CASP-supported person and see him/her so dedicated and content in his/her job, they say to themselves: "I should feel the same [way] about my own job and also do excellent work."[30]

Given the success of the supported employment program at BCP, both the bank and CASP have been interested in increasing the number of supported employees in Lima and expanding the program to BCP branches in the provinces. The most important constraint in expanding the number of students involved has been the lack of adequate funding for CASP to pay for training and job coaches; in 2005 most job coaches were volunteers and parents of the supported employees. CASP also lacks the funding to cover a broader geographic area, which would require training and supporting staff in the provinces. As a result, to date the placement of students outside of Lima has been rather slow.

Avoiding the Traps That Prevent Effective Training

The training policies of the companies profiled in this chapter were extremely diverse, ranging from informal, on-the-job training where workers learned from their coworkers to formal sessions and courses, such as those offered at Isola. In most of the companies we profiled, training consisted of a mixture of both formal and informal opportunities in addition to complementary courses, such as ESL.

The motivations for implementing the training policies varied from one company to the next. Isola used training to upgrade its employees' skills to enable them to keep their jobs postmechanization. Dancing Deer and Novo Nordisk emphasized the importance of English-language classes to improve communication and productivity. Banco de Crédito del Peru and CASP used training and support to pave the way for individuals to work in jobs they otherwise couldn't obtain.

Regardless of their initial motivations, these firms found that training was a means of improving employee recruitment, retention, and motivation, as well as productivity. The employees we interviewed appreciated having these skill-building opportunities and repeatedly spoke of how training increased their commitment to stay with the company.

It seems self-evident to say that more highly trained employees are more productive, and that they therefore benefit the company. Workers who acquire more skills will clearly improve their job performance. However, although it can be advantageous, training is not cost-free. It requires companies to invest, by both covering the costs of the classes when formal training is provided and granting the time to attend classes that are conducted during working hours.

What has prevented companies from offering more training opportunities to workers at the bottom of the corporate ladder? First, many companies have mistakenly assumed that they will not reap any benefits from doing so. The companies we interviewed provided clear counterevidence, ranging from the benefits of ensuring that all employees at a bakery can communicate in a common language, to the benefits of improved numeracy and literacy skills for factory workers as companies mechanize their production.

Second, many companies have assumed that they cannot provide education to their employees. The companies reviewed in this chapter clearly illustrate that small and large firms alike can do so. While a company's size may influence the economic feasibility of providing training internally versus contracting it to an outside agency, firms with fewer than fifty workers to over 140,000 employees worldwide are clearly capable of offering training opportunities to all of their employees.

Third, companies worry that they will not reap the benefits of their employees' increased skills if their trained employees leave, taking their skills with them and putting them to use at another firm. Though some employees who had obtained skills took advantage of advancement opportunities offered outside of these firms, the companies' financial rewards in terms of increased productivity and employee loyalty still exceeded the costs of training.

So what does it take for a company to turn training into profits? First, the company needs to be clear on what kind of training will bring the greatest benefits to the firm and to its employees. The right type of training varies substantially from company to company based on the specifics of the sector and setting in which it operates. Language training is useful in settings that have a diverse immigrant labor force where employees speak multiple languages, or in multinational companies where there are differences in the language abilities of entry-level employees and company management or home offices. Basic skills training, including literacy and numeracy education, is valuable in settings where employees have not previously acquired these skills, since workers are increasingly required to read written documentation as well as work with basic mechanical devices. As we will discuss in greater detail in the next chapter, on career tracks, advanced firm-specific training is particularly useful when it is linked to advancement opportunities.

Second, companies need to structure their training in a way that encourages the targeted employees to complete it successfully. The least-advantaged workers frequently have limited formal education because of barriers they faced in their previous educational opportunities. These barriers range from financial and time limitations to learning disabilities or differences. For training to be successful, it is critical that these same barriers do not prevent further learning opportunities. When time is provided for training during the workday, employees are more likely to be able to make use of it. When these opportunities are provided immediately before or after employees' shifts, they cut down on transportation time and make it more feasible for employees to participate. Free or low-cost training is essential for employees with limited income. To reach populations whose learning differences have previously prevented them from succeeding in school, language or basic skills training may be needed, and using methods that have been demonstrated to be effective with populations with a wide range of learning differences is essential.

Third, for training programs to succeed, it is crucial to have buy-in from all levels of management. In the companies we studied that had well-designed training programs and commitment from upper management, problems commonly occurred when support was lacking from middle management. Even when CEOs were convinced of the economic returns of providing training, middle managers' support was needed in the details of implementation. For example, these firms were often aware that training should be provided during the workday to make it accessible to employees, yet middle managers seeking to reach and exceed their productivity targets were often reluctant to release employees from their shifts to attend training sessions.

Finally, even when training opportunities are made available, employees' motivation to make use of them may vary, particularly when training requires putting in extra hours at work. Making training as accessible as possible is clearly a major factor. Novo Nordisk offered its language training at the plant and in Tianjin, where most of its workers lived. Creating a culture where training is appreciated also plays a role. At Isola, one of the plants experienced a much higher level of success with its training programs, in large part because leaders in the community took part in the classes. Most important, employees must recognize the benefits of the training. Motivation for training is higher when the new skills, such as language proficiency, enrich employees' lives both at work and beyond, and when they lead to more interesting or advanced opportunities at the firm. As the following chapter explores further, establishing career tracks gives employees a much greater incentive to pursue training opportunities.

6

Establishing Career Tracks for the Least-Advantaged Workers

ONE OF THE MOST significant yet ironically least common ways of ensuring good working conditions for the lowest-level employees is to provide them with advancement opportunities. Most jobs for employees with limited formal education lack clear career paths and the potential for upward mobility. Nearly one hundred thousand articles have been written on career paths, but when you search academic databases for articles focusing on career tracks for employees with lower levels of formal education, less than 1 percent of articles address these needs.[1]

All workers have the capacity to learn and acquire new skills; the desire for advancement is not bound by class or level of previous educational attainment. Although some employees at every educational level are content with their current positions and have no desire for the additional responsibilities that accompany promotions, others have a great desire to advance, take on new work, and adopt leadership positions. While near constant attention is devoted to the career paths of employees with a higher education, few companies pay similar heed to those with limited formal education. In many cases, there is a complete division between the career paths available to those entering the company on the "management/executive" side and those entering on the "labor/employee" side of the business. For most workers with limited formal education, low-paying jobs do not lead to better jobs.

In the context of our global study of firms employing workers with limited formal education, we interviewed employees on every continent about their career trajectories, including employees in vastly different industries, ranging from customer support to cement production. The service and manufacturing sectors received particular attention, given their traditional role as two sectors that regularly employ large numbers of workers with lower levels of formal education. To reflect the many facets of manufacturing, our studies included companies that manufacture everything from pharmaceuticals to cardboard boxes, apparel, roofing supplies, cement, and seatbelts. We also sought to include a variety of service sector companies, including retailers, financial services, and customer support.

When we interviewed working adults on six continents, they made it painfully clear that one of the most important and costly consequences of the structure of the labor market at the bottom of the corporate ladder is the limited availability of opportunities for career advancement. But in our research on innovative companies, we were able to study firms that had made dramatic departures from this trend and created career tracks for workers who entered their firms in the lowest-level jobs.

The companies presented in this chapter were selected because of their documentable opportunities for advancement. Xerox Europe offers training and advancement opportunities that are structured to ensure that individuals do not get stuck at the level of their first job. Costco provides the opportunity to move from entry-level positions working on the warehouse floor to high positions in senior management, and the company virtually requires senior managers to have experience in entry-level positions. We examined both senior management's and the least-advantaged workers' perspective on career opportunities in these companies. The companies provide different but equally important models: one model enables a higher percentage of entry-level employees to attain advancement, and the other is structured to provide the opportunity for multiple levels of advancement to those with the highest demonstrated ability and effectiveness on the job.

Xerox Europe: Making Advancement Accessible to All

Attracting and retaining staff was the biggest challenge faced by the Xerox service center in Ireland. Its business model considered a 30 to 40 percent attrition rate to be "acceptable," in part due to the high turnover rates in the call center industry, which have been estimated as averaging 40 percent.[2] Still, it was hard to achieve this retention goal. When we visited the service center in 2006, the center was located in a business park outside Dublin, alongside an abundance of other multinational companies, including Google, Yahoo!, and eBay. Business processing offices and call centers competed for workers, and Xerox managers were aware that their employees were frequently informed of openings at neighboring companies.

To improve employee retention, Xerox tried to make the Irish site a welcoming work environment. Signs all around the building announced company activities such as picnics and other outings. As at many of the top companies we visited, the offices of the general manager, Bob Horastead, and other executives were designed with an open concept, with large walls made of glass.[3] The call center was built around a large, multistory atrium, at the base of which was an Internet café where workers could gather during their breaks.

Providing advancement opportunities was an integral part of Xerox Europe's recruitment and retention strategy. While there were employees for whom Xerox was just a job, and as likely as not a short-term one, those who stayed longer did so because of the career development opportunities. Justiina Nieminen was just one of many employees for whom this was true. With only a secondary education, she had been at Xerox for one year and had already been promoted to acting team leader. She explained that one of the main reasons she stayed with the company was that Xerox would pay 100 percent of her tuition for a work-related degree such as business or accounting.[4]

In 2006, Xerox operated in over 160 countries and had 53,700 direct employees worldwide.[5] A wholly owned subsidiary of the multinational, Xerox Europe employed approximately 19,500 people, 1,900 of whom worked in Ireland. Xerox Europe had been looking to save on labor costs by consolidating its European services at one site. Ireland was an attractive location for several reasons, including its low corporate tax rate. Crucially, Dublin was seen as a desirable place to live; therefore Xerox knew it would be able to attract staff and management from Europe. When the company first arrived in Ireland, the country's salaries were lower than in many parts of Europe. By 2007, that was no longer the case since competition with other large firms had driven up salaries. Still, Ireland had long-term political stability, and its labor laws were perceived as flexible for employers, since companies could more readily upsize and downsize in response to economic conditions than elsewhere in Europe. At the time, it was hard for India to compete for the call center services due to the wide range of European languages required to deliver customer service across the continent.

The European Shared Services Division of Xerox in Blanchardstown supported Xerox operations in western European countries, employing approximately 1,500 employees in 2007. This division included the European Welcome and Support Center (WSC), a call center that provided technical support and reordering services for Xerox products; the Financial Services Operation (FSO), which handled customer accounts and billing; and Xerox Office Services (XOS), a relatively new area of operations that contracted with corporate customers to reduce their printing costs, committing to providing them a certain percentage of savings and remotely managing all models of copiers, printers, and faxes. WSC and FSO agents were organized into teams according to language. Language teams included Spanish, Italian, Portuguese, Dutch, English, German, Swedish, Norwegian, Danish, Finnish, and French.

Not surprisingly, given its language needs, Xerox hired employees from across Europe to work at the Xerox Shared Services Division. At the time of our visit in 2006, 72 percent of the WSC agents were non-Irish, including American, Austrian, Belgian, Brazilian, British, Danish, Dutch, Finnish, French, German, Italian, Norwegian, Portuguese, Spanish, and Swedish workers.

Training and Advancement as a Tool for Employee Retention

As the previous chapter made clear, having access to training opportunities is fundamentally important to most workers. Training provides particularly great leverage for those who are least likely to receive it at work: employees with low levels of formal education. Employees at the WSC, many of whom were young and early in their careers, appreciated the training opportunities at Xerox. While Mark Doherty, a WSC agent, valued the fact that the company put a lot of effort into improving employees' lives by offering good shifts and organizing social events, he felt that having the option of taking courses was what compensated for the mundane and difficult nature of his work.[6]

Xerox provided several kinds of training. Its on-site Virtual Learning Environment (VLE) was open twenty-four hours a day, offering hundreds of business and information technology courses. Employees could also take the Cambridge English exam and the MS Office Specialist certification test free of charge.

XOS Manager Lorlene Duggan told us how she counseled her staff to take advantage of the opportunities provided by the VLE:

> You really have to make people make time for [training]. Because the demands of business will counteract that desire to go and lock [themselves] into a room for two hours to do some project management course when they're sitting there going, "I've got a project to go through. I haven't got time to learn how to do it—I just have to do it!" . . . But I think [the VLE] is a motivating factor, particularly for people . . . starting [out].[7]

But not all middle managers were equally encouraging. Employees, particularly those at the WSC, frequently mentioned the difficulty of fitting VLE training into their schedules. The employees we spoke with made it clear that while some managers encouraged their staff to make time for training, others did not; it was ultimately up to the employees to schedule their own training sessions. Barbara Doelen had moved to Ireland from the Netherlands a year and a half before our interview. During that time she had completed the team leader training. She told us that employees often took part in training, but did so mostly outside of shift time and sometimes completed it at home.[8] Gabriel Diefendorf, a WSC technical agent, completed what Xerox termed "yellow belt" training within months of his arrival at Xerox and planned to take more VLE courses at home. He wanted to be prepared to transfer out of WSC after completing the mandatory six-month period working in the call center. He planned to remain at Xerox as long as it offered good career paths.[9]

Xerox's commitment to training went hand in hand with its policy of providing employees with advancement opportunities. New jobs were first offered to existing employees, and those who had undertaken training had the best chances of success in the internal hiring process. The firm recognized the importance of keeping employees informed about the training and experience required for advancement. In response to employee interest, Xerox created an internal Web site that provided employees with information on potential career paths within the firm. All job postings were easily accessible online and employees could browse the new listings at the on-site Internet café.

The employees we spoke with were well aware of these resources and felt that advancement was attainable. Seamus Dunne, who had a high school education, had been at Xerox for six years, having begun in the mailroom and worked his way up to team leader. He explained how he felt about the company and its advancement opportunities: "There's a lot of opportunity, but you have to keep your head down. If you're good at your job, you'll be recognized, but it might not be fast. You need to stay focused . . . Overall, I found the company [to be] a great place to work because of what I *could* have as opposed to what I *do* have . . . The training is there if people take the initiative."[10]

Call center employees could seek promotions within their own division as well as transfer to other divisions. The FSO and XOS departments generally did not hire entry-level workers, and many of their employees had started off in the WSC. Employees generally preferred the FSO to the WSC since, although the work was still phone-intensive, the majority of the calls were outgoing rather than incoming and many of the tasks could be done from home. FSO employees therefore had more freedom and flexibility in scheduling their work. They had more responsibility and were able to develop a more complete understanding of their clients' needs. Positions in XOS, with their focus on designing better approaches for corporate customers and related flexibility in work design, were also seen as more desirable than WSC. According to XOS manager Lorlene Duggan, positions in this department were seen as a "career path [and] an endpoint."[11] As a result, the XOS had an extremely low turnover rate. Duggan proudly announced that out of approximately seventy employees, only two help desk workers and one account manager had left the unit since it opened in 2002.

In 2005, 20 percent of entry-level Xerox employees in Blanchardstown received promotions, and an additional 20 percent were transferred to new departments to which they had applied. Overall, there were 246 internal transfers and promotions over the course of the year, the majority of which were received by employees in entry-level positions. There were seventy-five promotions within the WSC's technical support unit alone, with approximately 28 percent of technical support agents taking on new roles such as team leader, escalated technical support, technical mentor, process mentor, XOS account rep, and customer administrator. Given the call center industry's high turnover rates, the WSC's 30 percent turnover rate in 2005 was relatively low. Moreover, most employees who left the company did not join Xerox competitors. A large proportion of them returned to their countries of origin; 45 percent of WSC and 44 percent of FSO employees who left Xerox also left Ireland, and others left the call center industry altogether. If Xerox employees were unhappy in their positions, they had the option of changing roles, transferring departments, or relocating to another Xerox location around the globe.

Challenges: A Lack of Support from Middle Management

While Xerox's commitment to advancement led to companywide returns through improved retention, the associated costs were borne by localized teams. As a result, Bob Horastead explained, they had encountered roadblocks within the company in implementing the policy. It had been difficult to get middle management on board to provide educational and career opportunities to the lowest-level employees. As the immediate supervisors of these employees, midlevel managers sometimes felt that training interfered with their need to reach their phone-response targets and that promotions and transfers prevented them from holding on to their best employees. Horastead explained that sometimes midlevel managers "are parochial and don't realize they will lose these employees anyway," even if they don't encourage training and advancement; he knew that it took "brave managers" to successfully implement these mechanisms for the company to retain employees.[12] At the time of our interviews, Xerox didn't yet have a system of incentives in place to encourage immediate supervisors to ensure that their employees took advantage of the educational and advancement opportunities.

Having worked for a small firm in Italy, Carlo Rossi had come to Xerox because he wanted to work for a big multinational company. He described his belief that "companies like Xerox or IBM" would offer more long-term career opportunities.[13] He had begun to study economics and was focused on developing a career in business. His salary of 1,600 euros a month at Xerox was not as good as he had hoped, but it was better than the 1,200 euros he had made working at a call center in Italy and the 1,300 euros he had earned in a low-level position at a small bank. Rossi mentioned that the turnover in his department was hard on him and on the company; it increased everyone's workload and decreased their chances of receiving a bonus for strong team productivity. His primary concern was getting more access to training. Due to the high turnover rates, his supervisor allowed him only one hour of training a month. He was looking forward to the summer months, when he had been promised the opportunities would be greater as the call volume was expected to slow down.

Open Communication and Employee Involvement

Training and advancement policies were part of an overall plan to make Xerox Europe an appealing place to work. The company also encouraged open communication between management and employees. Describing his own management style, Horastead stated: "My way is two-way." He told managers that employees deserve responses to their requests, and he always made sure to write back when he received e-mails from his staff. He also believed, however, that there was nothing wrong with saying "no, and here's why [not]." As he put it, "We're in a competitive environment [and] our job is to be competitive."[14] Horastead was committed to visiting every section of the firm at least two or three times a year so that he could personally observe the way things were being done. He also held regular roundtable discussions with different groups of employees in order to hear their concerns. It was part of Xerox's corporate policy to have management be responsive to employees' suggestions. Horastead explained: "At any time, if they come up with suggestions that they feel would be good for them personally and their team and their coworkers, if it doesn't have a huge cost implication, we'll implement any extra benefits that people are looking for."[15]

Employees confirmed this openness and accessibility: "You can make your voice heard pretty easily here. There are roundtables with senior management, and you're on [a] first-name basis with everyone. It's a nice environment in that way."[16] Management sought recommendations from employees on how to make the service center a better place to work. Some suggestions were fairly simple to accommodate, such as the request to have the canteen open earlier in the morning. Horastead explained that this small change had made a big difference to those who worked the early shift. Many employees were won over when they saw management respond to their needs. Other suggestions were more complex and required more systemic responses, such as the request to improve employees' mobility between jobs.

Benefits for the Company

Employees repeatedly stated that the availability of training and advancement opportunities influenced their decision to stay with the company. Like many of the senior executives we spoke with at other companies, when asked what the main motivation had been for setting up these policies,

Bob Horastead spoke of both values and gains: "I can't honestly say whether it's mainly because we care about the employees or mainly because we see the benefit it gives [the company]."[17] Richard Dunphy, the controller, explained that their employees were their major investment: "There's [always] a heavy emphasis . . . on staff, because staff is our biggest cost . . . We're a 'people' organization. Between people and IT and facilities, that's it. There really isn't anything else . . . so we can focus all [our] time on what we want to do to really retain people. So that's what we do."[18]

Costco: Career Trajectories Without Strict Ceilings

Andrew Harris, a single father with two children, had been working at Costco for twelve years. He had a high school education and had worked in the food service industry before joining the company. He came to Costco because it was recommended to him by his brother, a Costco employee. Harris started off pushing shopping carts, and after taking on a variety of jobs, he had become manager of the food court. He told us how rewarding he found his current job, appreciating that it "never gets boring or dull or quiet. Time goes by quickly."[19]

Thomas Hill, a father of two children aged five and eleven, had worked at Costco for seventeen years. His previous jobs included working at a video store and a grocery store. He had initially come to Costco because his cousin worked there and the company offered good salaries for entry-level positions. Hill had started with the lowest-level job: pushing shopping carts in one of the stores. In 2006 he was an assistant manager and he planned to spend the rest of his career at Costco. In a few years, he expected to be promoted to warehouse manager. Although he didn't yet know exactly when or where this promotion would take place, he was optimistic that the company's commitment to promoting from within would ensure numerous advancement opportunities.[20]

In 2007, David Collins was the warehouse manager at one of the Costco locations in Washington. He supervised 475 employees and oversaw over $100 million in sales every year. Collins began working at Costco by chance. In 1988, he was living in his hometown, working as a produce stocker and weekend checker at a local grocery store. He transferred to Costco mainly due to its convenient location across the street from his parents' house. He began stocking food in the warehouses. He took advantage of every mentoring and advancement opportunity, moving up the ranks to different managerial positions. After a year and a half at Costco, he was promoted to an area manager, then to a staff manager for four years and to an assistant manager for another four years. In 1995, he became a warehouse manager in Alaska, where he stayed for eight years before being transferred to Washington in 2003. Collins got to know Costco's business inside out; he was well aware of the challenges faced by his staff and of the supports they needed. Costco's philosophy of providing training and career opportunities for all employees was deeply ingrained in his management style.[21]

Embedding Commitment to Careers in the Company's Management Strategy

As these stories illustrate, Costco's opportunities for advancement were tangible and available to workers at all levels. Some employees went from entry-level positions to senior management, and many others moved into midlevel supervisory positions. Costco stood out from its competitors in its belief that all of its workers had the capacity to learn and grow in their positions and should therefore be given opportunities to advance.

Managers were taught to help entry-level employees think through their options and plans for advancement. Dave Haruff, vice president of regional operations, explained the company's approach:

> That's part of our job: to look at the employees and know which [ones have the desire and skill to advance]. That's one of the questions I ask when I walk in the building: "Who's next in line? Who are the folks that you guys have recognized that could be department managers, assistants?" . . . You're asking those questions six months out, because you want people to be ready. We want to make sure that we're looking ahead, that we've got people ready to go into those positions. I think that's the biggest thing, is the open-door policy. That's probably the one thing I talk about most at our employee meetings, that our managers are very much approachable. You as an employee, if you're stocking or cashiering, you could walk up to your manager at any time and say, "You know, I really want to be a department manager." And we will literally sit down with you and say, "This is what you're going to have to do to get there." You don't have to wait for a posting. I mean, that's our job.[22]

Costco's focus on advancement was solidly rooted in its business needs and principles. First of all, the company believed that employees with experience working in lower-level jobs made better leaders. Mark Stalwich, director of personnel, explained: "If you don't have a feeling for what it's like to get up at 3 a.m. and throw hundred-pound boxes, driving a forklift, receiving merchandise, if you're not attuned to ringing up a cash register . . . for eight hours a day, if you're not ready to stay until ten o'clock if we have to go back [to finish work] . . . It's pretty hard to support someone if you don't know what it's like."[23] Costco saw providing opportunities for advancement as essential to sustaining the company in both strong and weak economic times. Stalwich explained how the company had been expanding, opening approximately twenty to thirty new locations a year. This meant that it needed to hire about twenty-five warehouse managers, fifty to a hundred assistant managers, and many more staff-level managers and entry-level supervisors each year. The only way to find enough people with an in-depth knowledge of the company who were capable of filling these management positions was to train and promote them from within. The director of employee development, Vito Romano, summarized: "If we don't grow our people, we don't grow our company."[24] At the same time, having experienced managers strengthened the company's ability to respond to difficult economic times because of the knowledge base they brought from the warehouse floor.

Costco's policy of promoting from within was evident at all levels of management; 68 percent of warehouse managers had started off working as hourly employees. Stalwich claimed: "I don't think we have ever brought in an outside person to run a warehouse."[25] Employees who had been managers in other retail stores were brought in as floor staff or lower-level managers so they could learn about the company before advancing into other positions. The emphasis on promoting from within also extended to positions in corporate headquarters, where nearly all the positions were occupied by employees who had at one time worked in the warehouses. Jim Sinegal put it simply when he said he didn't want "this building," corporate headquarters, to be "self-sustaining." The warehouses were the central hubs of the company; they dictated the company's success or failure. It had therefore been crucial to the company's success that the senior management have personal experience in the warehouses. Sinegal explained that this even applied at the CEO level:

> We don't exist for ten minutes if you shut those warehouses down . . . That's what we're all about. Everybody who's going to be anybody in

this company should have very close, intimate contact with what's going on in those buildings. I just cannot imagine anyone . . . [doing my job] . . . who hadn't worked in those warehouses, probably as warehouse manager. He or she would have had to have had that job, in my view, [before being appointed to] . . . four or five key [executive] positions that we have in our company.[26]

The required warehouse experience had been deeply operationalized. Stalwich explained:

> I think it's valuable to have . . . warehouse experience. In fact, we pre-fer that anyone coming over to the home office have at least a year in the warehouse. And if we get a call from somebody with . . . a master's degree? It's like, "Hey, great, come work for Costco! Here's the ware-house!" In terms of highly skilled positions, like maybe financial accountant, IT positions, networking—[for] those we do find some people on the outside who come directly in, but if you want to work your way into human resources or merchandising, or any of those other ones, you'd better go to the warehouse first, because you need to have that experience.[27]

It wasn't that Costco didn't welcome people with advanced levels of education. In fact, many of its part-time workers were students at local colleges. When the company opened a new location, the local university was always one of the first places it would recruit employees. Costco hoped that a significant number of these students would continue with the company after graduating. Jim Sinegal explained how the company would try to retain student employees after graduation by offering them attrac-tive careers within the company:

> If I could take you through our managers, I'd show you people who started pushing carts out in the parking lot twenty years ago and now are vice presidents of the company. You'd say, "Well, how's that possible?" But it is possible because they're smart kids; they're obvi-ously industrious enough to want to go to school and work at the same time, and many of them haven't [yet] made a choice of where they're going to work [or] what they're going to do with their lives . . . [If] we're a company that provides a career path, it becomes attractive [to work for us].[28]

That being said, unlike warehouse experience, college and graduate degrees were not a requirement. John McKay, vice president for regional operations in the Northwest, described the balance the company had sought to achieve with respect to education:

> A lot of our people start [working here] when they're in college. And they like to stay with us, so we certainly have some college-educated people with us. And people have joined who have college degrees, but . . . a lot of our executives . . . [have] succeeded without a college education. I think the skill set is much more important than the education . . . Education is *part* of a positive skill set. Certainly the ability to communicate, to think through, problem solve . . . are generally aided through education, but they are not necessarily defined by education.[29]

Costco's advancement policies have not been without controversy. In 2004, a group of female Costco employees filed a sex-discrimination suit against the company. The suit alleged that Costco's promotion system relied on a "tap on the shoulder," where senior executives would select candidates for assistant manager and general manager positions at the warehouses, and that this system resulted in discrimination against female employees. The suit was granted class-action status in 2007; Costco subsequently appealed this decision, and this appeal was on hold in 2009.[30] Whether it is found that the culture permitted some of the thousands of managers to make biased choices, whether unequal advancement will be found to have resulted from requirements to work long shifts differentially affecting working caregivers, or whether the claims will be found to be unwarranted, both the female and male employees we interviewed spontaneously made clear how real they felt career advancement opportunities were at Costco.

Laura Moore worked in marketing at one of the warehouses. Her youngest child was starting college in a year and she looked forward to re-thinking her career plan at that time. "The sky is the limit here," she summarized.[31] Christine Carter was the mother of three children aged thirteen to twenty-two, and she had been working at Costco as a part-time cashier for three years. Her impression was that you needed to work there for two to four years "before they start looking at you for advancement."[32] During those two to four years, your salary continued to rise. She was looking forward to the chance to move into a supervisory position. Melissa Guzman summarized the intentions of many employees when she told us that she did not "plan on going anywhere. There's so much opportunity here. If you give them your hard work, it will come back to you."[33] She had started out as a cashier and now worked in the membership department. She had already cross-trained for several different positions. Before coming to Costco, she had worked at an Albertsons grocery store. Guzman said she was "happy she moved to Costco" and wished she had done so sooner. These sentiments were reinforced by statistics: after employees had been with the company for a year, turnover dropped to less than 6 percent, a remarkably low rate for the retail industry.

Providing the Training Required for Career Tracks

Costco's training programs were integral to its policy of providing career tracks for employees and hiring internally for many management positions. Employees could prepare for their careers at Costco by pursuing the wide variety of training opportunities offered by the company. Instead of providing avenues for employees to leave, when combined with Costco's commitment to career tracks, this training encouraged workers to remain with the company long-term.

Training at Costco began with cross-training, which entailed teaching workers how to perform a variety of tasks in different departments. The cross-training gave managers increased flexibility when they needed to find someone to fill in for an absent employee, and it allowed employees to apply for jobs in different areas of the company. Regional operations manager Dave Haruff explained: "You've got to have people cross-trained. We certify all our forklift drivers, gas station folks . . . deli people . . . You can't just throw somebody in the deli and say, "Make these things." It's all about training. That's what we do a very good job at."[34]

Employees would then develop a career plan with their managers and establish the type of training that was required to achieve their objectives. The company referred to its more formal training program as "Costco University." This program consisted of courses on a range of topics, including diversity, career development, performance management, and sexual harassment and discrimination. These courses took place either in virtual or real classrooms, through conference calls, or in person. They could demand a significant time investment; for example, the eight-week Leadership Development 101 course for managers and supervisors lasted thirty-two hours.

Further training and advancement often depended on individual employees' levels of interest, motivation, and initiative. The opportunities were available to everyone, but it was up to individual employees to develop their own career plans and pursue the necessary training. The onus was on them to apply for different job postings or talk to their supervisors to figure out what kind of training they needed in order to fulfill their career goals. When we talked to David Collins, the warehouse manager in Washington, he explained how he felt his central role in managing employees was to show them that they were in control of their future at the company. It was fine if they were happy with their current positions, but if they wished to advance, there would be opportunities to do so.

One of the workers we met exemplified how Costco employees felt about their career plans. Paul Evans, a father of five children between the ages of five and twenty-four, had been working at Costco for eleven years. Prior to joining the company, he had completed one year of college and had worked in manufacturing and as a youth counselor. Like so many others, he started off pushing carts. Evans was now working in the marketing department of a warehouse, and he told us he could see himself staying at Costco until his retirement. He was clear about his expectations to advance within the company and had developed a plan and timetable to help him meet his goals. He knew that many executives had started off in the warehouse, and this made him confident in the advancement opportunities available within the company. Evans appreciated the fact that everyone at Costco had to start at the bottom and that there were real possibilities for advancement.[35]

Profiting from the Expertise That Warehouse Employees Bring to Management

Costco's policies and emphasis on offering career tracks and advancement opportunities were closely linked to its economic strategy and were central to its dynamic growth. Costco's first warehouse opened in Seattle in 1983, and the company grew rapidly over the next ten years. Essential to its successful growth had been ensuring the best management possible for each warehouse and the well-executed replication of its model from the first warehouses so that consumers could learn to rely on the Costco brand. Creating effective career paths for internal advancement enabled the company to select, train, and promote employees who knew how to make the Costco model work. Costco merged with PriceClub in 1993;

Price Costco operated 206 warehouses and had $16 billion in annual sales. In 1997, Price Costco was renamed Costco Wholesale. By December 2008, the company operated 550 warehouses in eight countries, was the fifth-largest retailer in the United States, and was the eighth-largest in the world. Sales had increased steadily from $41 billion in 2003 to a record $70.9 billion in 2008, while net income had remained consistently above the $1 billion mark since 2005.

Costco operates on a "club" model, which means that buyers must purchase a membership to shop there. There are three types of memberships: Gold Star individual membership ($50/year), business membership ($50/year), and executive membership ($100/year). There are more than twelve hundred warehouse clubs in the United States and Canada. Costco's main competitor is Sam's Club, which belongs to Wal-Mart. At the end of 2005, Costco had 45.3 million members and an 86 percent renewal rate, the highest in the industry and a testimony to its high levels of customer satisfaction. Membership fees constitute 60 percent of the company's profits. Consumers become members because they like the brand. Here too, the quality of employees is an essential component. The career advancement opportunities attract a highly competitive pool of men and women to work in the warehouse, and the quality of their work in turn leads to high customer satisfaction and membership renewal rates.

Costco spent more money on its workers than its competitors, but it also earned more money per worker. The numbers made this clear: Costco had higher annual sales per square foot ($795 vs. $516) and higher annual profits per employee ($13,647 vs. $11,039) than Sam's Club.[36] The key to the company's productivity was having a highly motivated workforce and managers who truly understood operations.

Employees at Costco corroborated the links among the working conditions, the career opportunities, and the quality of their work. Alan Hill was a "utility player" who filled in for different positions—forklift driver, membership clerk, cashier, and so on—as needed. When he started at Costco, he didn't know much about the company except for the fact that it paid well. He told us: "They've been good to me and so I've tried to be good to them by working smarter and safer."[37] Susan Clark, who worked as a greeter, decided to work at Costco because two of her children worked there and praised the work environment. She told us: "The people—supervisors, managers, members—make your day, and you try to make theirs. It's a good feeling."[38] Paul Evans, who had told us about his plans for advancement, explained his dedication to the company: "I would do anything humanly possible for this company because they do that for me."[39]

Costco's central mandate was clear in its mission statement: "To provide our members with the highest quality goods and services at the lowest possible prices." Its strategy of focusing on quality included having a mix of lower-priced and higher-end items. An external report comparing Costco's strategy to those of its main competitors stated that while "Wal-Mart stands for low prices and Target embodies cheap chic, Costco is a retail treasure hunt, where one's shopping cart could contain a $50,000 diamond ring resting on top of a 64-ounce vat of mayonnaise."[40] Providing higher-quality service than most of the "big-box" retailers and wholesalers, Costco was also better able to bring in customers who had more money to spend. While these customers could financially afford to shop at a higher-cost retailer, Costco's high-quality service left them no incentive to go elsewhere. As a result, Costco was able to sell both high- and low-value goods, and this significantly contributed to its higher profit per square foot and per employee.

Having a higher sales volume was a central element of Costco's economic strategy of ensuring low prices as well as higher-quality foods and fresh goods. High volume is the objective of any retailer or wholesaler, but how did Costco achieve this goal? There were four elements to its strategy: low prices, higher-volume packaging, limits on stock-keeping units (SKUs), and good service. Having supervisors and managers who knew exactly how the warehouses operated and employees who were committed to the company made it easier to achieve its high sales volume.

From the start, basic goods such as toilet paper and diapers were packaged in large quantities. Costco had, after all, begun as a wholesale club. The sale of larger- volume units was an essential component to being able to offer low prices. Equally important was the decision to limit the number of SKUs on a warehouse floor. Offering fewer models of hair driers and fewer brands of food processors ensured that it would sell a higher volume of each model and could negotiate a better price. The products sold in each warehouse were selected by the warehouse manager. It was therefore essential to have managers who understood their business well, who knew how the company functioned, and who were familiar with local consumer preferences. Costco CFO Richard Galanti told us, "If we had roughly four thousand items in the warehouse, then Sam's had about fifty-five hundred. Now that's compared to forty thousand at Albertsons or

Safeway."[41] The smaller number of items resulted in savings because Costco could negotiate a better price on quantities of each item purchased. Buying fewer items also meant lower costs because fewer employees were needed to negotiate deals. Finally, stocking fewer items lowered warehousing costs because most items could be stocked by machines. Costco had been able to sell fewer items effectively because it kept this goal front and center when purchasing goods. Galanti described Sinegal's reasoning during a budget meeting: "If the most expensive [model] that does it all . . . is $79, and most of them out there are $99 and $129 at Walgreens, just sell one and we keep it simple."[42]

Whereas the average markups are 25 percent in supermarkets and 50 percent in department stores, Costco's markups did not go above 15 percent of branded and 14 percent of private labels. According to Jim Sinegal, "The traditional retailer will say: 'I'm selling this for $10. I wonder if I can get $10.50 or $11. We say, 'We're selling it for $9. How do we get it down to $8?'" This strategy attracts customers both during recessions and in times of prosperity.

When Costco's sales volume on an item went up, it—like other buyers—was able to negotiate a better price with the manufacturer. However, whereas other companies kept their sales prices the same when their own purchase prices dropped and pocketed the profit, Costco's policy was to drop its sales prices as well so that it remained within the 14–15 percent markup range. Costco's repeated lowering of prices had fueled dramatic growth both in its membership and in the extent to which members bought almost exclusively at Costco. When necessary to keep its prices below a competitor's, Costco charged less than the 14–15 percent maximum mark-up it had set. This contributed to a virtuous cycle. Low prices enabled Costco not only to achieve high sales volumes but also to purchase large quantities, which enabled it to lower prices even further.

Product quality was as important to Costco as low prices. Managers cared about every part of the shopping experience. They wanted employees to greet customers warmly; wanted to make sure the parking spaces were big enough so that peoples' cars didn't get nicked in the parking lot; wanted chickens cooking in the rotisserie until closing time so that customers coming in at the end of the day were able to find what they were looking for; and didn't want anyone to find trash on the floor. Some of these decisions, such as making the parking spots wider than at other discount retailers, were made by corporate headquarters. Most managers in corporate headquarters had firsthand experience working in the warehouses and could better foresee what changes would be important to customers. The majority of the elements that determined the quality of the shopping experience were a direct result of how well warehouse employees and managers did their jobs. How well customers were greeted, how clean the stores were, how few problems customers encountered in finding goods, and how well any problems were resolved all came down to the quality of the Costco labor force.

In short, opportunities for employees at the bottom of the ladder to advance from line jobs in the warehouse to supervisory roles and senior management played an essential role in the company's economic success.

Throughout its history, Costco has seen that good employee practices are good for business. In the words of Jim Sinegal: "The net results of the thing, which I can repeat like a mantra [and] which many people seem to miss, is that it's just good business. Hiring good people, giving them good jobs, and keeping them with you and developing your company is good business."[43] In the end, Costco's management was equally proud of its economic and its human accomplishments:

> We're just trying to provide good jobs and build a good company. I don't think there's anything inconsistent about that. The fact that we can do it, and—and I have to be careful how I say this, I don't want to sound arrogant—the fact that we can do it, pay the wages that we can and have the best prices of anybody in the country, just says "we can do this." There's a sense of pride in having accomplished that. Everybody likes to work towards excellence, to have excellence as a goal. Obviously there's a distinction with perfection, but excellence is a laudable goal.[44]

Effectiveness Linked to Organizational Culture

While Sinegal led from the top, his goal was to ensure that Costco's approach was so ingrained in the organization that he or any other individual employee could leave and the values would still be maintained. Costco's code of ethics was enforced at every level of the company: "1. Obey the law; 2. Take care of our members; 3. Take care of our employees; 4. Respect our suppliers; and 5. Reward our stockholders."[45] All managers at Costco could recite the core elements of the company's mission and strategy. Dave Haruff explained how the code of ethics informed every decision: "Every business has one, but we actually *live* it. Any decision we make, we go down that checklist."[46]

Principles 2 and 3 of the code of ethics were central to both the economic strategy of the company writ large and to decisions made on a daily basis. Middle and top managers alike were expected to find ways to treat employees well and help them succeed, and to turn the fruit of their investment in employees into higher-quality service and lower-cost goods for their customers. The increased business that resulted from their success enabled them to achieve objective number 5: rewarding Costco stakeholders. The company took for granted that it had to play by the rules in doing so, which meant obeying the law and treating suppliers decently so that they wouldn't go out of business.

To be truly successful, Costco had to implement its philosophy at every level of the company, from the employees in the warehouses to senior management. Getting the company's culture to truly permeate an organization with over 140, 000 employees has been an extremely challenging task.

In fact, the biggest challenge for many of the companies we visited in our five-year study of companies seeking to succeed economically by transforming their work practices was finding the "right" middle management as their companies grew. The CEOs, COOs, and other top executives shared a vision of economic success that stemmed from building on all employees' skills—including those at the bottom of the corporate ladder. The success of the C-level executives depended on their ability to ensure that their approach was carried out by middle management. At many companies, the performance-based incentive systems for middle management focused on higher production and lower costs. As a result, even in companies that in theory recognized the economic benefits of investing in line workers, many middle managers commonly responded to their incentives by lowering their employee compensation and raising their demands.

Of the companies we studied, Costco had one of the most effective systems for ensuring that its strategy permeated all levels of the organization. Performance was measured by profits and by the satisfaction of customers and employees, not simply by cost cutting. Middle managers were selected based on their experience in the warehouse, their "people skills," and their ability to manage large organizations. Dave Haruff explained: "Really, the biggest thing I look at in our managers is people skills . . . and the second thing is making decisions." He described the importance of employee-management relations in successfully running a warehouse:

"When I was a manager at Kirkland, we did our first million-dollar day. That was a big deal for me. The *Seattle Times* came down, and they said, 'How do you manage a building that does a million dollars a day?' And I said, 'Well, it's very easy: I have 450 employees that manage it.' That's what every manager thinks about. It's not how good you are as a manager; it's how good you are at teaching."[47]

Middle managers were given an enormous amount of autonomy. Each manager was responsible for all warehouse staff and stocking decisions, since products varied by region. Senior managers stepped in if problems arose, and they had real-time access to sales and expenditures for each warehouse so that they could calculate profits and oversee middle management. They took it seriously when poor management led to morale problems, as John McKay described:

> We certainly, at times, have struggles . . . We have managers who fall out of favor, or people [who] don't feel that they're [being] treated well. And we listen to that. When we start getting more and more calls from a building, then we have to figure out . . . how to get through to [the] manager [in question] and get them in tune with the concerns of the employees. Or, sometimes you have to remove the manager if they're not effective in leading people . . . Certainly, if you have a building that has morale problems, they are probably fairly nonproductive, or at least less productive than the other buildings; these things go hand in hand. If they're not happy, they're probably not working hard. They're thinking about the problems around them [and] they're not focused on their jobs, so the service level drops . . . We go through those struggles, but the trick, obviously, is to tackle those morale problems.[48]

At the same time, Costco had visible mentoring in place right up to the top. Jim Sinegal visited all the warehouses, and he was famous for the intense pace of his trips. His goal was to ensure that Costco's values were known and understood by everyone in the organization. He strove to simultaneously educate warehouse managers how to teach by example and show line workers what it meant to care about a product.

> The message is a very consistent one . . . Any manager that doesn't recognize that at least 80 percent of their job is teaching doesn't get it! That's what it's all about: teaching. It's so fundamental to . . . the

job . . . And it's not just formal classroom teaching. It's teaching every day in what you're doing. If I see a piece of paper on the floor, I pick it up because I guarantee you every time I do it, an employee notices that I do it. And I do it because, I must tell you, it's a knee-jerk reaction, and I've been doing it all my life. The people respect that. If they see a customer ask me a question, and I say, "I think it's back there someplace," that's the way they think they should conduct themselves. If they see me say to the customer, "Let me see if I can help you find it," it sets a whole different tone for the business. If people see that . . . our manager out there is genuinely interested, they take that same attitude towards their own employees."[49]

Galanti explained with admiration: "Jim thrives on the fact that he [currently] tries to visit 470 warehouses in eight countries twice a year each. And he almost does it—[visiting] probably 80 to 85 percent [of them]. And his idea of a fun week is work." Galanti then went on to describe a recent trip during which Sinegal had attended the quarterly board meeting in New York and then visited Costco warehouses in New York and New Jersey, attended the opening of a new Costco in Indianapolis, and visited Costco warehouses in Washington, Idaho, Montana, Michigan, and Nova Scotia, plus ten U.K. locations, all in eight days.

That's how he thinks. His view is managing retail, not analyzing numbers behind a desk all day. It's visiting the competition, walking the floor with the warehouse managers, mak[ing] sure that [the managers are] running the business as you would, if you [were] the owner. "What is the competition up to? What's hot . . . , what's not? What are [we] overstocked in? When did we go to $11.99 on Tide detergent? Why are we at this price on this item? I think Sam's is beating us on this." That [sense of urgency] trickles down . . . to the fifteen manager[s] doing the hour walk with Jim, and it trickles down to the senior EVPs of operations and [to] the senior VPs of operations.[50]

Different Approaches to Creating Career Tracks

While the number of upper-level positions in a company is related to what the firm needs to accomplish, it is simultaneously a function of how the company chooses to organize its activities. Having more advancement opportunities does not have to mean having more middle managers, although multiple levels of supervision and management are a common means of both organization and advancement. Costco employed multiple levels in its supervisory structure and demonstrated how entry-level employees without extensive formal education can transition to supervisory roles in such a structure. But advancement opportunities need not require shifts from service or line manufacturing positions to supervisory roles. They can also consist of transfers to departments that require higher skill levels and that have more attractive opportunities. For example, Xerox Europe is structured in such a way that one of its service departments builds largely on employees who have gained experience in other departments.

Although all companies have some intrinsic limitations to the advancement opportunities they can offer, in many settings both managerial and union policies have needlessly stood in the way of improving those opportunities. Management has often required that employees complete advanced formal education before being hired if they are ever to be considered for upper-level positions; degrees are frequently seen as an easy way for human resource departments to segregate ambition, commitment, and talent. Unions at some companies have negotiated for contracts that prioritize seniority over quality of work to an extent that markedly restricts companies' ability to reward productivity and effectiveness with advancement opportunities.

Management's decisions about how to fill upper-level positions are at least as important as their decisions about the number of such positions. What stood out most about the companies highlighted in this chapter was their willingness to provide advancement opportunities for their least-advantaged workers. It is a self-fulfilling prophecy at many firms that employees who enter with less advanced formal education are not able to successfully carry out higher-level jobs. The culture at these companies prescribes that higher-level service or manufacturing positions require the most advanced formal education. As a result, managers simply do not consider other candidates for these types of positions. At the same time, they do not provide opportunities for their lowest-level employees to obtain advanced education.

This stands in sharp contrast to the firms we studied that had successful career tracks for all employees. Notably, these firms understood what skills were really necessary for the advanced positions. They were able to test and measure these skills themselves as opposed to relying on external validation or certification. Xerox Europe had created supervisory reports rating employees' skills at lower-level positions. They also provided the training required to fill any existing skill gaps so that workers who were interested in and committed to pursuing advancement could demonstrate that they had acquired the necessary skills. Similarly, employees at Costco had the opportunity to demonstrate their ability to advance. Whereas at Xerox this primarily took place at a formal training center, at Costco it generally occurred through on-the-job training.

Most jobs at the bottom of the corporate ladder fail to offer career paths. Too many companies assume that there are no advantages to investing in training and advancement for these employees, and consequently those who lack a higher education are restricted to a limited number of positions and opportunities. Yet, as this chapter has illustrated, countering this trend can bring demonstrable benefits to firms and employees alike.

7

Engaging Employees in the Company's Profits and Their Own

THE IMPORTANCE OF EMPLOYEE motivation has often been under-appreciated. While it has been seen as self-evident that highly skilled professionals such as lawyers and consultants perform better when they care about their work, the importance of the engagement of workers at the bottom of the ladder, be they factory workers or customer service representatives, has been less widely recognized. It has often been assumed that the nature of their work is so routine that employees having input into the process and caring about the outcome is not essential.

Yet the evidence on the benefits of employees valuing their company is persuasive. In 2006, Towers Perrin published research comparing companies with high and low levels of employee engagement. Researchers found that operating income for companies with high levels of engagement improved by 19.2 percent, while income declined by 32.7 percent among low-engagement companies over the same one-year period. Companies with higher levels of engagement also saw a 13.2 percent average increase in net income growth, compared to a 3.8 percent decline in net income among companies with lower engagement. High-engagement companies demonstrated a 27.8 percent increase in EPS (earnings per share) growth, compared to an 11.2 percent decline in EPS for low-engagement companies.[1] Towers Perrin has linked increased employee engagement to increased customer satisfaction, financial performance, overall business performance,[2] and commercial sales.[3] The importance of employee engagement and its impact on higher productivity, profitability, customer satisfaction, safety, and employee retention is upheld across countries.[4]

Other studies have similarly shown that greater employee involvement leads to higher productivity and quality and to lower error rates in production. A U.S. Department of Labor report found that these "high-performance practices" (including employee involvement in decision making, performance compensation, and extensive employee training) are linked to increased quality and productivity.[5] This was demonstrated in a study of *Fortune* 1000 companies that had implemented at least one workplace practice that gave employees greater responsibility and involvement in decision making; 60 percent of these companies reported a resulting increase in productivity, and 70 percent reported improved product quality.[6] A review of empirical studies conducted across a variety of industries including paper mills and apparel, automobile, electronics, and telecommunications manufacturers, among others, found that adopting work practices that led to greater employee engagement resulted in higher productivity and production quality.[7] Another report presented the differences in production quality and turnaround time between traditional "mass production" and "flexible production" automobile plants, which frequently incorporated work practices such as offering extensive employee training, using work teams and problem-solving groups, implementing employee suggestions, and decentralizing quality control. "Flexible production" plants had higher quality, with a substantially lower rate of defects per vehicle (an average of 0.5 defects per vehicle compared to an average of 0.8 defects per vehicle for "mass production" plants); "flexible production" plants also had lower production times (twenty-two hours to assemble a vehicle compared to thirty hours for a "mass production" plant).[8]

In addition to its impact on quality and productivity, engagement also leads to lower turnover rates. In the United Kingdom, the Chartered Institute for Personnel and Development (CIPD) found that engaged employees are less likely than disengaged employees to take sick leave or to leave their employer.[9] Findings from Towers Perrin ISR's Global Workforce Study support the latter assertion: 51 percent of engaged employees had no plans to leave their current employers, compared to only 15 percent of disengaged employees. Similarly, only 4 percent of engaged employees were actively looking for another job, compared to 28 percent of disengaged employees.[10] BlessingWhite found similar results worldwide: in the United

Kingdom and Ireland, 76 percent of engaged employees reported planning to stay with their current employer through the next year,[11] and this figure increased to at least 80 percent in Asia and the Pacific region (compared to less than 41 percent of disengaged employees).[12] In North America, 85 percent of engaged employees "definitely" intended to stay with their current employer through the next year, compared to only 27 percent of disengaged employees. In addition, less than 1 percent of the most engaged employees reported having plans to leave their company within the next year, compared to 22 percent of disengaged employees.[13]

Employee engagement is important for different reasons in different economic climates. When the economy is doing well, decreasing turnover is particularly important since employees who are not happy at the company will have plenty of other employment options. When the economy is doing poorly, the threat of turnover is naturally reduced; however, employee engagement remains essential to having higher productivity than competitors.

Finding ways to motivate employees is a subject that has occupied many human resources specialists. Chiumento, an HR consultancy, found that as many as 23 percent of surveyed employers admitted to having low levels of engagement among their staff (36 percent reported high levels of engagement).[14] In one study, a majority of employers seemed to consider staff engagement a priority: 72 percent reported that they were "actively addressing engagement." However, a third of these employers reported no improvement over the past year.[15] While employers are aware of the importance of engagement, they may be uncertain about how best to increase it.

In this chapter, we look at examples of companies that have policies designed to increase the engagement and motivation of employees at all levels. These companies operate in different industries and countries: one is a manufacturing company producing cardboard boxes in Canada, another is a roofing supplies company in Norway, and the last is a small bakery in the United States. What they all have in common is that they recognized the value and importance of employee engagement and sought to increase it in different ways.

Employee engagement was not one of the initial focuses of this book, which originally concentrated on areas essential to the financial and practical survival of employees at the bottom of the ladder such as wages, assets, and leave and flexibility policies. However, once we started visiting companies and talking to managers and employees, the vital importance of engagement and motivation to all areas of their operations became increasingly clear.

Great Little Box Company: Achieving Employee Engagement

Great Little Box manufactures cardboard boxes and packing supplies in British Columbia, Canada. The company emerged in 1982 with a 5,000-square-foot plant and only three employees. It grew steadily, with a series of moves into larger facilities. In 2006, it moved to its current 250,000-square-foot facility on Mitchell Island. Most Great Little Box customers are manufacturers and wholesalers; the company aims to meet all of their packaging and shipping needs. To diversify, in addition to corrugated boxes, the company opened a moving supplies division in 2004 and a label and plastics division in 2006.

In speaking with managers at the Great Little Box Company, it was evident that employee engagement at every level was a central concern for the company. The firm recognized the strength it could gain from employee engagement; it wanted workers to care about how the company was doing and to feel personally invested in its success. The firm had set in place a number of policies designed to make employees feel committed to the company. These employee engagement policies were a combination of providing workers with the right rewards and incentives, the information they needed to be engaged effectively, and the forums for them to be influential. Openness was at the core of the company's policies. Great Little Box believed that open-book management provided employees with the information they needed to work more effectively. As part of its efforts to keep employees informed, the company held employee meetings every month during which all workers were given detailed information about how the firm was performing financially and about any prospective changes in company strategy or investments, including updates on Great Little Box's development of new manufacturing lines and acquisitions of new companies. Employees at all levels of the company actively participated and asked questions throughout these meetings.

Open-Book Management as the Key to Engagement

Central to Great Little Box's management style was the belief that the only way to get people engaged was to have open-book management. For workers to be truly engaged, senior management argued, line employees needed to know what was going on within the company. Research supports this belief. An Ernst & Young survey found that 59 percent of workers would be more motivated if they knew how their jobs affected the bottom line, and that 77 percent of managers agreed that their employees would perform better if they were informed about their organization's critical numbers.[16] Great Little Box considers itself an open-book management company in which financial information is shared with employees who are also taught how to measure business success and offered real incentives to improve performance.[17] Though many companies agree on the importance of open communication, few have followed through on its implementation. *CFO*, a magazine for senior financial executives, estimates that approximately 1 percent of U.S. companies truly adopt the idea.[18] While such transparency is rare overall, given the extent to which it benefits economic success, it makes sense that it has been observed much more frequently among companies experiencing faster growth. A 2005 survey of the *Inc.* 500 companies—the fastest-growing private companies in the United States—showed that 40 percent of these businesses used some form of open-book management.[19]

As part of its open-book management approach, Great Little Box holds monthly staff meetings during which employees are informed of all aspects of the firm's performance. The stated purpose of these meetings is "for management to inform employees of 'what is happening and why it is happening.'"[20] The meetings feature leaders from different departments who share information on their results for the previous month. CEO Bob Meggy explained that keeping employees informed is central to keeping them engaged: "People want to know what's going on. It's really hard to feel you're part of something if no one tells you what's happening. So that's one reason we really like the open book here, 'cause we always let people know what's going on in the company."[21]

During our visit in March of 2009, we attended the staff meetings where they shared information about the company's February performance. Two staff meetings were held on consecutive days, the first for office staff and the second for plant workers. Although these meetings were held separately, both included the same level of information and details about the company's performance. The main difference between the two was that the first staff meeting included more details on sales, which the sales staff could influence, and the second meeting included more details about aspects on which the plant workers had greater impact, such as incorporation of new equipment.

Both meetings followed the same structure, with employees seating themselves at the lunchroom tables. All department heads, including senior managers, the CFO, and the CEO, got up to present the last month's results. These meetings were strikingly similar and quantitative in nature. All aspects of the company's operations were addressed, and numbers regarding the company's performance were provided. February's performance was compared to that in previous months and in the previous year. The information provided was extremely detailed and clearly linked to employees' performance. VP of manufacturing Nick Reiach talked about the fact that there had been 254 days without time lost due to accidents. Christine Bilodeau from the sales department talked about who had made the sales targets and which were the top accounts. She also compared sales in February with those in January and with the previous year, and noted that they were slightly below target. James Palmer gave an update on an upcoming acquisition. Carrie Dawson from On Time Delivery noted that 99 percent of deliveries were on schedule. Christine Meggy, the customer service manager, shared the trends data, which showed a decrease in "fivers" or identified errors. In addition to summarizing the facts, managers explained what these figures meant for the company's overall performance, and why certain problems occurred. For instance, Miguel Hernandez-Moncada, quality and safety manager, reviewed in detail the dollars lost due to errors, specifying which were occasional errors and which were systemic errors that had to be corrected. He explained that part of February's largest losses were due to two bad checks, and he introduced a new policy dictating that Great Little Box would not accept checks unless the customer was already in the system.

The meetings also served as an occasion to inform employees about the general direction of the company and what they could expect in the future. Given the economic climate in 2009, the numbers were not encouraging. In fact, in terms of sales, February had been the worst month in five years. The balance sheet revealed a net loss for February but also illustrated the financial strength of the company, which showed almost twice as many assets as liabilities. After reading the final part of the mission statement: "increase value of the company," CEO Bob Meggy noted that although this goal had not been accomplished that month, company value should rise in the intermediate term once acquisitions made during the economic downturn began to pay off.

Throughout both staff meetings it was clear that employees were very engaged in the information they were receiving. While it is often assumed that employees at the bottom of the ladder are less interested in corporate financials and strategic goals, if anything, plant workers seemed more engaged in the updates about the company's financial situation and plans for the future than the office staff had been the day before. Everyone in the lunchroom listened attentively as James Palmer talked about a company that Great Little Box was in the process of acquiring. When he finished, Liu Mulan, a factory floor worker, asked what the acquisition of a new company would mean in terms of space on the factory floor, clearly already thinking ahead in terms of what the company's expansion would mean for her job performance. Later in the meeting, everyone listened closely as Robin Tozer, protective packaging manager, described a new machine that would soon be installed on the factory floor. Truong Danh, a machine operator, wanted to know more about how this particular machine operated. Although he was currently part of the production crew that used another machine, he wanted to know the details so that he'd be prepared should he need to work with the new equipment.

Meetings included detailed information about the company's financial situation and its investments, but there was no open discussion about acquisition choice and the company's strategic plans. Though company leaders maintained control of large strategic decisions, they sought and acted on suggestions of how to improve operations. Throughout the meeting, employees actively participated. It was quite evident that the staff did not see the meeting as a mere formality.

Shared Ownership Through Profit Sharing

Great Little Box's profit-sharing program went hand in hand with its open-book management approach. In the words of CEO Bob Meggy: "When you run open book like we do here, you can't have open book and not have profit sharing."[22] In his view, what made the company work was the combination of its profit-sharing and open-book policies; one could not work without the other.

Great Little Box's profit-sharing program was designed to foster a sense of shared ownership, where the welfare of the company translated into direct financial benefits for employees by rewarding all workers when the company performed well. There was no vesting or waiting period to qualify for profit sharing. The only employees who did not participate in the program were managers who had separate profit-sharing benefits as part of their contracts, salespeople who earned on commission and therefore already received a larger salary when company performance improved, and employees who hadn't completed their three-month probation period. Each month, 15 percent of the company's pretax profit was divided equally among all employees.

The program was designed to provide immediate rewards. Every employee would see the numbers regarding the company's performance at the monthly staff meeting and would then see the corresponding reward in his or her paycheck. Profit sharing was set up so that everyone who benefited would receive the same amount regardless of wage or position. The amount obviously varied by month, but when the company was doing well, it had been approximately C$300 a month.

Profit sharing was in no way meant to substitute for wages. Great Little Box paid regular wages in addition to profit sharing, starting at C$11–$12 per hour for new plant workers, and rapidly increasing to C$17 an hour. Experienced plant workers could earn up to C$24 per hour. Managers we spoke with were clear that they did not want workers to see profit sharing as part of their wages. As CFO Margaret Meggy explained: "The profit sharing, you know, I don't want to think of that as part of their basic compensation, because it's not. It's variable; it's a 'thank-you'; it's intended as an incentive to buy them in."[23] It was apparent when talking to employees that they did not count on the profit sharing as part of their wages; workers explained to us that while they considered it a nice "bonus," they would not take it into account when planning their expenses. Kathy Stevenson, who had been with the company for over seven years, told us: "I know what I'm going to bring home. The profit shares, they're a bonus."[24] Brian Clement, a machine operator and the cochairman of the safety committee, told us: "Profit sharing . . . when it's there, it's there. It's nothing I ever count on."[25]

Additional Rewards

Great Little Box had established additional rewards programs aimed at motivating and engaging employees. Every year when preparing the budget, CEO Bob Meggy would set a high but realistic goal for the company's profitability, called the Box Goal. If this goal was reached, the entire staff would go on an all-expenses-paid trip. These trips were another way that everyone either won together or lost together. The trips were also seen as a great opportunity for employees working at different levels and in different areas of the company to get to know each other and increase their ability to collaborate. In Bob Meggy's words: "[In] the past seven years, we have been to Las Vegas twice, to Puerto Vallarta, and to Cabo San Lucas . . . The entire company [has gone]. We pay the whole shot for everybody for everything. The bonding ability of that is tremendous . . . You can't beat something like that."[26] The last trip was to Mexico in 2006. Three years later, employees were still repeatedly bringing it up and pointing out what a great experience it had been: "Can I tell you my absolute favorite part? Bob flies the company down to Mexico. I mean, how much does that rock? I mean, profit [sharing] is wonderful, that's great, but you know what? If we reach our goal, we all get to go and it is so much fun! Honest to God. We have a lot of fun when we go to play!"[27]

Great Little Box also introduced rewards for employees who came up with ideas for cost savings and increased efficiency. The company instituted the Idea Recognition Program. Employees who came up with an idea that might cut costs would bring it to their supervisors, who would review it. Once the ideas were evaluated, promising ones were implemented. For successful proposals, employees received a financial reward based on how much the company would save from their innovation. Knowing their ideas were valued made a difference to employees, Pang Vithara explained:

> I had an idea last month on just the way we tag things. If I pick an order, I have to label it so we can find it. This is a whole warehouse, right, [so we] have to be able to store and find [objects] efficiently. But there were some things missing from that label that I thought should be on there. They took that idea, implemented it, and now I'm going to receive like C$10. It's not a big deal, but it's just the incentive to encourage you—"We want your ideas so much that here's some money."[28]

The program usually received around ten ideas per month. Financial rewards to employees had ranged from as low as C$10 to as much as C$2,500 for a particularly effective cost-saving innovation; the average amount was C$50. As Pang Vithara's experience above illustrates, the recognition mattered even when the financial reward was small. For the most part, cost-saving ideas provided relatively small savings; however, some ideas were significantly more important and increased the economic value of continuing to implement the program. Nick Reiach, VP of manufacturing, told us how the month before our visit, one of the plant workers had come up with a way to adapt one of the machines so that it would produce thirteen-inch boxes in addition to the twenty-inch boxes it was already producing. This would be a substantial improvement, since it increased the use that could be made of this particular machine and increased flexibility in production. This innovation was being tested at the time of our visit to see if it worked, but so far it looked very promising. If it was implemented, the worker who made the suggestion would receive a financial reward.

Quality control was another area where Great Little Box introduced rewards. Production workers were in an optimal situation to detect any mistakes that had been made when placing orders. The company had placed a C$5 reward, which they called a "fiver," for catching a mistake. Although a small sum, the immediacy of the reward encouraged workers to pay extra attention and try to check the details. Miguel Hernandez-Mondaca told us how when a mistake occurred, he would meet with the crew to determine the reason for it and how to address it. He explained how the "fivers" meant people would take more time to read a work order carefully and make sure that there were no mistakes.

In addition to monetary incentives, Great Little Box made an effort to publicly recognize employees' performance. At the monthly staff meetings, supervisors and colleagues frequently named employees who had performed particularly well. Everyone nominated by peers or supervisors for an award was publicly recognized; the person with the greatest contribution was selected as employee of the month. This kind of nonmonetary recognition was seen as extremely important for employee motivation. In Bob Meggy's view, recognition was the central element to having a good relationship with employees and having them feel invested in the company: "When they do surveys of employees, [the] needs and wants of people, they all . . . say number one is recognition or appreciation . . . We spend a lot of time recognizing people doing well in many categories. [It] doesn't matter if it's sales or production or piece per hour, doesn't matter, but we work on that very much. It creates a very positive atmosphere because people say: 'Number one [is] recognition.'"[29]

Challenges of Getting Incentives Right

Great Little Box was deeply committed to setting up programs that motivated employees. However, managers were also clear about the fact that implementing the right incentives required time and attention. Many of the incentives in place at the time of our visit had been the result of trial and error; the initial structures had been modified when it became clear that they were not leading to the desired outcomes. It was particularly important to avoid incentives that could have negative consequences. For instance, Great Little Box did not offer incentives to increase the speed of production, since there were concerns that this could lead to a disregard for safety and result in higher accident rates.

Some incentives programs had been abandoned because they were not producing the right results. Nick Reiach, VP of manufacturing, explained how it was important to recognize that programs could have good intentions but lead to unintended consequences. He gave us an example of how incentives for productivity had resulted in data manipulation and employees' abuse of the system:

> The obvious one, the one that you would think would work, was: we used to incentivize people on productivity. So each machine had its own target, and if 7 out of 10 machines hit their target for a month, everyone would get C$25, or twenty-five points to use towards cash or prizes in a showcase. And they could accumulate those points and win Playstations and things like that. If 8 out of 10, or 9 out of 10, or 10 out of 10, then the points just escalated. Which sounds like everyone's doing their part and carrying the weight of this program. I started to notice that data was being manipulated, going into the computer to make the graph look better than the machine was performing. So it became easier to manipulate a graph than to figure out how to run the machine to do what you were actually saying it was doing.[30]

Sometimes finding the right policy structure had required several modifications. For instance, the profit-sharing program had been restructured several times before taking on its present form. It had initially been calculated as a percentage of employees' salary, but that had provoked dissatisfaction from employees who felt work on the factory floor was undervalued. Then, profit sharing was calculated based on seniority. Here, too, it inadvertently discouraged new workers. Finally, the firm decided to divide profit sharing equally among all employees to demonstrate the value that all employees were instrumental in the company's success. CFO Margaret Meggy explained this process:

> We struggled, looking at it [in] different ways: a percentage of salary, or different departments would get different incentives, and that was raising animosity. People thought: "Well, I contributed; aren't I as worthwhile as . . . ? So we went to a different profit-sharing plan and we've stayed with that since probably '93, I would guess; we've been with the same plan [of equal profit sharing] and that's been quite successful. People understand it and they feel that's fair.[31]

The company also believed that immediacy was the key to success in motivating employees. Managers made sure that employees were recognized for their performance and contributions as quickly as possible. Bob Meggy's view was as follows: "Anything to do with recognition, anything you ever read about it [is that] the more immediate [it is], the better. With everything [that has to do] with thanking somebody, later just doesn't work."[32]

Paying the profit sharing every month was one example of this immediate reward system. If the payments took place only at the end of the year, employees would have no sense that they were being rewarded as a result of their efforts in a particular month.

Measurable Outputs and Indicators

Central to Great Little Box's employee engagement strategy was its ability to accurately measure productivity, performance, and return on sales. As immediately became clear during the staff meeting, all aspects of the company's performance were linked to measurable indicators, and this information was shared with employees. Having measurable results was essential to having an effective way to link open-book management, incentives for enhanced contributions, and employee performance.

Translating Employee Engagement into Results

Open-book management and incentives and recognition programs were aimed at ensuring employees knew they were an important part of the company and that they had a personal stake in its success. The goal was for all employees to feel that, as one plant worker put it, "If the company does well, we all do well."[33]

Managers believed that openness translated into improved productivity and results in a number of ways. First, individual employees worked harder as a result of the incentives and recognition they received. To facilitate their success, they received performance reviews with explicit information about how they could improve, since every aspect of their performance was measured.

Second, in addition to working hard, people wanted to make suggestions on how to improve productivity and reduce costs. It was clear when attending the staff meeting that employees were keen to voice suggestions and ask for clarification if there was something they did not understand. Kathy Stevenson explained how employees were motivated to go out of their way to help improve the company's products: "Especially during times when we're not getting profit shares, when we're fighting our way back up, I tend to be watching for things like quality, to make sure quality is there. And it's not my job to check for quality, but I do find myself doing it, and I think other people do it too."[34]

Third, as was the case in other companies, people did not like to see their coworkers slacking off, since any reduction in productivity and performance would be felt by everyone at the company through a reduction in profit sharing or the loss of the all-inclusive, expenses-paid trip. As Bob Meggy put it: "People know [when] somebody is not working hard. They notice it, [and] people care."[35] Miguel Hernandez-Mondaca, quality and safety manager, talked about how employees' sense of ownership translated into improved performance: "We have a huge work ethic among the guys. They have been in the company for so many years that they want to see the company grow . . . When they do a step, they're thinking [of] the company as their *own* company. That's very important. Everybody [with] . . . over five years [of] seniority in the company has that mentality."[36]

Finally, open-book management and employee engagement increased workers' incentives to cooperate and work collaboratively with one another. One of the central purposes of Great Little Box's many social events such as trips, tournaments, and barbeques was to foster relationships among employees so that people felt more comfortable working together as a team. As factory worker Susan Brennan explained: "We have a lot of things that we do together. There's golfing and there's picnics; there's a Christmas party; and we have a luncheon every so often for safety (after so many days we've been safe). So we have more things to do with each other than just work, you know. So it's really a bonding process for everybody."[37]

Having committed employees who cared about the company's productivity was central to Great Little Box's success. The firm's faster turnaround time from receiving an order to sending it to a customer allowed it to compete effectively with bigger companies who had slower turnaround times. The quick turnaround time was very much driven by experienced, flexible employees on the factory floor. Great Little Box's high level of employee engagement was central to this performance.

The company put a great deal of effort into hiring the right people. It wanted to make sure that the person was not only capable of doing the job, but was also a good fit for the company as a whole. Nick Reiach, VP of manufacturing, explained: "We're looking for someone who has a good work ethic. They may have very limited skills on paper, so it's not so much about what their education is or their past experience; it's about how they actually perform and fit with the organization."[38]

Once Great Little Box had hired these quality employees, it did its best to hold on to them and ensure that they remained motivated and engaged. As Bob Meggy explained: "Your employees are your biggest asset. You know, a good employee . . . can make you three more times their income back."[39] High employee engagement contributed to low turnover rates. Managers repeatedly mentioned how they had almost no turnover after one year of employment. The workers we spoke with repeatedly emphasized how much they enjoyed the work environment at Great Little Box compared to previous places of employment. Machine operator Brian Clement was typical when he described the policies that mattered to him:

> It [is a] very open-door policy. You can go up and talk to the owner anytime you want. [We] get a lot of extra things outside of work that are trying to keep the members together, such as trips to Mexico, picnics, golf tournaments, barbeques, a lot of bowling—a lot of things like that that you get your family involved in. I think in comparison to other plants that do the same thing, I think that [the wages are] a little less than what they're paying, but we're not unionized, but on the same side the company does a lot of extra things for you too, so it kind of balances itself out. I've turned down some jobs where I'd be making almost double what I'm making [in order] to stay here.[40]

The company has also received numerous awards for its employee and management practices. Great Little Box was listed as one of Canada's Top 100 Employers in 2005, 2006, 2007, and 2008, as well as one of Canada's

50 Best Managed Companies in 1995, 1999, and each year from 2004 through 2009 when we visited. The resulting publicity was an important asset when it came to establishing the company's brand name and increasing its name recognition in the region. While touring the company, managers stressed the importance of brand recognition when it came to sales. When making cold sales calls, it made a great difference if people already knew the company's name. They explained that although paid advertising was one way to achieve this recognition, people remembered what they saw in ads only for a short period of time. Instead, the press coverage the company had received for its many awards and different incentive programs had had a much longer-lasting impact.

Response to the Economic Downturn

Open-book management had been beneficial for the company during good economic times. At the time of our visit in 2009, it was also making it easier to adjust to tough economic times. Employees who had access to detailed information on the firm's financial situation were more understanding of any difficult decisions that had to be made to adjust to the poor economy. Profit sharing had not been paid out for several months due to the economic downturn, but CFO Margaret Meggy explained that there had been few negative responses as a result, since all employees saw the sales and financial numbers every month and understood why this was happening. In the words of Nick Reiach:

> I think it does a lot for the psyche that the books are open and that you benefit when times are good. If we didn't have [open-book management], there would be a lot of rumors and suspicions about how profitable the company truly is and they might base [their opinions on] what car the [company] owner drove [and on] how extravagant our parties were, in terms of profitability, which could cause all sorts of problems. For them to know made it a lot easier to approach them with a four-day work-share program, to postpone certain incentives, [and to reduce] tenners to fivers. If they truly felt that they didn't understand those numbers, those sorts of concessions would be nearly impossible.[41]

Bob Meggy pointed out that employees had volunteered to forgo pay raises in an effort to help the company and to avoid layoffs. Employees also agreed to have a four-day work week (receiving partial unemployment on the fifth day) in divisions where this would prevent layoffs. Moreover,

Meggy described how employees were more engaged in these difficult economic times in coming up with ideas to help the company adapt.

Maintaining a Long-Term Vision

Long-term thinking was clearly at the core of Great Little Box's strategy with regard to employees as well as investments. Managers felt that being a private company made it easier to take this long-term approach. While public companies have to focus on short-term goals, Great Little Box could make long-term investments and implement policies such as profit sharing for all employees. CFO Margaret Meggy explained the company's focus on long-term growth:

> There's a huge advantage in being a private company: it's that you don't have to manage quarter by quarter. If you think about public companies, they have to report every quarter and their share value depends on those financial quarterly reportings, which is a huge negative. And I think it's a huge drag on the North American economy because you get CEOs managing for the next quarterly report. We're investing a lot in technology and in new equipment, and this is dragging down our quarterly earnings. It's dragged down our annual earnings for this year, next year, and last year—and we're not looking for good financial performance for this year and next year. We're looking ten years out. And the acquisition that we're looking at making is going to drag down our profit even more this year. It's going to be a huge drag on resources. It's going to lose money until we get it cleaned up. But I think that's the advantage of being a privately owned company: we can manage our own objectives, and our long-term objective is what's most important to us. So that's what we're looking for, is the future.[42]

In addition to the expenses of acquiring the new machines, the company incurred costs associated with training employees to use the new technology. Acquiring new companies also entailed the additional costs of incorporating these employees into Great Little Box. The company did everything it could to ease the transition for employees, but there was always an adjustment period. Similarly, investing in employees by having rewards and incentives such as profit sharing and expenses-paid trips did not always result in immediate returns. Fostering employee engagement was a continuous process with long-term benefits. Great Little Box's investments in machinery and employees always had the objective of encouraging long-term growth.

At the time of our visit, Great Little Box was in the process of acquiring a company with C$4 million in sales. Throughout the past ten years, acquisitions had been one of Great Little Box's strategies to diversify production. The company's move toward labels and packaging had proven to be beneficial during the economic downturn since sales were diversified, and a greater decrease in one area could be offset by an increase or smaller decrease in another. The company continued to expand even in an economic downturn. As Bob Meggy explained, whereas many companies found themselves in trouble because they had been growing too rapidly and running up too much debt, Great Little Box's financial situation was solid. Managers explained that they wanted to keep acquisitions to half the size of Great Little Box at most, a size they considered to be manageable. Margaret Meggy was clear about the challenges involved in acquiring a new company:

> All the companies that we've acquired have been sold for a reason, usually because they are in financial straits. Often they're managed by people who don't have the skills to manage them. Perhaps they're a salesperson who knows how to sell the product but doesn't know how to manage a company, or they're a company started up by a production person who understands very well getting a good product at a good cost, but can't market it. All the companies that we've acquired have had problems, so you're taking on those problems when you're acquiring a company. You're taking on additional problems—employees of that company are undergoing stress because their lives have been changed [and] they have very little control over it. There's a huge time investment in working with the employees.[43]

The firm took advantage of the slower demand during the economic downturn to give employees time to prepare for acquisitions of new machinery and companies. When production demands decreased, employees focused on cleaning equipment, preparing the factory floor for expansion, and training in new production techniques to prepare for rapid expansion during the anticipated economic recovery.

In planning for the future, one of the challenges that was often mentioned by managers was the issue of leadership and succession. Great Little Box's corporate culture and policies drew strongly on CEO Bob Meggy's personal beliefs. When he retired, whoever took over would need to share this commitment to the company's management principles. Great Little Box had grown significantly over the past decade and this growth had also presented new challenges. The company had recently moved to a larger facility, but the executives wanted to maintain their small-business style of management. Doing so would require a significant effort and commitment. In addition, the new workers who were brought in when Great Little Box acquired new companies also needed to become familiar with the company's corporate policies and culture.

Isola: Moving to a Teamwork Method of Production

Great Little Box sought to increase engagement through open-book management and incentives. Isola took a different approach by restructuring production to increase employee decision-making power and autonomy.

As described in more detail in chapter 5, as it mechanized production, Isola simultaneously began to implement a teamwork production system. The shift to the teamwork approach entailed a central change in the structure of leadership and production that granted workers much greater decision-making power. Isola began researching the teamwork approach in 2000 and implemented the new structure in January 2002. This change was motivated by the belief that it would increase production efficiency. Managing director Erik Withbro explained:

> Instead of taking all decisions at the top, we wanted to move the power to make decisions into the organization, and we wanted that the workers or employees should use their competence better. They shouldn't be told to do that or those things; they should, by themselves, find out what's needed. We wanted a common responsibility to [meet] the targets, and we wanted that the employees should be managed by themselves. And we wanted a new style of management that would be advising and helping instead of [having middle management] giving orders.[44]

What Teamwork Entailed

The switch to teamwork entailed a complete restructuring of production. Under the new structure, workers were organized into groups of six or seven employees, and each group had a leader selected by management. The team leader position rotated every two years, and all workers could apply for the vacancies. Bent Brekke, the director of human resources, explained that while in the past they would have had a foreman and under-foreman working between the plant manager and the workers, the leader of each team now reported directly to the plant manager. The new system eliminated a significant portion of middle management and meant that workers took increasing responsibility for their own roles in production. In an effort to build leadership from within the workforce, Isola emphasized internal advancement by favoring internal applicants for team leader positions. As Erik Withbro explained, "It was essential for us to find internal candidates for all team leader [positions] even if we should have not as good persons . . . as we could get outside. We thought it was very important to start with internal people, and I think that has been one of the successes we've had."[45] Isola built on the internal candidates' firm-specific expertise and provided them with the training required to fill any skill gaps.

Bent Brekke explained that the shift to the teamwork system had been negotiated with the unions. Workers who had previously been foremen and underforemen did not experience decreases in their salaries. Management and labor agreed to a three- to four-year salary freeze for these workers as they went back to functioning as line workers, until the salaries of the other line workers had caught up. More than the practicalities of the agreement, Erik Withbro noted the two-year process leading up to the shift to the teamwork system. Although it had been time consuming, it had allowed workers and their representatives to be significantly involved in designing the teams. In the end, the system provided team members with greater responsibility and engagement than operators had previously experienced.

Before the move to teamwork, Isola's production structure had followed a hierarchical model where operators reported to a work group foreman, who in turn reported to a foreman, who reported to the production manager, who then reported to the production director, who reported to the CEO. After the implementation of a teamwork system, the structure was much more straightforward. Team members worked together, with one operator functioning as a team leader. The team leader reported directly to the factory manager, who then reported to the CEO.

The Impact of the Shift to Teamwork

The results of the move to the teamwork approach were positive. According to an analysis conducted by Isola in 2004, teamwork had contributed to greater cooperation and participation in goal setting, and to more employee involvement in decision making.[46] Employees benefited since they found the work less monotonous and more independent. Teamwork also led to lower absenteeism as employees felt a greater sense of responsibility toward their team members, which also helped increase productivity. Comparing absenteeism figures between 2002 and 2005 reveals a substantial improvement. Absenteeism figures from 2002, the year in which Isola first began to implement the teamwork system, showed a monthly maximum of 12.1 percent total work days missed; in contrast, the highest monthly number for 2005 was 7.4 percent. The lowest monthly number for 2002 was 6.2 percent, whereas the lowest monthly absenteeism rate in 2005 was down to 4.4 percent.

One of the team leaders at the Isola plant in Platon, Norway, spoke to us about what the shift to teamwork had meant for employees:

> In team organization, the ideals are a positive view on the human, and the human capital level within the company. When workers get increased responsibility, the tasks are more interesting. There's the possibility to get new challenges at work that they didn't have before . . . Five years ago, I would have had a lot of complaints, but the team organization addressed a lot of these issues. Now, I'm mostly concerned with helping to develop teamwork and moving forward.[47]

While the shift to teamwork had a significant positive impact on Isola's production and work environment, the company would have some challenges to consider as it looked to the future. The rotating nature of the team leader position was advantageous since it gave more workers a chance to acquire leadership experience; however, it also meant that line workers did not have the opportunity to permanently move into management positions. Had the new teamwork structure not provided workers with more autonomy, responsibility, and input solicitation, it might have led to increased turnover as employees sought permanent advancement opportunities elsewhere.

Dancing Deer: An Informal Approach to Structuring Engagement

As described in more detail in chapter 4, Dancing Deer Baking Company produces cookies for the high-end market. Given the company's size and scale of production, it would not be feasible for it to compete on price;

instead its strategy was to target a niche market that was willing to pay higher prices for higher-quality products.

To make the best products available, Dancing Deer needed employees with a high level of commitment to the company. CEO Trish Karter explained that since they could not afford to pay higher salaries, they opted to give employees a stake in the company by setting up a profit-sharing program in which all employees participated. This had been a matter of principle for Karter, and it was also aimed at making employees feel invested in the company's success. The belief was that employees who felt that they had a stake in the company's performance were likely to be more engaged and committed to their work and more likely to actively participate in improving production and efficiency.

Trish Karter also tried to foster an open environment that encouraged active employee involvement and participation. Reflecting the company's emphasis on open communication, no one at Dancing Deer had a private office—not even the CEO. The administrative offices, which were located one floor above the production area, consisted of a large space with workstations for eighteen full-time and four part-time employees and no walls. The conference room, lunch room, and restrooms were the only enclosed spaces. The rationale behind the openness of the office space was that it encouraged collaboration and teamwork among the administrative and management staff.

Production workers were encouraged to participate and bring their ideas forward. Karter was very clear on the type of work environment they were trying to build: "This is an environment where everyone is expected to be constructively critical all the time."[48] Production manager Lissa McBurney told us: "People on the floor do come up to me. They'll say, 'Lissa, you know, this is a problem and I feel very strongly about it,' and they'll pull in a friend to translate. So they feel if they're working with a supervisor and it's not working, they can come straight to me and I can help them."[49]

Open communication and employee involvement resulted in improvements in production. Production workers were clearly aware of what changes were needed and what could best increase productivity and the quality of production. In return, Dancing Deer management was willing to listen to employees and to implement their suggestions. They reaped tangible benefits from doing so in terms of increased production and sales.

Just one example of instrumental input from workers was advice on how to improve packaging, as described in chapter 4.

To be effective, widespread participation also required a structure that allowed for feedback to be used constructively. Dancing Deer created teams to handle the free flow of ideas and ensure constructive communication among the production staff. It can be challenging to effectively take action on a cacophony of conflicting recommendations on a wide range of issues. Some companies have responded to this challenge by simply stifling input from their employees. Instead, Dancing Deer sought to establish a coordinated dialogue. Controller Keith Rousseau explained:

> There's kind of extremes of everything, and you can't have everyone talking about one particular problem. What we do is we set up different groups that are typically very diverse within the office and with downstairs, and we talk about a project just to get different opinions, to get people working on the packaging. Because that's the kind of feedback that usually is helpful and produces the best and quickest results to grow the business or make a process faster, or streamline things, to get a better product to the customer, which is our ultimate goal: to do it as quickly and efficiently as we can.[50]

Dancing Deer has been very successful in creating an open environment and in drawing benefits from workers' participation.

The company's management style largely depended on CEO Trish Karter, since it was her personal philosophy that informed the firm's working conditions and business model. Rousseau explained: "You can't differentiate Trish's philosophy from Dancing Deer's philosophy because everything that she's about and everything that she is just flows through Dancing Deer really quickly."[51] The fact that the company's philosophy was based so firmly on Karter's personal beliefs was both a strength and a liability. Her deep commitment to these policies was an asset in terms of helping to make sure they were successfully implemented. Dancing Deer prided itself on its positive work environment and considered this to be one of the company's major achievements. Maintaining this environment required a committed leader. Karter was clear on the need to pay constant attention to these issues:

> I mean, you can lose it overnight. You can absolutely lose it overnight. You can take your sights off it, you can change your policies, you can

hire managers who don't get it and not care, and we've had instances of that. We've had instances of people that have come in and weren't with the program, and it's trouble. It takes a long time to fix. I don't think you can stop thinking about how you're dealing with people for one day. You can't afford a day in which you don't think consciously about, What are the impacts of my actions and my words and policies? Does somebody need help? Is there trauma or strife in the organization that I'm not aware of?[52]

The accompanying risk came about because Dancing Deer had not set up formal structures for employee input and participation; instead it relied mainly on workers having informal access to managers. The lack of formalized paths for input meant that Trish Karter's personal style and accessibility determined the extent to which workers could share their ideas. Clearly, if Dancing Deer's corporate values were to be maintained in the long run, future leaders would need to share Karter's dedication to these ideals.

Another important challenge was the fact that Dancing Deer was growing quite rapidly. One of the advantages of the Dancing Deer workplace was that all employees felt they had access to Karter and could bring their concerns to her attention. As the company grew, it became more difficult for Karter to provide personal attention to all employees and aspects of production. In Karter's words: "We're getting bigger and I have less direct contact with [employees]. It's just a mathematical truth. It is not possible for me to have as much contact with every person who works here."[53] It might not be possible to maintain this very personal leadership style once the company expanded. This raised the question of how to make sure that new managers were equally committed to the company's values and equally invested in maintaining them.

Employee Engagement in Diverse Contexts

The companies featured in this chapter had very different approaches to employee engagement. Regardless of their differences, some commonalities emerged in terms of what was needed to motivate and engage employees in the workplace.

First, it is necessary to have mechanisms in place that enable employees to easily communicate their ideas and concerns. More formal structures can include specific programs for encouraging employee input, such as the Idea Recognition Program at Great Little Box. Mechanisms to facilitate input can also be established as part of the production structure, as was the case with the teamwork system at Isola. A more informal approach can also be used, like at Dancing Deer, where employees regularly talked to the CEO and other senior managers and communicated their ideas.

In addition, workers need to believe that their input is valued and may be acted upon. People will be less likely to share their opinions and ideas if they don't believe they will be taken seriously. The three companies presented in this chapter clearly valued workers' input and provided examples of innovations resulting from employees' suggestions, such as a new way of packing cookies at Dancing Deer, or a modification to a machine at Great Little Box. Engagement increases if employees feel that their input has a real impact. With Isola's new teamwork production system, workers were able to make a range of decisions that had formerly been left to middle management. The company found that employees' sense of responsibility for their work increased after they were given more autonomy.

If employees are to be engaged, they need to care about the outcomes of their ideas. When employees are rewarded for their productivity, they are also rewarded for making the organization succeed. Fostering common goals and a sense of teamwork is another way of making workers more invested in the results of their ideas. Isola sought to create a greater sense of cooperation and common interests when it set up the teamwork system. Companies can also set up extrinsic reasons for employees to get engaged in their work. Dancing Deer set up a stock options program to increase employees' investment in the company. Great Little Box offered profit sharing as a form of shared ownership and established a rewards programs linked to cost-saving ideas and to error detection.

Ultimately, for companies to increase employee engagement, they need to believe that it is a worthwhile investment of time and resources, believe that it is a feasible goal, and find a way to make it work effectively within their company. The research evidence summarized at the beginning of this chapter makes a compelling case for the importance of employee engagement and its potential benefits for companies. The experiences of the three companies featured here also make a compelling case for the feasibility of improving employee engagement in different industries and economic contexts. Finally, these companies also make clear that firms will have to work at finding and implementing the right model. Increasing employee engagement is an evolutionary process that is individual to each company. Firms must be committed to continuing the process even when it does not produce immediate results, and they must be ready to make the necessary adjustments, whether that means changing the structure of their incentives or reworking their mechanisms for soliciting input from employees.

8

Reaping Returns from Community Investments

SINCE MEMBERS OF THE community often constitute a company's labor force in addition to its customer base, support from the community can facilitate both production and sales, just as opposition can significantly impede expansion. As a result, a company's relationship with the community can be a critical determinant of its economic future.

Global competition has brought new dimensions to community involvement. As companies expand their sales and production to new locations in different countries, their need to operate effectively in diverse settings grows, and their attachment to single communities diminishes. Yet no matter how globally structured a company may be, its production always takes place in specific locations that shape and are shaped by the company's presence and corporate behavior.

This chapter tells the story of two very different companies' approaches to community involvement. The first is a manufacturer operating in a rapidly developing economy with uneven infrastructure, and the second is a wholesaler that began in one of the world's largest and most industrialized economies. These case studies demonstrate how companies can invest in communities during both stable and turbulent national and global economic times. The manufacturer began investing in Indian communities during the global economic depression in the 1930s and maintained its investments through decades of boom and bust; the retailer invested in raising American salaries and lowering prices for consumers during periods of rapid expansion as well as some periods of recession.

Both influenced the social and economic base of the communities in which they operated.

ACC India: Building a Country and a Company Hand in Hand

Associated Cement Companies Limited (ACC) is India's largest cement producer. As it expanded in the mid-twentieth century, it faced difficulties commonly experienced by companies in extractive industries: setting up production in poor, rural areas that have extremely limited infrastructure. The primary ingredient in cement is limestone, of which India has many large deposits, but these sources are frequently situated in undeveloped areas that lack basic public works, including roads, water, and electricity. During our visit in 2007, Nand Kumar, ACC's head of corporate social responsibility and head of corporate communications[1], explained the reasoning behind setting up production in these rural areas:[2] "Since limestone is the principal raw material [in cement], it is [more] economically viable to set up cement plants exactly where your deposits are so that you save on transportation . . . For one ton of cement, you would need one and a half tons of limestone."[3] In fact, transportation can account for up to 20 percent of the cost of cement production.

Kumar explained that ACC saved enormous amounts of money by developing manufacturing operations next to natural sources of limestone. However, not only did these areas lack basic infrastructure, but their populations often had little if any formal education or experience working in factories, having primarily been engaged in subsistence agriculture. ACC needed to invest in infrastructure development, including basic services such as water and electricity, if it was to reap the benefits of producing near the limestone sources.

Company History

ACC's corporate history is inextricably linked with the history of India. The company formed in 1936 when four competing Indian holding groups—Tata Sons Limited; Mulraj Khatau & Sons; Killick, Nixon & Company Limited; and F. E. Dinshaw & Company Limited—merged the ten cement firms under their management. The primary objective of this collaborative venture was to pool resources and knowledge and to become more competitive vis-à-vis foreign-owned companies.

Nand Kumar explained the context of the merger: "India was under British rule at that time. So as it happens, between the two wars, there was a surplus of cement in the world, especially in Europe."[4] This was no surprise given the global economic depression that had decreased the amount of construction worldwide, and consequently depleted the demand for cement. The European firms "created for themselves a nice little comfortable market in India with fairly discriminatory taxes and policies tilting against domestic cement so that domestic cement companies were forced to be reduced in scale and size."[5] With a growing nationalist spirit, the Indian cement companies banded together in a fight for economic survival since they could not survive independently. This was, as Kumar pointed out, "a merger between business rivals . . . You don't normally see that. And it was a *voluntary* merger." It was considered unique in the history of business in India as the first and only example of a voluntary merger by all of the most competitive companies in a given industry.[6]

While attempting to develop an organizational structure in which none of the merged companies felt marginalized, ACC had to build a corporate culture that reflected the shared values of its new partnership. In this process, it had to develop its own brand name, since its products were still known under the names of the merged companies. ACC's corporate commitment to the communities in which it operated became emblematic of its brand.

ACC's Contributions to the Community

Like all companies, ACC had the opportunity to decide what kind of corporate citizen it would become. When the newly formed Indian cooperative went into rural areas in the preindependence and early postindependence years, it was confronted with a severe lack of infrastructure; these communities needed roads, electricity, water, schools, and medical clinics. There were clear economic incentives for ACC to build public works since it needed the infrastructure in order to facilitate production and attract workers. The company was also influenced by the nation-building spirit that infused the country during and immediately following the long struggle for independence. A sense of responsibility toward the new India had emerged, creating a commitment toward the social and economic development of the nation as a whole.

As one of India's largest cement manufacturers, ACC played an important role in national development—beyond supplying 14 percent of all the cement used in nationwide construction, ACC built housing and schools near all of its factories. Head of human resources Paramjit Pabby explained: "Because our plants were located in areas where not much housing was available, where cities and towns were not close by, we felt that we needed to provide housing to our own employees."[7] Company secretary A. Anjeneyan provided an overview of the history of ACC's involvement in the community:[8]

> Most of the manufacturing locations are situated away from the cities or places where anybody would actually like to live. So if the company has to attract and retain the basic minimum talent required to run the factory or the works, it has to create a certain kind of infrastructure for a person to come and live there with his family . . . you require roads, you require transport, you require a school, you require houses, you require banks for service. All the basic necessities that go with any township. In short, what companies like ACC or the Tata Group companies [did was] they recreated a mini township, . . . starting with [creating a] water facility, . . . hospital, [and] schools . . . If a person has a family, if he wants to live, all the facilities that he needs were provided by the company. That was necessary to attract and retain . . . talent. And over a period of time, it became evident that if the facilities are of certain standards, the people [will] not want to [leave].[9]

ACC has provided water access to seventy-five villages in seven states: 4 in Himachal Pradesh, 30 in Jharkhand, 17 in Uttar Pradesh, 2 in Karnataka, 9 in Orissa, 6 in Madhya Pradesh, and 7 in Rajasthan.

Although investing in infrastructure was a business necessity for ACC, the company consciously decided to expand these investments to benefit its workers and the community at large. Instead of building a school only for the children of ACC management, the company built schools for all employees and the surrounding communities. It provided water for the communities in which its workers lived, and provided health care for families as well as staff members. Building infrastructure for the community as a whole became part of the company's corporate identity. Anjeneyan explained:

> It is obvious that if you provide good facilities, you attract good talent . . . Once a person comes into our factories, he works. He does not have to worry about what his family is doing in the house. There is

somebody to look after all his needs—medical, transport, school. Whatever is needed, there is an infrastructure created to look after [it]. A person will go to the plant, work with full concentration, and come back [the next day]. So the company automatically gets a benefit by providing these facilities. And maintaining it and improving it over a period of time becomes a . . . motto or a sort of creed for the organization because you realize it's not [only] one person who benefits; you are creating an infrastructure which would last beyond any single person's lifetime.[10]

The company aimed to provide fairly equal benefits and infrastructure in all of its locations; however, given the diversity of living standards across different regions in India, some locations had significantly more severe gaps in infrastructure than others.

One of ACC's most significant contributions to the community has been the provision of well-compensated jobs in rural areas where there previously had been few employment opportunities and where most people had lived on subsistence agriculture. Wages at ACC were well above minimum requirements. In Himachal Pradesh, the factory's wages for daily workers began at Rs. 100/day (US$2), compared to the state's minimum wage of Rs. 70/day (US$1.40). For permanent employees, the lowest-level salaries were equivalent to approximately Rs. 300/day (US$6). Of the nine thousand workers employed at various ACC locations across the country in 2007, sixty-five hundred labored in production. ACC spanned the country geographically, operating in states at diverse levels of economic development, including Chhattisgarh, Himachal Pradesh, Jharkhand, Karnataka, Madhya Pradesh, Maharashtra, Orissa, Rajasthan, Tamil Nadu, Uttar Pradesh, and West Bengal. Moreover, ACC was providing a number of financial benefits along with salary packages, including allowances for inflation, modest housing costs, off-site education, laundering the company uniform, purchasing periodicals, and paying transportations costs, as well as productivity bonuses as part of a companywide efficiency-enhancing program. In addition to these benefits, the Indian Payment of Bonus Act required the company to pay a bonus to employees. For most employees, ACC's bonus was well above the minimum amount required by law (8.33 percent of the salary). But ACC's economic impact on surrounding communities extended beyond those who were directly employed by the company. The head of human resources at Gagal, for example, estimated that a total of twenty thousand families were directly or indirectly dependent on the plant to make a living.

GAGAL PLANT IN HIMACHAL PRADESH

The Gagal plant in Himachal Pradesh provided an example of the kinds of benefits ACC offered. The majority of the low-level employees at the Gagal plant were from local communities, and many of them spoke to us about how the company had improved infrastructure in the region by building roads and schools and providing access to water. The site had a housing colony that provided lodging for managerial staff and employees. Most low-level employees at the Gagal plant lived in their own homes in surrounding communities, but some workers lived in company housing. The sports club on the premises could be used by all employees, regardless of whether they lived in the colony.

The benefits of ACC's investments in education were not limited to ACC employees; the on-site school at the Gagal plant had twenty-five teachers and 780 students, half of whom were children from surrounding communities whose parents did not work for ACC. The school in the Gagal colony offered a subsidized rate of Rs. 250 (US$5.00) per year for employees' children, and the company paid half of this amount. Parents therefore ended up having to pay only Rs. 125 (US$2.50) per year. This particular educational subsidy was offered only to parents whose children attended the school in the colony; if children attended a school outside the colony, their parents had access to the educational allowance of Rs. 500 (US$10) in their salaries.

In their interviews, employees across the country repeatedly raised the importance of the health care ACC provided. The company ran clinics at all of its sites where employees and their families could obtain free health care and medication. The on-site clinics also provided free hospitalization to employees. All of the on-site clinics had a pharmacy and a pathology lab, and most also had x-ray facilities. ACC also provided preventive health care.

Almost all the employees we interviewed at the Gagal site reported health care as a major advantage of working at ACC. In rural India, where infrastructure was severely lacking, the clinic had three doctors and three nurses, x-ray and ECG facilities, and a computerized pathology laboratory. Its birthing center had not been used recently since most of the employees were past childbearing age; at employees' request, it could be used free of charge for the birth of their grandchildren.

The Gagal clinic provided free health care for ACC employees and their families, and nonemployees were welcome to pay for the clinic's services and medication. Several staff members told us that most locals preferred the ACC clinic to other treatment options. All employees at the Gagal plant had a yearly health checkup to address health risks before they developed into problems. When an employee became ill or injured, if the on-site clinic could not provide the required treatment, the company paid for treatment at regional centers. Employees had the option of seeking services outside the ACC clinic for privacy or other reasons even when these services were offered on-site. Those who chose to do so could be reimbursed up to a total of Rs. 18,000 over three years (approximately US$445).

ACC's first step in setting up production in new locations was acquiring land for its mines and factories. Purchasing land owned for generations by local communities can often be a difficult process. For the Gagal factory in Himachal Pradesh, as elsewhere in India, ACC provided monetary compensation to families who sold their land as well as at least one job per household.

Sanjay Mistry had completed his studies through grade 9. When we spoke with him, he was working as a painter at the ACC plant in Gagal while raising his sixteen-year-old daughter and five-year-old son. At first worried about how he would feed his family without a small plot of farmland, in the end he welcomed the transformations that ACC brought about in his life. Before the company arrived, there was hardly any infrastructure in the village. Sanjay Mistry's family was pleased with the facilities that ACC had put in place in Gagal: "I will say that the company is doing a great deal for us . . . The company gave us water. We didn't have [access to] water. Once the company drilled [wells for] . . . water for all the villages around here . . . The roads didn't come this far . . . Whenever there is something or if there is a problem, they are [there for us]. The company has spent a lot for us. [They] made [a] school."[11]

Prakash Yadav, another worker in Gagal, had been working for ACC for twelve years. He had completed his studies up to grade 8, and had previously worked as a farmer tilling the fields. His parents, respected elders, had been sad to part with their land, but when they saw many jobless people around them trading their land for money and work, they decided to follow suit: "At first . . . it was very painful. The land was in a way like our mother. [But] there was no force [used]. [At first] our elders refused [to give up the land], but then . . . the majority of the people gave up [their land] . . . [and the elders] were in the minority. So I gave up our [land] . . . [In return] they gave [us] money as well [as a job]."[12]

Yadav was given a job as a *mazdur*, a laborer, in the ACC plants. He had worked his way up over the past dozen years to become a machine attendant. The transition to factory work hadn't been easy, but he believed that he and his family were better off than they had been before the company's arrival: "I feel good about it because we are getting everything here. Getting water used to be quite a hardship; it is no longer a hardship. Morning, evening . . . and midday—three times a day—the company provides water. Lack of roads used to be a problem; that too has been taken care of. The biggest problem was school. The company made [a] school also for us . . . all the way to '10 plus 2.'"[13]

It is not uncommon for companies or governments to buy or expropriate land for mining, manufacturing, or dams. What made ACC's land transfers unique was the company's ongoing commitment to developing the community by building better educational and health supports while providing long-lasting economic opportunities.

Economic Returns for the Company

To keep up with the increasing demand for cement, companies in India have needed to find new sources of limestone. For them to set up production near these deposits, land owners had to be willing to sell their land, and communities had to consent to the mining. Although in recent years some cement companies have had difficulty obtaining this consent, ACC has fared well in this regard. Its reputation for investing in community health and education has made it a welcome partner throughout much of India, facilitating expansion to new locations.

HR head Paramjit Pabby described the ways in which the company profited by providing these benefits to its employees. For example, by providing on-site housing, commuting time and other problems associated with transportation were reduced since employees lived closer to the factories, and employees were loyal to the firm because the housing had been provided at very low cost. The same applied to the other benefits ACC provided, such as education and health care. Managing human resources for such a large company, Pabby was well aware that there were clear returns on investments in the community. Lower rates of attrition and higher employee satisfaction led to lower recruitment and training costs and higher productivity. He explained the reasoning behind these initiatives: "One was definitely a selfish motive: that you can hire employees and you can keep them closer to the factory. The other was also an opportunity or a philosophy that if these people do not have housing, where will they go? . . . If you are having a satisfied employee whose housing needs are met, obviously he is more productive at the workplace."[14]

At some of the older sites that have been operating for decades, where ACC is employing the second and third generations of families, the company is directly benefiting from its investments in education. Operating with a good reputation in small communities as one of the few employers, it is not surprising that children of ACC employees have sought jobs with the company upon entering the workforce. Harvesting the benefit of providing these children with better educational opportunities, ACC now has a more highly educated workforce.

ACC not only has lower turnover, but in a country known for the frequency of its labor strikes, it also has less labor unrest. The 1990s were a particularly turbulent time for labor relations in India. The combination of economic liberalization with an economic downturn, a slowdown in construction, and frequent cutbacks in wages and benefits resulted in many labor strikes. Yet, with its good working conditions, ACC experienced hardly any strikes. N. Shembavnekar, a senior manager in human resources, recounted: "For around fifteen years, we haven't had a single instance of work stoppage in our twelve cement manufacturing units."[15] He attributed this to all the services the company provided to its employees, ranging from good wages to benefits to health care.

Pabby summarized ACC's belief in the economic benefits of community investment:

> There are proud families which say, "I am the fourth-generation employee working for ACC" [or] "I'm the third-generation employee working for ACC" . . . Pride comes out of a sense of satisfaction of working together with the company, feeling that the company's been a good employer. It's taken care not only of me as an employee but my family [too]. My children have gotten educated in this company's schools. Sometimes they have been trained in [the] company's technical institutes and thereby maybe given an opportunity to work with the company. So this is a cycle. And this satisfaction index, if you really analyze it, at the end of the day, it has helped us in having industrial harmony, very few strikes, less disruption of work and a higher

productivity as well, because a satisfied employee and his family definitely contributes happily in the workplace . . . Even if he leaves you, he still speaks well of the company as a good, forward-looking, enlightened employer. So at the end of the road, this is what we get."[16]

These initiatives wouldn't have been maintained if they weren't an asset to business. Behram Sherdiwala, head of organization management, noted that business always had to be the first priority. As he put it: "[Only] if my business is running [smoothly] . . . can I provide you with bread and butter."[17]

Beyond yielding good relationships with communities and employees, ACC's community investments helped it build strong relationships with customers. Unlike in the United States, where few home owners are familiar with cement brands and manufacturers, in India there is a high level of cement brand recognition since homeowners purchase their own cement. Kumar explained:

In an average Indian . . . lower-middle-class home, the share of expenditure on design or the aesthetics would be a very small share . . . They are simple homes where [people] can't even afford plaster on the walls. That means they would use cement as a binder for bricks to create walls and rooms and ceilings . . . When money is scarce, the homeowner is very anxious to see that he spends where he is assured of durability and cost-effectiveness, which means he gets involved [in the purchasing process]. And how does he get involved? [Through] word of mouth . . . There are recommendations of experts and other influences like an architect or a civil engineer or a contractor or material supplier. Or it could be some village elder . . . or some senior person like a headmaster or a postmaster or a doctor. Those are the kinds of recommendations that a normal villager or a small townsman would pay heed to. So I guess that's why [certain cement] brands are so popular."[18]

The ACC brand had become well known among teachers, physicians, village leaders, and all those providing services for the communities near ACC's manufacturing sites. The company's civic engagement had brought just as much recognition to its brand name as the quality of its product.

While these programs grew out of a combination of economic necessity and efforts at nation building, they were maintained due to their economic viability. As managing director Sumit Bannerjee explained: "For me [it's] a no-brainer actually, because nothing . . . ultimately gets sustained without economic benefit."[19] ACC reported profits of Rs. 1.23 trillion (US$28 billion) for the fiscal year ending in December 2006.[20] It had previously reported a profit of Rs. 544.18 billion (US$12 billion) for the three quarters ending in December of 2005. The *Wall Street Journal* noted that ACC shares had risen 85 percent in six months by May of 2006.[21]

The four main groups that had formed ACC in 1936 eventually dissolved. The members of the Tata family were the principal owners of the company until the late 1990s, when they sold their stake to Gujarat Ambuja Cement. In 2006, Gujarat Ambuja sold shares to the Swiss firm Holcim. At 36 percent, Holcim became the largest single shareholder in ACC, and in 2006, ACC was in the process of merging its systems with the Holcim global network. Though Holcim has established some new priorities, most notably a concern with environmental sustainability, ACC has retained its distinct identity, and the majority of its board members are Indian.

The availability of limestone in India has shaped the rapidly growing economy's choice of building materials and helped create a national industry in cement production. By 2007, India had become one of the largest cement producers in the world, second only to China.

ACC's Long-Term Vision

Managing director Bannerjee's strategic approach was far-sighted, and it was consistent with that of the company's founders, which had led them to make sizable investments in the community:

> Another CEO may think: "Let me build the company now . . . I know [there are problems]—I am aware of it—but let me look at today's earnings and let me look at the future later." It always happens . . . I mean just go to a mine . . . completely denuded . . . This is just an example that you know. We are all, most of the time, short-term oriented. I think this return or the business case for this is obviously long-term, very long-term—very, very long-term. But my sense personally, and I think that of Holcim and ACC, is [that] we have to create a good reputation rather than do damage control when a bad reputation is created.[22]

Like the company's leaders who preceded him, Bannerjee found ACC's consideration of its long-term social and environmental impacts to be a competitive advantage. In contrast, other companies and industries in

India and elsewhere had followed very different paths. During the period in which we conducted our interviews at ACC, Nigeria's oil industry was once again in the news, this time for the kidnapping of an executive's three-year-old child. Strife had surrounded the oil industry in Nigeria for decades; oil companies had gone into poor areas of the country to extract oil, and they had left these areas in even worse condition. The environment had been ravaged, and local communities had benefited little from the billions of dollars in company profits.[23] Political and economic unrest had led to militant attacks against oil companies, resulting in significant disruptions in production and financial losses. It has been estimated that well over one hundred thousand barrels of oil production a day were lost as a consequence of the most recent spate of militant attacks in September 2008, in addition to an estimated loss in capacity of six hundred thousand barrels a day from previous attacks.[24]

ACC executives also compared the business to the IT industry, only half with ironic humor, when they heard our next destination was Bangalore. They spoke of how, despite the explosive growth in the IT industry, the companies had failed to invest in the city infrastructure. While the IT companies were not coming into poor rural areas as ACC had, their business in Bangalore had led to dramatic growth that the city did not have the capacity to support. Yet the IT companies had not made the parallel investment in Bangalore that ACC had made in rural communities. As a result, in 2007, all the basic facilities in Bangalore were overwhelmed. Whether or not this was a fair encapsulation of the role of information technology in Bangalore, the point of the parallel was clear: investing in the community where you grow is profoundly important for the long-term economic and social outcomes across industries and geographies.

ACC was now facing a new challenge in addressing the environmental impact of its manufacturing process. This became a more pressing issue after Holcim, a European company concerned with environmental sustainability, became its largest shareholder. Cement manufacturing is an energy-intensive process and is responsible for approximately 5 percent of all greenhouse gas emissions globally.[25] ACC would have to make significant investments in order to address this issue. Bannerjee spoke about ACC's plans to invest in renewable energy and environmental sustainability:

> We have to consume energy, but we can do a lot [to contribute] on renewable energy . . . I think by October we will have our first wind

farm ready. In Holcim it will be the first, [but] in India of course it is not first. There are other cement companies who have done it already. Smaller cement companies. We are bidding for hydroelectric projects in the north . . . We are looking at now broad-basing our basket and not just generating all our power using coal, and that's going to be more and more our contribution to mitigating this . . . I think the cement industry globally should spend a lot more money on hydrogen fuel cell . . . research as their contribution.[26]

For ACC, investing in the community's needs was clearly not a symbolic gesture or a one-time decision but rather a repeated examination of roles, opportunities, and responsibilities.

Costco Wholesale: Investing in Jobs in Advanced Economies

As a wholesaler founded in the United States in the 1970s, Costco faced an entirely different set of community issues than ACC had confronted when it was founded in India in the 1930s. Roads and schools already existed in all the communities in which Costco operated; the problem the community members faced was not whether there was a primary or secondary school for their children to attend, but whether they would have the opportunity to go to college—and if they did, whether they could afford to finish their degree. Similarly, the problem wasn't that health care facilities did not exist, but rather, that too many community members lacked adequate health insurance and decent pay and could not afford to make full use of the existing hospitals and clinics. As the cost of health care spiraled upward in the 1980s and 1990s, so did the number of inadequately insured and uninsured people in the United States, and the problem only worsened.

During the 1980s and 1990s, communities in the United States increasingly felt that one of the greatest threats they faced was the loss of quality jobs. First, globalization led many of the best-paid manufacturing jobs to leave the United States for lower-wage countries. Then, as the rise of low-cost instantaneous communication made it possible to move business operations overseas, an increasing number of middle-class office jobs were threatened. Call centers and accounting offices, among others, went overseas. There was a marked decline in the availability of jobs that offered any hope for Americans with only a high school education to reach the middle class.

In this environment, Costco played a different but still important role in the communities in which it operated throughout the United States. Costco provided good health insurance so that employees could afford to fully utilize clinics and hospitals; it provided jobs to college students so that they could afford to finish school; and it supported workers who chose to return to school part-time while working in Costco warehouses.

Although the company's decision to pay good salaries and offer strong benefits was based on an economic strategy to attract, retain, and motivate employees, it also had a lot to do with the beliefs of the company and of its CEO, Jim Sinegal. Lee Scott, CEO of Wal-Mart, had argued that retail could not create a middle class in the twenty-first century as manufacturers such as GE had done after World War II.[27] Costco CEO Sinegal argued just the opposite:

> Well, I think any organization can and should strive to provide those types of opportunities for their employees. Absolutely. This is not the eighteenth century! This is the twenty-first century, and we should be looking for ways to improve things like that. We're part of the fabric of the society where we live! We're part of looking at this great country that has lots of opportunities. Why shouldn't an employee who works in retail have the feeling that they can afford to get married and have children, that they and their spouse can have a house, that they can send their children to school [and] provide for them? Aren't they entitled to that? What, are they supposed to be subhuman beings?[28]

Sinegal's values weren't based on abstractions. Born and raised in Pittsburgh, Pennsylvania, his father had worked in the coal mines until he was injured, at which point he became a salesman who carried boxes and wares from one sale to another. He died of emphysema, his condition undoubtedly having been exacerbated by his work in the coal mines. After his father died, sixteen-year-old Sinegal was sent to live on the West Coast with his uncle, a commercial fisherman. Attending San Diego State University, he began working at Fed Mart on weekends, unloading delivery trucks. Sinegal worked his way up in the company before starting his own business. He knew from experience how hard low-level jobs could be.

In one community after another, Costco became one of the firms helping to fill the critical gap in quality jobs for those with only a high school education. As noted in chapter 1, by 2005, the starting wage for cashiers at Costco was twice the minimum wage and for truck drivers, three times the minimum wage.[29] More important, with rapid salary increases in their first years of employment with the company, employees with a high school education could earn $43,000 a year after working as a cashier for only four years. This was more than double the national mean annual wage for cashiers in the United States, which was only $18,380.[30]

When Costco needed to develop new services for its employees, it worked hard to build them collaboratively with community organizations in ways that would benefit local residents as well as Costco employees. For example, the company partnered with the Bellevue Community College to help build a day care facility in Washington. The day care center reserved 50 percent of its 175 spots for Costco employees. Sheri Flies, a senior manager in the legal department, explained: "We have a lot of new programs that we think are really helpful for parents with children . . . We put together a collaborative model that is being replicated, and now communities are doing it . . . We're hoping that [this] could be a way to get the whole community involved in community child care . . . Any community we're in, they know we'll treat [them] well."[31] Fundamentally, Costco saw itself as a member of the communities in which it operated.

Benefits for the Company: Community Support

Just as ACC needed to buy land to build new limestone mines and cement factories as it expanded to new communities, Costco needed store sites in new locations as the company expanded. Building the "big-box" stores often required zoning variances and community permissions. Other firms that sought to open large retail and wholesale stores, including Wal-Mart, Costco's closest competitor, faced great opposition in obtaining these permissions from small communities.

The media has underscored how communities have strongly opposed the opening of new Wal-Mart stores because "they are just not very good community citizens," but have more readily accepted retailers with a better reputation, such as Costco and Target.[32] Residents have worried that the new Wal-Mart stores would lead to the loss of quality jobs in small local stores that would be put out of business, and that these jobs would be replaced by poorly paying jobs without insurance or future opportunities.[33] Moreover, Wal-Mart was seen as burdening public services rather than helping to build them. Lacking health insurance, many

Wal-Mart employees landed on government-funded programs that were designed to serve the poor.[34] In Maryland, state legislators attempted to pass legislation requiring the company to increase spending on health insurance for its employees, with the goal of decreasing the cost to the government of the health care the company failed to provide.[35]

Like any big-box store, Costco occasionally faced concerns from community members who were worried about the impact of a large new warehouse on traffic and quality of life, but it faced far less opposition than Wal-Mart. Communities were more welcoming of Costco since the company created well-paying jobs with long-term career opportunities and health insurance.

What Kinds of Community Investments Pay Off?

In the context of rural India, where there was virtually no existing infrastructure, ACC had focused on building a system of public works in order to facilitate production. Operating in a different economic context, where this basic infrastructure was already established, Costco's community involvement was very much influenced by its identity as a major wholesaler in a globalized economy. In spite of their differing sectors, economies, and approaches, there are crucial similarities between these two companies. Like ACC, Costco's long-term goal was to provide a good working environment with good wages and working conditions that would attract workers and encourage employee loyalty and commitment. Costco has contributed to the building of an economic base in a context where well-paying jobs with advancement opportunities have been one of communities' greatest needs.

The approaches taken by ACC and Costco had many differences. ACC operated mines and factories, whereas Costco ran a chain of wholesale stores; ACC began operating in an emerging nation-state, whereas Costco came of age in an economy that was undergoing profound changes in the context of globalization. But beyond their differences, these two companies had one important factor in common: while both had a strong social conscience, their community involvement and good labor practices were initiated to meet business imperatives.

Both Costco and ACC greatly benefited from their contributions to communities. Both had easier access to the community real estate they sought. Costco had encountered decreased community opposition, and in

India, communities had been more willing to sell their land and provide access to the natural resources that were essential to ACC's operations. Both companies benefited by increasing employee productivity and retention. In the short term, initiatives such as providing health care, transportation allowances, and support for child care centers meant that employees were better able to focus on their work and were less likely to be late or absent. In the long term, their investments in education meant that they were able to draw on a more qualified workforce. Finally, both profited from the ways in which their reputations in the community enriched the value of their brand.

For companies in extractive industries, investing in local communities may well be a necessity since they may not be able to produce if they don't build basic infrastructure. Moreover, companies that use local resources without providing any benefits to local communities foster resentment, which can lead to serious disruptions in production along with accompanying financial losses. Even companies that simply need to set up stores or factories in certain locations may find it much easier to do so if there isn't significant local opposition.

The essence of community involvement is taking the community's needs into account. Some of ACC's initiatives, such as building roads and bringing electricity, were based on the company's need for infrastructure; however, other measures, such as building schools, were needed by the community but were not immediately required for the company to function. While these measures benefited the company in the long run, their immediate benefit was for the surrounding communities.

Why don't more companies take communities into consideration in their strategic plans? In the nineteenth and early twentieth centuries, some locally based companies invested in the communities in which they were headquartered. They saw the need for these investments, since these communities were the source of the production and quite often the consumption of their products. CEOs were more readily aware of the nature and importance of the community's needs when they resided in the same community as their workers. With the rise of multinational corporations and of national companies with branches in multiple locations, companies less frequently have strong ties to a single community, and the community base is less obvious. Yet as the case studies in this chapter have shown, there are returns on community investments for companies across industries and levels of development.

To address communities' needs in a way that is profitable to communities and companies alike, executives need to be strategic long-term thinkers. While this should come naturally since long-term strategy is essential to the growth and profitability of any major firm, as Bannerjee pointed out, the lack of long-term thinking is often the biggest barrier when it comes to community engagement. Once firms are committed to long-term engagement with the community, there are three essential steps to ensuring significant mutual benefits. First, company executives need to understand the community's greatest needs and identify whether there are economically viable ways to address them. Second, the company must determine which improvements are instrumental for the company to accomplish its own core goals, as opposed to its peripheral objectives. Third, the company needs to determine what kind of expertise it brings to the problems and what capacity it has to resolve them.

A company may be significantly more willing and able to invest when communities' critical priorities also have the capacity to greatly increase the firm's productivity. Similarly, when community needs lie in a firm's area of expertise, the company may be particularly well suited to address them. ACC needed roads to facilitate transportation to the poor communities just as much as the communities themselves needed them. The same was true for the firm's investments in water and housing. Although ACC did not have any particular expertise in providing education or health care, maintaining employees and operations in remote, unserviced areas necessitated these investments. The mutual benefits helped forge a strong relationship between the company and the communities. Similarly, the communities in which Costco operated needed strong employment opportunities, and bringing in good jobs was one of Costco's areas of expertise. In both cases, the complementarity of community and company needs led to a far deeper and more meaningful engagement than many other companies' typically small community contributions.

Thousands of companies give a very small fraction of their profits to local community organizations, but these gifts are frequently more symbolic than transformative. These companies' financial engagement and commitment to successful outcomes is limited since they see these investments as utterly peripheral to their core objectives. This stands in stark contrast to firms that see the healthy growth of the communities in which they operate as essential to the core of their business.

9

Creating Good Working Conditions Throughout the Supply Chain

COMPANIES PRODUCING IN HIGH-WAGE countries repeatedly face the question of whether they should move some of their operations abroad to lower-wage locations. Companies that already have a portion of their sales in one or more low-income countries inevitably need to address whether it makes more sense to move some of their production closer to the site of their sales. Regardless of the origin of a company developing a multinational presence, any organization that is working across borders needs to answer a fundamental question about the nature of the work environment, wage and benefit policies, productivity and quality control. If a company from a high-income country has an operation in a low-income country, which aspects of the work environment should be similar to other local work sites and which should be similar to those in the company's headquarters?

China has become one of the most popular destinations for multinational companies setting up production facilities overseas because of its combination of lower-wage labor, investments in transportation and communications infrastructure, and large potential sales market. In setting up production in China, companies simultaneously face two important dilemmas: whether to provide only the minimum standards and benefits required by Chinese law, even if they are lower than those required in their countries of origin; and how to ensure adequate quality of their products.

Long recognized as an important issue, this second dilemma received increasing attention in 2007, when a series of foreign firms' products manufactured in China posed serious health risks.

Novo Nordisk: Manufacturing in China

Novo Nordisk is the world's biggest manufacturer of insulin pens for diabetics. At 35 million cases, China has one of the largest diabetic populations in the world, second only to India. Although Novo Nordisk produces insulin in Brazil, it manufactures the "durable devices" used to inject the insulin in China. Novo Nordisk's decision to set up production in China was largely motivated by the country's lower production costs and the size of its local market. The company opened a sales office in China in 1994 and initiated production there in 1996. It moved its facilities to the Tianjin Economic-Technological Development Area (TEDA) in 2003, where it could benefit from improved infrastructure and lowered taxes. By 2005, the Novo Nordisk factory began expanding its production. As of May 2007, its site in Tianjin had 218 employees, many of whom only had a middle-school education and technical training.

When Novo Nordisk began manufacturing in Tianjin, like other firms, it had to make two important decisions: Would it implement its Danish company culture and workplace policies at its site in China, and how could it ensure the high quality of its products, given the precision required in the pharmaceutical industry. If the company had solely been seeking the cheapest sourcing, it could simply have offered the local minimum wages and benefits and set up a traditional hierarchical management structure. Instead, it chose to bring its own global standards to its production in China.

Implementing a Consistent Global Approach

As part of these efforts, Novo Nordisk brought in two senior managers from its Danish headquarters to manage the expansion process and implement the company's management philosophy. Christian Larsen, senior manager for economy and logistics, believed that effective management included ensuring that employees were adequately rested and healthy, spending more time listening to and valuing employees' contributions, and providing development opportunities and career paths for all employees. These three central concerns were translated into workplace policies that often differed greatly from those that employees had experienced in their previous manufacturing jobs.

1. VALUING EMPLOYEE CONTRIBUTIONS: THE C-LEAN PRODUCTION PROCESS

As a central part of its search for the highest possible standards of quality, Novo Nordisk found it essential to systematically seek employee input. The managers firmly believed that if you asked line workers the right questions, their knowledge could be used to optimize operations. Short for Current Lean Manufacturing Process, the Novo Nordisk adaptation of the c-LEAN process made employee engagement a central part of production. During our site visit in 2006 Lars Nielsen, senior manager of durable devices, explained that the lean manufacturing process, adapted from Toyota's, also incorporates "one-piece flow," where one item at a time is moved between operators within a group. This enables flaws or errors to be detected rapidly and corrected instead of accumulating.

As part of c-LEAN at Novo Nordisk, all employees were involved in problem-solving activities. The company ran regular c-LEAN workshops during which employees were asked a series of questions referred to as "the five why's" in order to get their feedback and ideas on how to improve the quality and efficiency of production. The goal of this process was to find the source of the problem and then work together to find a solution. According to Nielsen, "Challenging ideas is the only way to improve things."[1] The underlying philosophy at Novo Nordisk was "Don't work harder, work smarter."

The c-LEAN workshops had been highly successful, with an approximately 50 percent increase in efficiency rates since the process began. Nielsen felt that the ideas that had been generated through the workshops had been extremely valuable: "We can actually transfer some of the ideas back to Denmark, and make Denmark more efficient."[2] Larsen gave us an example of the c-LEAN "five-why's" approach to problem solving. If a machine was not working, leaders would ask: Why is the machine not working? Because there is no grease. Why is there no grease? And so on, with at least five rounds to get closer to the root cause of the problem.

To be successful, the c-LEAN process required workers to be willing to speak up and voice their opinions. Line workers in Novo Nordisk's Tianjin factory were initially surprised when management requested their input. Larsen explained: "A couple of months ago, we were running a c-LEAN workshop. We invited some new operators who were shocked that they would come upstairs [to the management floor] and be a part of the workshop, because at their old jobs no one would listen to them."[3] Although management was initially uncertain whether workers would openly offer feedback, employees had been enthusiastic about participating in the workshops. According to Nielsen: "They are very eager and willing to come up with suggestions about how to do it, [as well as] criticism about how things were being done."[4]

The company also wanted employees to participate and contribute feedback spontaneously, outside the context of the workshops. Novo Nordisk placed a suggestion box in the company cafeteria where employees could drop anonymous comments and recommendations. A factory worker explained this process: "Every month there is one suggestion day and all the suggestions received are read to the whole group. Then they all discuss the ideas and they choose together which ideas to take."[5] Novo Nordisk also obtained feedback through surveys that measured employee satisfaction. Employees who had been working at any location for at least one month were given a survey to find out if they had been taking advantage of the company's various benefits and whether the company's values were evident in the workplace. Staff who had been at the company for three months or more were given additional surveys to determine whether they were satisfied with the company's mission and values and to obtain their opinions about their managers and the work environment.

2. ESTABLISHING GLOBALLY CONSISTENT BENEFITS

Novo Nordisk provided many of the same benefits in Tianjin that it provided in Denmark, including paid maternity leave, medical insurance, disability insurance, unemployment insurance, yearly bonuses, health checkups, lunch allowance, transportation, vacation, sick days, overtime pay, and wedding and funeral leave. The company believed that it was both feasible and advantageous to do so even if local regulations did not require it. Managers repeatedly mentioned that they felt that for factory workers to perform well at the firm, it was important for them to have a good work-life balance, leave work at a reasonable hour, and take vacation. The average work week on the factory floor was between thirty-six and forty hours, depending on whether employees worked the day shift (five 8-hour days a week) or the night shift (three 12-hour nights a week). Nielsen understood that stressed, unhappy workers would not be as productive and would not remain at the company for as long as those whose lives had a healthy balance between work and leisure time. Less had been achieved by Novo Nordisk in normalizing the hours of its professional staff.

In developing its policies for its operations in China, Novo Nordisk supplemented the Chinese labor laws with certain benefits that they felt were important to workers everywhere, as well as others that they felt Chinese workers might value in particular. The company expanded on the Chinese legal requirements for medical insurance, sick leave, public holidays, unemployment, housing, pension, disability, and parental leave. For instance, instead of offering the five annual paid sick days required by law, Novo Nordisk allowed up to twenty. Although Chinese labor law did not require paid holidays, Novo Nordisk offered between fifteen and twenty days of annual leave. The company also offered a variety of benefits that were not required by law, such as free transportation from Tianjin city, free lunches, annual salary increases, breaks during the day, and generous yearly bonuses equivalent to three months' salary.

3. PROVIDING DEVELOPMENT AND ADVANCEMENT OPPORTUNITIES

Managers repeatedly stressed that they saw advancement opportunities as a crucial component of their workplace policies. Christian Larsen pointed out that advancement opportunities not only motivated individial employees but also changed the entire work environment at the factory. Without these opportunities, even the better employees would lose motivation, and he argued that this loss of enagegement would spread to the rest of the workforce."[6]

Since the company needed workers with skills and expertise in production, it made sense to invest in basic training and language courses that would facilitate advanced training in production techniques. Nielsen explained: "We try to develop people in order to make them more capable of acquiring new knowledge . . . by educating them in English—all operators have English training—and also by educating them in our systems."[7] The training had direct effects on improving quality and efficiency of production. Providing training was also a strong recruitment and retention tool. The line operators we interviewed were immensely enthusiastic about these opportunities. Learning to speak English meant that more employment opportunities would be available to them both at Novo Nordisk and elsewhere. While companies such as Motorola provided classes for their managers, Novo Nordisk made training available to all employees, including workers with the least formal education. Advancement opportunities within Novo Nordisk included four levels of machine operator on the factory floor as well as career paths that kept employees motivated.

Benefiting from a Consistent Global Approach

As a pharmaceutical company, Novo Nordisk knew that ensuring the highest-quality products was an economic necessity, since any mistakes could result in high financial liabilities. It was therefore essential for the company to be able to recruit, train, and retain motivated and able employees. Moreover, excessive fatigue could lead to costly production errors.

Senior managers were well aware of how important so-called low-skilled workers were to the quality of their products. In the words of Lars Nielsen: "Actually, low-skilled workers are probably those that can influence [products the most] because the quality that our products have in the end is a combination of the persons that make the actual product, and of course the tests that we do afterwards."[8]

Novo Nordisk's reputation as a good employer facilitated recruitment. While outsiders often describe China's labor force as being limitless, with its hundreds of millions of workers, that is not the local reality. In China as elsewhere, manufacturing companies need to be able to attract and retain the most capable operators. The millions of workers emigrating from the Chinese countryside often had limited experience working in factories, and although the "low-skilled" jobs at Novo Nordisk didn't require an advanced formal education, they required an enormous amount of practical skills. Several workers mentioned the company's benefits and workplace culture as one of the main factors that had motivated them to apply for a job there. One employee told us: "The most important reason [I came to work at Novo Nordisk] was . . . because of the friendly and caring atmosphere. I have worked at three pharmaceutical companies before coming here and this is by far the best of them all."[9] Other workers said: "The benefits are far better here than at other foreign-owned companies" and "I left my last job because of too much overtime. There was not time for vacation. There was too much pressure at work and there were not enough benefits."[10] Novo Nordisk had clearly distinguished itself from its competitors.

Novo Nordisk's good working conditions also translated into reduced turnover rates. From April 1, 2006, to April 1, 2007, the company's turnover rates of 9.3 percent for office employees and 5 percent for operators were much lower than the average turnover for the pharmaceutical industry in China (24.1 percent) and in Tianjin (15.5 percent).[11] Christian Larsen talked about how the company's high standards of quality made employee retention extremely important: "Caring for our employees is very important to us. There is a business side to this as well . . . Because we are a pharmaceutical company, we are evaluated [on the quality of our products]. We save money by having people stay, even with a pay raise. We carefully find employees who want to stay. This is why we treat the workers well."[12]

The company's low turnover rates reflected employees' high levels of satisfaction with the company, which also increased the quality of their work. Workers told us: "I really like working here . . . Every day I am happy to be here."[13] Liu Jianbo, a thirty-year-old Novo Nordisk employee, had previously worked for a state-owned steel factory. He felt that the quality of Novo Nordisk's work environment encouraged workers to care more about their work, and he believed that his colleagues were more motivated than they had been at their previous jobs.

The company has received numerous awards in the Tianjin Economic-Technological Development Area, including selection as the "Best Employer" in 2003. Like other European firms, Novo Nordisk reported a triple bottom line. More than simply a reporting requirement, this was also an economic strategy since the company believed that its positive social impact helped it attract and retain the best employees.

Challenges and Complexities

While there were great benefits from ensuring good working conditions, employee participation in production design, and training for the least-advantaged workers, Novo Nordisk faced real challenges in implementation. Deciding how high to set the bar for compensation and ensuring that employees felt free to use benefits and that local managers supported the process were far from straightforward.

SETTING THE BAR FOR COMPENSATION

While believing that cultural differences might make some benefits more welcome in one country than in another, Novo Nordisk understood that treating employees well and making them feel valued was important everywhere. Lars Nielsen explained: "We care about our employees and I think that that makes a difference. I think that it makes a difference in China and it makes a difference in the United States, in that you feel that where you work, they actually care for you and want you to have a good time."[14] As in many other multinational companies, there were debates about how high Novo Nordisk's standards should be set. Novo Nordisk needed to decide which standards to adopt and how to adjust them to the local context. These decisions were motivated by a desire to benefit employees while benefiting the company. Christian Larsen discussed this process: "We spend a lot of time on talking together and discussing what is the ultimate way to motivate people: [We] say, 'Should we do this? Does it have a benefit?' 'Cause of course there is no reason to do something if it doesn't benefit employees and . . . at the same time . . . benefit productivity. Because it has to go hand in hand."[15]

Novo Nordisk's policy was to set salaries in the fiftieth to seventy-fifth percentile of foreign pharmaceutical firms, which was already above the average for local Chinese firms and slightly above average for all foreign companies. Christian Larsen explained: "The worldwide Novo policy is that Novo does not go into a new country and start a salary spiral. We have seen other companies where they took an employee from another company and gave them a completely crazy high salary. We, however, are not part of things like that. We don't just want people to work here because they get a lot of money. We want people to work for Novo because they are engaged and want to be here."[16]

While offering a similar level of benefits in China, Novo Nordisk did not simply copy the benefits package from Denmark. It developed a unique package that combined Novo Nordisk's workplace culture with local practices. Christian Larsen explained:

> We come with our experience, and then based on what you . . . do in China, then we can come and say, "Well, we would like to give this benefit to our employees." . . . For instance, . . . look at the bonus scheme. Of course, salaries are a lot lower in China, but the bonus scheme is a lot better in China. So, there is a higher bonus in China than there is in Denmark because it is the culture here, but it is not the culture in Denmark. And the same thing with other benefits. If you feel that it is a good idea at the site, then you can implement it.

ENSURING EMPLOYEES MAKE USE OF POLICIES AND BENEFITS

Novo Nordisk's commitment to having good labor standards and greater employee involvement in problem solving did not mean that these policies were easy to implement. Part of the challenge was operational.

Opting to provide such long vacation leave can be a problem for production if it is not carefully planned. Line managers in particular are needed on the factory floor and they cannot all take vacation at the same time unless the factory shuts down.

Part of the challenge was ensuring that workers truly felt free to use their benefits. In Tianjin, Novo Nordisk's employees rarely took the full maternity leave that was available to them. Vacation leave was another benefit that was often not used. Lars Nielsen knew that workers were particularly unlikely to take vacation but he wasn't sure whether this was due to the cultural emphasis on work, to midlevel Chinese supervisors sending the message that it was better not to take vacation, or to workers' fear that using these benefits would affect their annual evaluations. One of the Chinese facility managers spoke to us about the cultural complexities that influenced employees' attitudes and behaviors: "[The plant] is owned by Novo Nordisk, but the director is Chinese, so he always said that a Chinese environment is like this. If you take a lot of vacation, you won't have good performance."[18] In an effort to encourage workers to use these benefits, management started regularly following up on employees' use of vacation time and considered closing the factory down for one or two weeks each year.

It was also difficult to get workers to provide unsolicited feedback. Though they were eager to participate in the c-LEAN workshops, it was still a challenge to get them to voice their opinions outside of this structured forum. One factory worker explained: "People are still not totally comfortable to speak out. It is our culture."[19] Senior managers made an effort to encourage workers to offer suggestions. To ensure that employees got in the habit of speaking up, Christian Larsen was considering introducing a new policy obliging every worker to provide at least two ideas per year.

GETTING BUY-IN FROM MANAGERS

Having support from all levels of management was essential for Novo Nordisk's workplace policies to be implemented effectively. While this is true for all companies, both managers and factory floor employees felt that as a Danish company operating in China, one of Novo Nordisk's major challenges lay in combining two very different management styles. Local management is critical in China in order to obtain the permits to build factories and run operations for a global market, as well as to produce effectively and sell to the local market. While Novo Nordisk recognized the importance of having local management, it also wanted to ensure that the factory in China maintained the Danish headquarters' vision and practices. For this reason, it temporarily sent two senior managers from headquarters to serve as advisors for the expansion process.

Both Danish and Chinese managers at Novo Nordisk observed differences between their historical management styles. A Chinese middle manager who had been to Novo Nordisk's Denmark headquarters discussed these differences: "I think that this gap between management and workers is large in Chinese culture. I didn't see this in Denmark, where the workers can say anything to the manager, and people smile and say hello. It is quite different in this factory; many Chinese people don't say hello. It is the Chinese culture. In Chinese history, you have officers, emperors, etc. People aren't used to feel[ing] equal. We have different levels and you must humble yourself."[20]

His description was similar to that given by Christian Larsen: "The biggest [difference] comes in the hierarchy. In Denmark, you try to make everything as flat as possible. You can tell the boss if you do not agree with him. In China, you never say you don't agree. I hear 'yes' all the time. It comes a lot from culture and history . . . Many people are happy about Novo's way where people are important and what they say is important. They like that we have removed the barrier and people can talk to us and we listen to them."[21] The Chinese workers and middle managers were largely enthusiastic, repeatedly mentioning Novo Nordisk's workplace culture as a major motivating factor in their decision to apply for a job there.

There had, however, been some obstacles in implementing these policies, since not everyone had easily been brought on board. These hurdles were as much due to differences among the Chinese managers as to differences between the Chinese and Danish leadership. Chen Qi, the first plant director, did not fully embrace the company culture, and this had impeded the efficacy of the new policies. Although he understood the rationale behind these policies, employees' testimonies and further probing revealed that he didn't truly believe in them and wasn't genuinely invested in their success. Chen Qi stated that career development opportunities for workers were important for the company, but he was unable to explain in detail how the company made sure that employees could take advantage of them. He simply stated that there was an individual plan for each worker.

The Chinese line workers and middle managers and the Danish senior managers were better able to provide detailed descriptions and examples of Novo Nordisk's development opportunities.

Chen Qi's lack of commitment to Novo Nordisk's workplace policies, in particular to encouraging employee engagement and input, was mentioned on several occasions by Chinese middle managers. As one facility manager said, "It is very difficult to persuade the Chinese boss to follow Novo Nordisk's policy." He went on to explain: "In Chinese culture, we don't challenge our boss. It is very dangerous for us, even if we don't feel satisfied. I am Chinese, so even though the Danish make the environment very open, I feel pressure to go the Chinese way. I report to my Chinese boss so I must follow his orders."[22] Other managers pointed out their lack of autonomy and control over departmental budgets; even the simplest decisions, such as ordering a pizza lunch to reward their department, had to go through the plant director.

When employees did make suggestions, tensions arose in the development of action plans based on these ideas. In accordance with Novo Nordisk's policy of promoting employee involvement and participation, these action plans should have been developed by teams of workers and managers. In reality, however, the plant director devised the plans alone and then had the head of HR announce them at the meetings. Middle managers felt that this significantly reduced the plans' effectiveness since it failed to take their knowledge and input into account. Christian Larsen candidly discussed these challenges: "Yes, there are a lot of challenges [in implementing new policies], especially when you have the top boss who is not able to see that doing things differently is good. That can be an issue . . . We've had incidents where there have been clashes like that here, but we have also had to put a lot of focus on [solving them]. We have talked these clashes out."[23]

As a foreign company, Novo Nordisk had to find a way to nurture local leadership while maintaining its global corporate values and standards. It eventually brought in a new plant director from Denmark, Preben Haaning, who was more attuned to the company's corporate culture. They put Chen Qi in charge of local affairs, taking care of relations with local government and organizations. Haaning described his efforts to transform the factory's management style: "I think it is very important for me to be visible and to be approachable for everyone so that I am not hiding at all. I am trying to be seen physically as much as possible to get a feeling of approximately what is going on, and also to break down this huge distance . . . especially between foreign people and Chinese, and also this [dichotomy] of the boss and the worker. Because in China, people are thinking very hierarchically."[24] One of the first steps Haaning took upon his arrival was to move his desk to an open area in order to encourage employees to come and see him. He also gave managers increased decision-making power over their departmental budgets.

Lars Nielsen pointed out that the factory floor operators had generally responded well to the benefits Novo Nordisk provided and to the company's participatory management style. The biggest clashes in the implementation process had taken place within management. Christian Larsen contended that the differences were partly generational: "China has changed dramatically in the past five to ten years and business management has changed . . . There is a huge generation gap happening in China and the management sometimes cannot understand. Young people come out of school expecting to be heard, whereas managers come out of long-time management roles expecting to be listened to."[25]

The operators had grown up in an age of rapid economic expansion, where there had been a dialogue about democratic openings. They wanted their opinions to be respected. Novo Nordisk believed that enhanced communication between levels of employees would improve production and make the company more competitive.

Multinationals and Labor Standards

In an era of low-cost transportation, instant communication, and increased accessibility to global markets due to falling tariffs and trade barriers, more firms are opting to produce overseas. As countries such as India and China continue to grow, more companies will be drawn by the size of their markets. At the same time, multinationals operating abroad have come under increased scrutiny and criticism regarding their working conditions and production practices. Yet as we saw with Novo Nordisk, multinationals can choose to establish good working conditions in all of their global facilities.

Why Are Labor Standards Overseas So Important?

Although quality standards are a particularly important concern in the medical field, companies in a wide range of industries can incur significant financial losses due to production errors. Companies ranging from those producing pet food to candy, toys, car tires, and toothpaste have had to recall products that were manufactured in China under poor conditions. As one example, in 2007, Mattel Inc., the toy company that sells Barbie, Hot Wheels, American Girl, and Fisher-Price toys worldwide, had to recall large numbers of products manufactured in China due to concerns about toxic lead paint. Over the course of several recalls, over 20 million Chinese-made toys were recalled.[26] The company spent $110 million on testing, advertising, and legal fees directly related to the toy recall.[27] Mattel CEO Bob Eckert was asked to appear before a U.S. Congressional Energy and Commerce Subcommittee in September 2007 to answer questions about the scope of the recalls.[28] The company posted a loss in the first quarter of 2008 and remains concerned about potential consumer lawsuits.[29]

The problems associated with poor product quality can readily outweigh the benefits of lower labor costs. Steiff, a German toy company known for its high-end teddy bears, decided to outsource one-fifth of its production to China in 2003; however, the company announced in the summer of 2008 that it would be moving production back to Germany, mainly due to concerns about the quality of manufacturing.[30] According to Steiff managing director Martin Frechen, it normally takes eighteen months to train employees to assemble the bears correctly. In China, as elsewhere, the factories with worse working conditions have higher turnover rates. High staff turnover meant that workers were not staying at the company long enough to learn how to properly fulfill the assembly requirements.[31] Producing in China also caused longer delays in the distribution of Steiff products to European markets, and this was a serious concern, given the short trends in demand in the toy industry. According to Frechen, the lower-quality bears produced in China resulted in "a significant loss of reputation" for the company. For Steiff, the trade-off between quality and cost was ultimately not a good deal.[32] The bottom line is that methods of reducing labor costs that result in poorer production quality can lead to financial losses.

ASSURING PRODUCT QUALITY AND PRODUCTIVITY

Companies are beginning to recognize the important link between working conditions and product quality and productivity. The Gap's 2005–2006 Social Responsibility Report noted: "We know that better working conditions improve the efficiency of our supply chain. Workers who are paid fairly, work a reasonable number of hours, and operate in healthy and safe environments tend to be more productive, deliver higher-quality work, and choose to stay with factories longer than those who are mistreated."[33] In contrast, research has repeatedly shown that disgruntled, unhappy employees are more likely to produce lower-quality products and negatively affect the nature of their coworkers' efforts. Employees who are tired due to excessive overtime or work-related stress are more likely to make mistakes. Studies have linked higher grievance and discipline rates with lower product quality and labor efficiency, and have shown that better employee attitudes are associated with greater labor efficiency and better product quality.[34]

As a result, direct impact on product quality and productivity is the first business reason that companies should be concerned about their working conditions overseas. Working conditions that ensure that employees are well rested, healthy, and have a positive attitude toward their work will lead to higher-quality products overseas as well as at home. As the examples provided illustrate, while some industries, such as pharmaceuticals, have particularly strict quality requirements, quality assurance is an issue that affects all producers, regardless of their domains. Poor-quality manufacturing can lead to financial losses due to massive product recalls and to damaged corporate reputations; even when the consequences are not as dire, customers in a competitive marketplace have little incentive to purchase poor-quality products.

Additional business reasons to be concerned about poor working conditions are their effect on turnover. Higher turnover rates are in turn linked with increased error rates and lower efficiency. If workers constantly leave the company after a short period of time, they do not acquire the skills to make better products. Research has shown that workplace practices that link compensation to performance and emphasize employee involvement, training, and education contribute to lower employee turnover and improved company performance. As discussed in chapter 7, a study of data from nearly one thousand U.S. firms found evidence that investments in all level employees including policies that support employee involvement, training, internal promotion, and compensation incentives, were associated with substantial reductions in turnover.[35] Though these studies focused on firms manufacturing in advanced economies, the practices they describe are just as important to quality and productivity in outsourcing as they are to production in a company's home country. The impact of employee motivation, training, and participation on productivity and quality is not limited to a specific geographic location.

PROTECTING CORPORATE REPUTATIONS

Building and maintaining a good corporate reputation is critical to success. In fact, surveys have shown that most CEOs consider their company's reputation to be their most important intangible asset.[36] With increasing public attention being paid to companies' global footprints, most firms at least state their intentions to be socially responsible. After a series of public relations scandals over goods produced under sweatshop conditions, more firms have begun to recognize the necessity of paying attention to working conditions in their operations in all countries.

The extent of the impact that a company's reputation has on its performance varies by industry; consumer goods companies are particularly vulnerable to negative publicity. The bad publicity of being associated with sweatshop working conditions can lead to serious economic losses. The CEO of Levi Strauss stated in 1994: "In today's world, a TV exposé on working conditions can undo years of effort to build brand loyalty."[37]

Customers' preferences can ultimately reward or punish a company for its labor practices. According to a 2005 poll conducted by the Program on International Policy Attitudes (PIPA), 74 percent of respondents believed that they had a moral obligation to ensure good working conditions for the foreign workers manufacturing the products they bought, and this percentage has remained almost constant since 1999.[38] According to four other polls conducted by PIPA and the Chicago Council on Foreign Relations (CCFR), 76.6 percent of respondents believed that the United States should ban products produced under unsafe and unhealthy working conditions.[39] In a 1999 survey conducted by PIPA, an overwhelming 86 percent of respondents agreed with the statement that American companies operating overseas "should be expected to abide by U.S. health and safety standards for workers."[40]

A company's corporate reputation can also have an impact on its employee recruitment at all levels of the firm, since companies with damaged reputations are less attractive to job seekers. A 1997 Walker Information Survey found that 42 percent of respondents considered a company's ethics when deciding whether to accept a job offer.[41] Case studies of campus recruitment have found evidence that firms with better reputations attracted more job applicants and could therefore select higher-quality candidates.[42] According to GlobeScan's 2003 Corporate Social Responsibility (CSR) Monitor, 70 percent of North American students said they would not apply at a company that was considered to be socially irresponsible.[43]

Steps That Companies Can Take to Improve Their Working Conditions and Those of Their Suppliers

Recognizing that working conditions within companies' and suppliers' facilities affect firms' bottom lines is clearly only a first step. Implementing change across countries and corporate entities is an enormous challenge. The following section reviews different possible approaches and addresses how firms can build an effective strategy that learns from the experiences of other companies.

1. Establishing Codes of Conduct: Setting the Rules of the Game

The most common way to establish ground rules is to develop a code of conduct that lays out the company's official requirements for its overseas facilities and suppliers. When creating these rules, companies must make many important decisions. First of all, they must decide what they are trying to achieve. What are the ultimate goals of these rules? What are their objectives with regard to their subcontractors' working conditions? Second, given the sheer number of issues surrounding labor standards in overseas facilities, what are the priorities for action? Factories can rarely address all necessary changes at once. Which improvements are essential and urgent, and which ones can gradually be improved over time? These decisions may require companies to evaluate their beliefs. Are they willing to compromise on certain standards with factories that have a long way to go before achieving their goals?

Some practices are much easier to change than others. Clearly, safety measures that require one-time steps, such as installing fire extinguishers, are easier to implement than broader changes, such as restructuring work schedules and payroll systems. Some companies argue that given the complexity of issues surrounding working conditions, it is best to have realistic expectations and start with easier changes, then build on them over time. Others contend that this means settling for lower standards rather than pursuing more ambitious changes. A critical question then arises: Is it better to begin with changes that are readily implementable even if they do not address the most pressing issues?

While all these questions apply to the full range of firms, small companies face particular constraints when it comes to ensuring good labor standards at their overseas suppliers. Their smaller purchasing power means that they have less leverage to pressure suppliers to make the changes they desire, and they have fewer resources to devote to monitoring and enforcing their regulations. One option for small companies is to work together with other like-minded firms and agree on a common set of standards to enforce. Small companies will benefit from increased leverage by joining forces to form a larger group. Groups of companies can also share information concerning factories' labor standards, thereby facilitating monitoring and enforcement. Barriers to the implementation of this collective approach include the difficulty of finding other firms with similar factory production needs and approaches to labor standards, the challenge of collectively negotiating without violating antitrust regulations, and the limitations it places on purchasing decisions.

An increasingly common feature of corporate life since the 1990s, codes of conduct are self-regulated and voluntarily established by individual companies. These codes have been promulgated by some companies as very real obligations and by others as mere formalities. Companies have sometimes established codes of conduct in response to public criticism or to major negative public relations events. Companies often make their codes public as a way to inform consumers about their official stance on certain issues or to head off calls for stricter regulations. Business organizations such as the United States Council for International Business have advised that "positive efforts on the part of business to confront legitimate concerns about social and environmental issues will also help blunt the efforts of trade unions and NGOs who seek to control corporate behavior in the pursuit of their objectives."[44]

Codes of conduct have varying degrees of efficacy in improving working conditions since they vary widely in their scope and strength. They can apply only to internal operations or regulate suppliers as well. Some codes of conduct simply dictate compliance with local labor requirements, while others go above and beyond local laws and establish stricter standards. To be effective, codes must be accompanied by mechanisms for education, integration, implementation, and evaluation. A 1996–97 U.S. Department of Labor survey examined the codes of conduct of forty-five top retailers and apparel manufacturers. The survey found that a third of factory managers surveyed at seventy-four apparel-producing plants in developing countries were not aware of their companies' codes of conduct; less than half of managers were able to produce a copy of their codes upon request; only 20 percent of the managers who were aware of their companies' codes had received training in their implementation; and only 20 percent of factories posted their codes of conduct at the workplace.[45] It remains to be seen how much the implementation of codes has improved with the increasing public attention paid to labor conditions globally over the past decade. Clearly it isn't enough to have policies on paper; codes of conduct need to be disseminated and integrated into a company's day-to-day activities.

2. Integrating Labor Standards into Company Culture

Codes of conduct set the rules for improving working conditions, but in order to achieve meaningful results, it is essential to integrate their principles into all branches of the company. Different departments may have differing perspectives and priorities regarding labor standards. For implementation to be successful, labor standards cannot solely be a concern of the Corporate Social Responsibility (CSR) department; they need to be integrated into central aspects of production, such as design and purchasing.

The difference between what companies' codes of conduct formally require of their suppliers and what their demands for lower prices and faster production effectively encourage is often reflected in differences in corporate culture within the company. For example, managers responsible for purchasing may be guided by different principles and targets than those in charge of CSR. When corporate buyers receive incentives from their supervisors to focus on immediate cost savings, longer-term values such as corporate reputations often fall by the wayside. Buyers may see those in charge of quality assurance, ethics, or even product safety as creating unnecessary hurdles that prevent low-cost purchases.[46]

One company we visited was paying top managers to design ways to improve the labor standards of its suppliers. However, when we spoke with employees who were not directly involved with the program, they knew little about its operations or the ways in which it related to their work. There was little integration between the company's approach to suppliers' labor standards, the firm's formal code of conduct, the ways in which purchases were made, and how the product department made design decisions. As a result, the company's efforts to improve working conditions had limited impact.

Purchasers have a central role to play when it comes to compliance with labor standards. Reports from Oxfam and the Catholic Agency for

Overseas Development have suggested that corporate buyers' increasing demands for lower prices and faster product delivery can undermine suppliers' capacity to comply with companies' codes of conduct.[47] Yet, just as corporate buyers can pressure suppliers to lower their prices and production times, they can also use their purchasing power to push for better working conditions. Sheri Flies, a senior manager in Costco's legal department, demonstrated how Costco had used its leverage as a large purchaser to provide incentives for a supplier in Vietnam to improve its corporate behavior:

> When they asked, "Would you be willing to buy from us?" we said, "Well, we will buy from you, assuming that your pricing is good, your quality's good, and you're in compliance with our Code of Conduct, which makes you in compliance with your local laws." And they said, "Well, nobody else asks that." And we said, "Well, we ask it," and they said, "So that's the condition for all companies selling to you? " And we said, "That is the condition. We will not buy from you unless you do that." So they said, "We need to become in compliance with our own laws so that we can be international, so that we can become part of this new global market? "And we said, "From our perspective, yes, you do."

Costco CEO Jim Sinegal explained: "If you think you're doing yourself any favors by driving down the price so low that the other guy can't make any money, you're making a tragic mistake. Because one of three things are going to happen, and they're all bad: if he's not making money, he's going to go broke; or he's going to start cheating in terms of the product that he's selling you; or he's going to start abusing the people who work for him."[49]

In short, the nature of the relationship between buyers and suppliers is central to ensuring improvements in working conditions. When retailers provide realistic notice when placing orders, suppliers do not have to rely on temporary workers to fill orders on time. When suppliers are able to predict their production schedules, they are also able to offer decent work schedules to their employees. When purchasing teams are asked to ensure compliance with the company's code of conduct and believe in the business case for improving working conditions, they are more likely to take longer-term reputational issues into account when making purchasing decisions. By improving suppliers' working conditions, companies can experience improved quality of production, efficiency gains, and reputational advantages.

3. Selecting Committed Factories and Suppliers

Companies can ensure that their suppliers have decent labor standards in two ways: by selecting suppliers that have a strong record and rewarding them for their higher standards, or by seeking to improve factories that have inadequate standards. This section focuses on the first strategy, and the next section will address the latter approach. It can be argued that firms' greatest power lies in their initial purchasing decisions—when they select the factories and suppliers for their products. It is a good investment to carefully assess the labor practices of potential suppliers before making any purchasing decisions, since favoring factories and suppliers that have demonstrated a commitment to decent labor standards rewards those that have already worked on improving their labor conditions, thereby functioning as a market mechanism to create incentives for good practices. This practice also greatly facilitates subsequent monitoring and enforcement of compliance.

While choosing the right supplier can significantly improve compliance for all companies, even for large firms with significant leverage to press for change, this approach is particularly beneficial for small companies that have more limited ability to change their suppliers' behavior. In countries with thousands of factories to choose from, companies can establish a policy of working with factories with good working conditions, thereby rewarding good labor practices. Since small companies also have limited resources for monitoring and enforcement, they can focus their efforts on selecting good factories.

Nearly as important as choosing *which* factories to source from is deciding *how many* factories to source from. Large multinationals have sometimes been accused of sourcing from hundreds or thousands of factories in order to purposefully obscure the sourcing trail, making it difficult or impossible to determine their suppliers' labor conditions. Whether or not these decisions were taken to obfuscate labor conditions, concentrating purchasing among fewer factories certainly makes it easier to monitor and improve labor conditions. While true for firms of all sizes, this is particularly true for small companies that can acquire greater leverage by sourcing more products from fewer factories.

4. Monitoring and Enforcing Labor Standards

Getting accurate reports about conditions in the factories from which they source is essential for all companies. As detailed in this chapter, good conditions confer reputational, quality, relaiability, and productivity advantages. Yet ultimately, the only way for companies to ensure decent working conditions when outsourcing is to have complete, reliable, and impartial audit information.

Company audits of suppliers and third-party evaluations are important tools for identifying problems in the implementation of corporate codes of conduct. These audits can also keep the public and consumers informed about companies' efforts to improve working conditions. Making these audits public can increase companies' credibility with consumers, resulting in positive publicity for demonstrated commitments to transparency and improvement. Sharing this information also presents challenges, however, since it may seem like companies releasing their audit reports have worse working conditions than others who do not disclose such information. At the same time, companies don't want to send the internal message that they would prefer to get less informative audits that reveal fewer potential problems. There must be an internal structure that ensures that auditors are not punished for producing an informative but less glowing report. Clearly companies have to be prepared to respond to the information they release to the public. If negative results are to be disseminated, companies need to have a plan for how they will address their weaknesses.

Accuracy of monitoring is crucial in order to reap the gains in quality and productivity that improved labor standards yield. While there is no guarantee of an audit's accuracy and objectivity, companies can try to make sure they get the best possible information. Companies need to ensure that audits are conducted by people who can talk to workers in the local language, conduct interviews with respect for privacy and confidentiality, and take the time to gain a comprehensive view of conditions in the factory. Audits need to be a prerequisite for firms to purchase from suppliers, and they should be performed randomly; factories mustn't be allowed to turn auditors away or refuse to let workers speak with them.

To gain reputational advantages, companies also need to care about the perceived objectivity of monitoring. Even when companies invest in accurate audits, if firms conduct the monitoring themselves, there are

often reasonable concerns about their objectivity since each company decides which labor practices will be audited by whom, and how the reports
will be structured. Third-party audits (Canada's Ethical Trading Action
Group's Transparency Report Cards is one example) are clearly seen as
more objective than self-audits. The credibility and accuracy of any evaluation process can be questioned without the existence of an internationally recognized body for independent reporting.

Though audits are a necessary step in the monitoring of labor standards, some companies believe that a collaborative relationship with suppliers regarding follow-up to findings is better than strict enforcement.
With such an approach, both parties agree on areas that need improvement and on how they should be addressed, including any technical assistance that may be required. Other companies believe that the traditional
"evaluate, critique, and respond" process is the only way to make progress.
In this approach, companies establish their requirements, suppliers agree
to comply with them, progress is monitored through audits and reports,
and lack of compliance is penalized through loss of business. Critics of the
collaborative approach contend that it is simply a rhetorical exercise that
does not lead to real improvements. Both sides can point to advantages
and disadvantages of either method.

Ultimately, the real question is which approach to use in different contexts. This decision necessitates assessing the barriers to progress in improving labor standards. If the barriers are based on a lack of will, then
incentives for improvement are needed, such as the risk of losing business
due to inadequate compliance. If there is a willingness to improve but
local obstacles are preventing progress, then it would be more effective for
the parties to solve the problem together. A successful collaborative approach is one in which companies work with factories and provide them
with the necessary technical assistance to facilitate compliance. Ultimately, this approach can be effective only when it is applied to suppliers
that have already demonstrated a substantial commitment to improving
their working conditions.

5. Supporting Countrywide Strategies

Even when companies prioritize compliance with their codes of conduct,
it can be challenging for retailers to monitor sourcing, since retailers often
purchase their goods from hundreds to thousands of suppliers. The National
Labor Committee estimates that Wal-Mart has sourced products from

over a thousand factories in China alone, and that Walt Disney products are manufactured in thirty thousand sites around the world.[50] Even when retailers have long-standing relationships with a few large suppliers, these firms often subcontract their production to smaller suppliers and home workers, creating a complex supply chain. The enormity of modern-day supply chains can make monitoring difficult as well as inaccurate. Given these challenges, some countries have sought to gain a nationwide reputation for improving labor standards.

By implementing national programs, countries can demonstrate their commitment to improving working conditions. Such programs act as countrywide codes of conduct. From a business perspective, such initiatives present the possibility of relying on national monitoring systems, instead of individual monitoring by every business of every factory and subcontractor.

THE BETTER FACTORIES CAMBODIA PROGRAM

The Better Factories Cambodia program provides an important example of such a countrywide initiative. Cambodia's garment exports grew to 50 percent of the country's total exports in the 1990s, with 90 percent of these products destined for the United States. Under pressure from American textile and garment manufacturers to restrict imports from Cambodia, the U.S. government placed the country under a quota system. The U.S.–Cambodia Trade Agreement (UCTA) guaranteed Cambodia a quota growth rate of 6 percent, with the possibility of annually increasing this quota based on its compliance with internationally recognized labor standards. This was an innovative approach, since the majority of trade agreements that contain labor provisions do so in the form of sanctions for noncompliance rather than incentives for improvements. The International Labor Organization (ILO) set up the Better Factories Cambodia program to monitor Cambodian factories' compliance with national labor standards. While factories were not required to participate in the program, the Cambodian government required registration in the program in order to export garments to the United States. The program was largely funded by the U.S. government, with a smaller contribution from the Cambodian government.

Better Factories Cambodia conducted capacity-building and training programs for government, unions, and management. Most important, it sent monitors to visit factories and speak with managers and workers in order to evaluate their compliance with a checklist of up to five hundred labor regulations. Their initial reports were sent to employers, who were given the opportunity to implement the recommendations themselves. The monitors would return to the factory six months later to assess the factory's progress in improving working conditions.

Although the program had some significant constraints, such as its limited ability to enforce recommendations and factory managers' potential to anticipate factory visits and prepare for audits, its results were largely positive. Working conditions substantially improved from the time of its inception. As a result of the progress made in improving labor standards, Cambodia was awarded a bonus quota of 9 percent each year between 2000 and 2002, 12 percent in 2003, and 18 percent in 2004. Although the quota system expired in 2005, it inspired labor programs that were maintained after its dissolution. Cambodia's strategy of positioning itself as a country with good labor standards had become part of its comparative advantage. In an interview with one of our researchers, U.S. Embassy Economic/ Commercial Officer Jennifer Spande said that "even if Cambodia faces some challenges in terms of higher costs and more limited skills, the garment industry is going to do pretty well. A huge part of that is its reputation for good labor standards."[51] Company leaders reported keeping their operations in Cambodia due to the country's commitment to a higher level of working conditions.[52]

6. Providing Consumers with Labor Standard Information Through Product Labeling

Although research has shown that the majority of consumers are concerned about manufacturing conditions, the lack of access to information on companies' working conditions prevents customers from making informed purchasing decisions. Labeling products with information on corporate labor standards is the most common mechanism for providing consumers with the ability to assert their preferences. A number of research projects have shown compelling evidence that consumers are willing to pay more for products that are manufactured with good labor conditions. A 1999 study by Marymount University's Center for Ethical Concerns found that 86 percent of respondents were "willing to pay $1 more for a $20 garment guaranteed to be made in a legitimate shop."[53] Since factory worker compensation is a small fraction of the cost of many consumer products, consumers' willingness to pay even modestly higher prices to ensure better factory conditions can translate into substantially increased wages and benefits for workers at the bottom of the corporate ladder. A similar result was found in a 2004 PIPA poll where respondents were asked to choose between purchasing a $25 garment guaranteed to have been made under sweatshop-free conditions and a $20 garment of unspecified sourcing; 61 percent of respondents said they would purchase the more expensive garment, while 33 percent would buy the less expensive one.[54] A 2003 study from Ghent University surveyed 808 Belgian citizens on the factors affecting their coffee purchasing decisions and found that Fair Trade labeling was the second most important determinant in their selection process, after flavor.[55]

It can, of course, be argued that people's *actual* behavior might differ from their responses on questionnaires. However, several experiments that tested whether consumers would pay more for products labeled as being "socially responsible" concluded that people were generally willing to pay more for such products. In 2005, Hiscox and Smyth conducted an experiment at ABC Carpet and Home, a Manhattan retailer of high-quality furniture that attracts an average of twenty-two thousand customers per week.[56] The store has established a reputation for being socially and environmentally responsible. Although all of the towels and candles used in the study were made under good working conditions, the researchers put labels on some products that read: "Made under fair labor conditions, in a safe and healthy working environment which is free of discrimination, and where management has committed to respecting the rights and dignity of workers." There was an increase in the demand for the labeled products, which were also assigned higher prices: a 10 percent price increase for the towels resulted in a 20.6 percent increase in purchases of labeled towels, while a 20 percent increase in price resulted in a 4.3 percent increase in sales of labeled towels. The demand for candles similarly increased with the labeling, even with the 10 percent higher sales price, though the demand for candles fell when prices increased by 20 percent. The total revenue increased for all goods with labeling and price increases.

A second experiment targeted less affluent consumers. Using eBay, Hiscox and Smyth sold almost identical sets of coffee beans and Polo shirts that had all been made under good working conditions. These items were auctioned with one set of beans labeled as "fair trade" and the other as "premium," and one set of shirts labeled as "ethically made" and the other unlabeled. Once again, the results indicated that shoppers were ready to pay a premium for products made under good conditions. According to Hiscox, "eBay shoppers were willing to pay a substantial premium for goods certified by label as produced under fair standards."[57]

While the research evidence shows that companies can gain by labeling their products as socially responsible, there remain some important challenges in this process. In the absence of a central authority, labeling can be confusing and of dubious validity. In 2009, most labeling initiatives were private and voluntary rather than uniformly administered by the public sector. Their impact has been constrained by the fact that only a small proportion of producers participate and relatively few customers are aware of them. A study by a team of sociologists at the University of Michigan provides an example of the challenges of labeling. The researchers labeled one batch of plain white athletic socks in a department store as having been made under "good working conditions."[58] Follow-up interviews with customers showed that 70 percent of consumers who had bought socks either didn't notice the label or didn't understand its significance.[59] Companies with good working conditions stand to gain from the creation of objective third-party monitoring and from labeling that becomes widely recognized through public awareness campaigns.

Benefiting From Better Global Standards

What is the best way for companies to guarantee the quality of their global production? What labor standards and practices should they adopt in their factories, and how should these standards be monitored and enforced?

There is significant evidence that consumers care about the labor standards of the companies producing the goods they purchase. The negative publicity associated with producing under bad labor conditions can have substantial economic repercussions, particularly for firms that have direct contact with customers who rely on their brand name. Furthermore, lower labor standards are associated with lower-quality work, and often lower safety standards as well. As recent examples have shown, this can lead to costly product recalls and negative publicity that can taint a company's public image. There are therefore significant economic motivations for companies to invest in the quality of their overseas working conditions.

As this and previous chapters have shown, providing better wages, scheduling flexibility, and health care and improving general working conditions can have significant benefits for companies in terms of increasing employee motivation, retention, productivity, and product quality. These benefits are as applicable to manufacturing or sourcing overseas as they are to producing at home. The main difference with global supply chains is that it becomes much more difficult to ensure good working conditions when companies are at arms' length from the workers manufacturing their goods. Outsourcing adds the complexity of ensuring good working conditions in factories that belong to suppliers over which companies do not have direct control.

When companies produce overseas in their own facilities, they can decide which standards they want to adhere to. Effective implementation requires making sure that local managers are fully on board with the company's labor practices and have the expertise to be able to implement them. Sourcing from external suppliers is considerably more complex. After determining labor standard objectives and having a clear sense of priorities, companies need to establish clear ground rules. Once the ground rules have been set, compliance requires a commitment on the part of the whole company. Improving working conditions must be a central component of the corporate culture throughout different departments and must inform design and purchasing decisions. Chances of success are shaped from the start by selection of suppliers—and whether the company considers labor conditions and commitment to improved standards in its choice. Monitoring and enforcement require thorough and objective audits as well as the will to respond to the information they reveal.

10

Developing a Blueprint for Changing Companies and Lives

I N LOOKING AT HOW companies, countries, and the lowest-level employees are faring in the current economy, it becomes clear that there is
a pressing need for corporate and government action. In countries around
the world, real GDP growth stagnated in 2008 and continued to decrease
even further in 2009. The United States' real GDP grew by 1.1 percent in
2008 and experienced negative growth during the first two quarters of
2009.[1] The majority of European countries likewise experienced negative
growth in the first half of 2009.[2] Even the economic growth of newly industrialized Asian economies slowed down.[3]

A Pressing Need for Action

The private sector has found itself in an increasingly vulnerable position.
The approach taken to increase firm and national worth failed in large
part due to the extent to which it relied on speculation as opposed to true
increases in value. In the United States, bankruptcy filings increased by
31 percent in 2008.[4] Bankruptcy filings for the first quarter of 2009 were
78 percent higher than those for the same period in 2008 and almost triple
those of 2007.[5] Moreover, the slowdown in economic growth and the
rise in unemployment significantly worsened the situation of those at the
bottom of the corporate ladder. The International Labour Organization's

2008–2009 *Global Wage Report* warned that the combination of slow or negative economic growth with volatile prices would result in a reduction of real wages for workers in many countries, particularly those in lower-income households.[6]

This will exacerbate the enormous disparities in wealth and income that were already at critical levels before the recession. Around the world, the wealthiest 2 percent of adults own more than 50 percent of all global wealth. In contrast, most men and women control almost no wealth, with the bottom 50 percent owning barely 1 percent of global wealth. Disparities in wealth and income are present within countries as well as between regions. Figures for the United States showed that the richest 1 percent of the population received 20 percent of the total income; meanwhile, the poorest 40 percent received only 10 percent. Wealth disparities were even more pronounced: the richest 1 percent of the population held 33.4 percent of wealth while the bottom 40 percent held only 0.3 percent.[7] In Australia, the top 5 percent of households controlled 32 percent of wealth, while the bottom 40 percent held only 4 percent. In Canada, the richest 10 percent of families held 53 percent of wealth, while the bottom 50 percent held only 6 percent.[8] The inequalities in income and assets are likely to be even more pronounced when the global economy recovers from the recession.

Moreover, even when the financial crisis has turned around, there will still be a crisis of confidence. Extensive coverage of financial and corporate mismanagement has increased public perception of companies as caring only about their short-term profits, without regard for their employees. On a survey measuring confidence in institutions, "big business" was ranked lower than nearly all institutions, including the military, the police, organized religion, the medical system, public schools, the Supreme Court, the presidency, the media, organized labor, and the criminal justice system. The percentage of respondents who said they had a "great deal" or "quite a lot" of confidence in "big business" has decreased over the past decade, from 30 percent in 1999 to 16 percent in 2009.[9] At the same time, the percentage of respondents who said "big business" will be the biggest threat to the country in the future increased from 22 percent in 2000 to 32 percent in 2009.[10] Unless companies change their practices, the loss of credibility is likely to have longer-term implications for the private sector than the financial crisis itself.

The companies highlighted in *Profit at the Bottom of the Ladder* have demonstrated ways of increasing the quality, quantity, and value of their products and services by investing in and improving the quality of life of those at the bottom of the corporate ladder. This has brought them rapid short-term gains, as demonstrated by the tripling of productivity within the span of a few months at American Apparel. Equally important, it has brought long-term gains, as demonstrated by ACC India's success in finding sites for limestone mining, in being welcomed by communities, in having an increasingly educated workforce, and in experiencing few labor disputes.

Transforming the ways in which their companies invested in and learned from their lowest-level employees demanded unique strengths on the part of corporate leadership. The CEOs were far more accessible than their peers. Jim Sinegal at Costco had an office without walls where he held most of his meetings, as well as a corporate office with walls where he held the relatively few meetings that required privacy. He visited nearly all the warehouses every year, providing and receiving direct feedback from warehouse managers and low-level employees, including cashiers and shelf stockers. Mike Jenkins IV at Jenkins Brick knocked down the walls of the old CEO's office so that his space would be open and people would come to him with their critiques and recommendations. Jenkins Brick CFO Tommy Andreades told us: "I can go in to [see] Mike right now and say, 'You're out of your dang mind!' And people in the organization can do that as well . . . I'd just tell him that to get him to really pay attention. We've had to do that in many cases, and we've talked every one of them out."[11] Similarly, CEO Trish Karter at Dancing Deer didn't have a private office, and she considered it an important part of her job to talk to bakers and packers to solicit their suggestions and constructive criticism.

Each of these companies took a series of steps.

A Blueprint for Change

The experiences of these and others companies we've studied around the world suggest a blueprint for effective change entailing ten important steps: five ways in which corporate leaders need to adapt their strategic approaches and five practical steps firms should undertake.

Five Changes Needed in Corporate Strategy

1. Leaders need to understand who performs the majority of the essential work at their firms. At professional services firms, this may be lawyers or paralegals; in surgical clinics, this could include

surgeons, nurses, technicians, paramedics, and individuals preparing the operating room; and in manufacturing, clearly those
working on the factory floor carry out most of the essential work.
Likewise, in call centers, the employees answering the phones are
central to the firm's productivity; for wholesalers or retailers, the
sales staff perform a central role.

2. Leaders need to realize that their firms' success depends on the
   quality of the work of those who carry out the majority of the labor.
   As obvious as this statement may seem, remarkably few firms currently structure their work environments to optimize the efforts of
   employees at the bottom of the corporate ladder—even when these
   employees are central to creating the firms' added value.

3. Leaders need to recognize that the quality and productivity
   of employees at the bottom of the ladder, like all parts of their
   workforce, depend on whether their employees are healthy,
   adequately rested, well prepared to carry out the tasks they are
   asked to perform, and motivated in their work.

4. Corporate leadership needs to realize that the line workers are
   often the ones who know best how to increase the efficiency
   of operations, either by increasing the quality or the pace of
   production.

5. As companies increasingly operate in distant locations across countries and continents, leaders need to recognize that the same factors
   will influence the quality of their production around the globe. The
   health, skills, training, motivation, input, and commitment of line
   workers influence the quality of production, whether the factories
   are in California and Quebec or in China and Bangladesh.

Once corporate leaders have transformed their companies' understanding of these key factors, there are clear steps they can take to profit
together with employees at the bottom of the ladder.

Five Practical Steps Necessary For Profiting Together

1. PROVIDE INCENTIVES AT THE BOTTOM OF THE LADDER

Employees will be more motivated if they feel involved in and know
how to measure the success of the organization. In mission-driven firms,

employees may intrinsically be motivated by the goals of the organization. But in many companies, financial rewards and prospects of career advancement motivate employees who would not otherwise be as dedicated to the organization's success. This is as true for the lowest-level as it is for those at the highest-level. The companies featured in this book devoted significant time and attention to finding the best ways to motivate their employees. Some companies opted to provide financial incentives for increased productivity. After implementing a teamwork system in which sewers were paid based on the number of garments produced by their team, productivity at American Apparel increased dramatically; output tripled from thirty thousand to ninety thousand pieces a day, with only a 12 percent increase in the number of workers. In the United States, average wages at Costco were approximately 42 percent higher than those at their closest competitor, Sam's Club, the wholesale branch of Wal-Mart. Though Costco had higher labor costs than its competitors, it also had higher productivity and lower turnover rates. Costco had higher annual sales per square foot ($795 versus $516) and higher annual profits per employee ($13,647 versus $11,039) than Sam's Club. While the high productivity wasn't solely due to employee incentives in either case, in both cases, financial rewards clearly fueled employee productivity.

In addition, some companies set up asset-building programs such as profit sharing and stock options, which increased employee retention as well as workers' sense of ownership and investment in the company's performance. For example, in addition to providing incentives for every aspect of production, Jenkins Brick set up a profit-sharing program in which employees became vested after six years. Managers pointed out that turnover decreased while productivity and product quality improved.

Career tracks also served as a powerful motivating tool for employees who took advantage of advancement opportunities that were not as readily available elsewhere. Xerox Europe emphasized career opportunities to decrease the high turnover rates that were characteristic of the call center industry. Managers pointed out that given the industry's estimated average turnover rate of 40 percent,[12] the Xerox Service Center's turnover rate of 30 percent for 2005 was seen as a valuable improvement. Moreover, a large portion of the workers who left Xerox did so to return to their countries of origin. Many employees specified that the training and advancement opportunities at Xerox were a major factor in their decision to remain with the company. Costco similarly went against the norm by providing career opportunities for employees at all levels. In fact, senior managers estimated that the company promoted from within its own workforce 98 percent of the time. Costco believed that its policy of growing and developing the skills and talent of its employees helped their recruitment, motivation, and retention of warehouse workers and improved the quality of management in the long term. Senior managers repeatedly emphasized that experience working in lower-level positions within the company provided an in-depth understanding of the company's day-to-day operations. Sixty-eight percent of Costco's warehouse managers had started out working with the company as hourly employees. Costco's commitment to providing career opportunities also led to a low turnover rate. After the first year of employment, turnover was less than 6 percent.[13]

2. SUPPORT THE HEALTH OF THE LOWEST-LEVEL EMPLOYEES

Companies need to care about the health of their employees. Investing in workers' health can lead to reductions in absenteeism and turnover rates, and to greater productivity. A comprehensive health promotion program at a large industrial company was found to lead to a 14 percent reduction in the use of disability days among blue-collar workers participating in the program over two years.[14] Studies looking at a range of company health improvement programs have found that program participation resulted in 3 to 16 percent reductions in absenteeism rates; furthermore, health improvement programs were a highly beneficial investment for these companies, showing a return on investment (ROI) of $2 to $6.40 for each dollar invested.[15]

There are elements of employee health care that only companies can provide. While governments may provide regulations and incentives, ultimately it is up to employers to ensure that they provide a safe and healthy environment by reducing harmful physical, chemical, biological, and social exposures. Among many other factors, companies determine whether toxic or safe chemicals are used, whether machines are set up ergonomically or in ways that are more likely to lead to musculoskeletal injuries, and whether contagious materials are separated to limit the spread of disease. The work environment can influence the probability of illness and injury as well as determine workers' ability to address their own health needs. Paid leave for working men and women to consult physicians and to recover from health problems is essential, and it ultimately needs to be implemented at the corporate level. Autoliv's leave and flexibility policies had a strong impact on its employee retention. After implementing these policies, turnover decreased from 15–20 percent to approximately 3 percent, thereby actually saving the company money. In addition, workers who remained at the company had very high levels of employment satisfaction, with 85 percent agreeing that "Overall, I am satisfied with Autoliv Australia as an employer."[16]

At American Apparel, in addition to providing affordable health insurance to all employees, workers' health was promoted through on-site exercise classes and massage therapy as well as more nutritious menu offerings at the company cafeteria. Managers pointed out that these programs resulted in employees being more energized and productive at work. In 2007, the company also set up an on-site clinic where employees could receive free health care without having to leave work for time-consuming external appointments.

When governments provide adequate health care, companies do not need to set up their own health clinics. The public provision of health care saved Isola money in Norway and cut costs for Great Little Box Company in Canada. It is clearly in companies' best interest to encourage governments to provide comprehensive preventive care as well as medical insurance. At the same time, when countries fail to provide adequate health care, companies often need to fill the gap in order to maintain a healthy workforce. Operating in South Africa, in a context marked by the HIV/AIDS epidemic and an overwhelmed public health care system, SA Metal chose to provide free access to HIV/AIDS treatment for its employees. The company spent approximately 88 rand annually (US$12 based on 2007 exchange rates) per employee to ensure coverage for all who needed antiretrovirals. This amount constituted only a small percentage of its total health care expenditures. Looked at per person receiving treatment, HIV/AIDS treatment never cost more than 25 rand a day (approximately US$3.50), whereas it cost 750 to 1,000 rand a day (approximately US$105–$140) when a truck driver and a truck were out of commission for health-related reasons.

3. TRAIN EMPLOYEES AT EVERY LEVEL OF THE COMPANY

Companies need to ensure that employees are prepared to perform their work effectively. As with health care, there are complementary roles for the public and private sectors when it comes to education and training. Some elements of training are so firm-specific that only companies can provide them, such as teaching workers how to operate a particular kind of machine, how to stock materials in the company warehouse, how to handle specific phone requests, and how departments should work together.

At the same time, the public sector is traditionally expected to take care of other areas, including the provision of quality basic-skills education as well as primary and secondary school. When companies are situated in countries that provide affordable advanced education, they benefit from having a workforce with a higher level of training. When corporate leaders support government investments in education, they benefit citizens and companies alike. Just as companies need to fill in when there are gaps in health care, so do they need to fill in when there are gaps in education.

Xerox and Novo Nordisk managers established training opportunities that were not available to low-level service and manufacturing workers in competing firms. While most of its competitors offered training only to managers, Novo Nordisk offered free and readily accessible language training to all its employees in China, including line workers. As a result, the least formally educated workers learned to communicate more effectively in English with their Danish managers, which was essential since the company put a strong emphasis on employee feedback. Xerox employees obtained skills they brought to new positions within the firm as they adavanced. In both cases, employee appreciation of training opportunities contributed to the firm's turnover rates. Novo Novodisk's turnover was well below average; from April 1, 2006, to April 1, 2007, turnover rates were 9.3 percent for office employees and 5 percent for operators, whereas average turnover for the pharmaceutical industry in China at the time was 24.1 percent, and 15.5 percent in Tianjin.[17]

Similarly, Dancing Deer, a smaller company with only one production facility in Boston, offered free ESL classes to its production workers. The company found that these classes improved communication between employees who had immigrated from a wide range of countries and who frequently spoke no common language upon their arrival. Their increased ability to communicate effectively with one another in turn increased the efficiency of their work.

4. ENGAGE LINE WORKERS AND ACT ON THEIR BEST RECOMMENDATIONS

Companies need to establish ways to learn from their lowest-level employees, who have the most expertise on the ways in which much of the work at the company is done and could be improved. Managers at Novo

Nordisk actively encouraged greater employee involvement because they felt that the workers manufacturing the products would have the best ideas about how to improve the efficiency of production. Workers would also be more motivated if they felt that their input was sought and appreciated. In Novo Nordisk's method of production, the c-LEAN process, employees provided feedback and suggested solutions for problems that arose. The results of c-LEAN were very encouraging, with an approximately 50 percent increase in efficiency rates since the program's implementation.

Isola restructured production into a teamwork system to provide workers with greater decision-making power. Instead of reporting to a foreman and underforeman, six or seven workers functioned as a group, with one team leader who reported directly to the plant manager. All employees could apply to become team leaders and take the team leader training course. Absenteeism was greatly reduced as a result of employees' greater sense of responsibility and mutual pressure by team members. Absenteeism rates declined from 6.2 percent of total work days missed in the summer of 2002 to 4.4 percent in 2005, and from 12.1 percent in the winter of 2002 to 7.4 percent in the winter of 2005.

Great Little Box had several different programs to encourage employee suggestions. The Idea Recognition Program was designed to encourage employees to come up with ways in which the company could save money. The firm offered financial rewards for ideas that were implemented. Although most of the ideas had resulted in fairly low savings, a few suggestions had been significant innovations, with payouts as high as C$2,500. Savings from employee suggestions could be substantial, with managers reporting cost savings of up to C$25,000. Great Little Box also offered small rewards, such as C$5 bonuses for spotting errors in work orders. These rewards encouraged employees to pay more attention to detail and to the quality of their work.

5. TAKE STRATEGIC STEPS THAT ENSURE COMPANIES AND COMMUNITIES PROFIT TOGETHER

With increasing globalization, companies may no longer be located in a single nation; however, they always have a profound impact on and are deeply affected by the communities in which they operate. As demonstrated by ACC India's long history, investing in the community's goodwill can be financially beneficial. Since limestone is the main ingredient in cement production and is costly to transport, firms benefit economically from building their factories in the rural communities where the limestone is located. ACC needed communities to be willing to sell their land for limestone extraction and cement production. These rural locations were poor and not yet developed, and the company built the physical infrastructure they needed, providing roads, water, and electricity. ACC went beyond providing these basic necessities and also invested in facilities for the communities, such as schools and clinics. As a result, the company was much more likely to be welcomed into new communities. By investing in health and education infrastructure, ACC had sought to entice workers to remain in their communities and work in their factories instead of migrating to the cities in search of economic opportunities. According to ACC managers, investments in community development and good working conditions had the added benefit of diminishing labor unrest during periods marked by high numbers of strikes at other companies. Furthermore, the firm's investments in health and education had long-term gains, since generations of workers were healthier and better educated.

Operating in a very different context, Costco didn't need to set up the physical infrastructure when it opened stores in the United States. Instead, the company was valued by the surrounding communities because it provided economic opportunities—jobs with decent wages, benefits, and advancement opportunities that were sorely needed but increasingly unavailable to workers with only a high school education. Starting wages at Costco were significantly higher than the minimum wage; in 2005, their cashiers started at twice and truck drivers at three times the minimum wage. Employees also had the opportunity to advance and receive salary increases in their first few years with the company. After working as a cashier for only four years, employees with a high school education could earn $43,000 a year, which was more than double the national mean annual wage for cashiers in the United States of only $18,380. As a result of its reputation for providing good jobs and investing in the community, Costco faced less community opposition than its competitors, such as Wal-Mart, when looking for new sites for its warehouses.

While ACC and Costco had very different approaches, they both saw the benefits of having good relationships with local communities. They both opted to provide what the local communities needed, whether this was roads and schools or good jobs. As a result, they benefited from not facing the kind of opposition to expansion that has often surrounded companies in extractive industries and big-box retail.

To successfully engage with communities, companies must have a clear understanding of each community's needs, of the economic feasibility of addressing these needs, and of how these needs relate to company objectives. Some improvements may be aligned with the company's priorities, while others may be less essential. Finally, it is important for companies to determine their capacity to address particular issues. Companies may be more able and willing to address areas in which they already have a significant capacity or that are essential for their operations. Costco had a long-standing commitment to providing good jobs, and ACC needed to build roads in order to manufacture cement in rural communities. It was therefore a straightforward decision to implement these solutions. Companies must also think long-term about their community investment. Some of ACC's investments, such as roads and electricity, were of immediate use to the company, while others, such as education, were beneficial in the long run by providing them with access to a more highly educated workforce.

Balancing the Roles of Companies and Governments

The companies presented in this book have taken an active role in establishing good working conditions that greatly benefited their employees as well as their businesses. At the same time, these top company executives called on governments to participate in ensuring benefits and social supports for workers. While it makes sense for companies to provide safe and healthy work environments, training opportunities, decent hours, and good wages, there are other areas where it is both more appropriate and cost-effective for governments to take a leading role.

Child care was one central issue where government involvement was clearly necessary. Companies were aware of the importance of affordable, quality child care for working parents, but they often felt they couldn't afford to provide benefits to all their employees in the absence of government support. Autoliv Australia's general manager, Bob Franklin, told us: "The one area we've never ever been able to address satisfactorily is child care. It's a big issue for our people. It's a huge issue, but it's also a very expensive issue."[18] Autoliv Australia's policy was to only offer benefits that it could provide to all employees, and since child care could not be provided in a cost-effective manner to all workers, it had been unable to implement this benefit. Instead, the company had settled on offering employees more leave and flexibility options that could be used to meet child care needs. In Franklin's words: "As time went on, what we started to realize is that a lot of women have a problem with child care, particularly production workers [and] manufacturing people. They don't earn the sort of money that will allow them to pay for child care. Child care is expensive. So we looked at that option and said, 'Can we do something there?' And in the end we said it's a little bit beyond our capability to do that, but let's provide some options."[19] Though the company's leave and flexibility options were helpful to working parents, they weren't the best solution. Franklin clearly stated that more should be done in this area, but he felt that the government needed to take a bigger role: "It's something that I've always been disappointed in; I thought there might have been something in last night's [Australian] budget presentation that might have gone some way towards addressing some of the school and child care issues that we've got. So there are still things to be done, still things that we haven't found a way to do. We certainly haven't finished, by any means."

Companies also understood the importance of health care for both employees and productivity, but they weren't always in a position to provide all the necessary benefits. Costco's Jim Sinegal talked about the need for government to take on a more direct role in ensuring health care provision:

> I think it's got to be a collaborative method and system . . . I'm going to start to get political here and I don't mean to, but you can't have 50 million people in the nation without health care and not have a serious problem on the horizon. And that 50 million today is going to be 75 million in a decade. Something has to be done about it. And I think it's going to take the efforts of everyone involved—the medical professionals have to get involved, the insurance companies have to get involved, the educators have to get involved, the government has to get involved, and employers play a big role.[20]

Although Costco offered health insurance to all its employees, it had increased employee contributions over the years in order to keep pace with the rising costs of insurance premiums. In fact, its efforts to keep health insurance affordable for its employees by not raising the dollar amount of employee contributions had gotten the firm in trouble with the market. As health care costs rose, the company had been paying for an increasing percentage of health insurance costs to an extent that was deemed by the market to be financially unviable. Finally, Costco had to reach a compromise, and it agreed to gradually increase employee contributions.

For smaller companies, providing health insurance benefits can be even more challenging. While larger companies can obtain lower rates through economies of scale, smaller companies do not have this option. Though Dancing Deer provided health insurance to its employees, managers spoke frankly about how challenging it was to obtain rates that kept the costs affordable, and they explained that some benefits, such as dental insurance, simply weren't affordable for a small firm.

Several of the companies in our case studies were willing to step in and provide services when governments failed to do so. ACC in India and SA Metal in South Africa saw the benefits of investing in community development and health care, and showed a significant commitment to providing services for their employees. However, they also believed that there were limitations to companies' capacity in these areas. Managers at ACC India explained that the company could not afford to provide health care services for the community at large, pointing out that this should be done by the government. In the words of Paramjit Pabby, head of human resources: "Our hospitals are definitely only [free] to employees and their families. They can't be made open to the world at large because we can't. Infrastructurally, we can't take that load." Pabby explained that initially ACC said, "We'll go beyond just our employees and our families and look at community. Although we understand it's government's responsibility to take care of medical needs [in the long run]."[21]

SA Metal's managing director, Clifford Barnett, spoke of the company's desire but inability to extend health care services to employees' families, and of the need for the government to take a more active role in this area: "Yes, that would be very nice [providing health care to employees' family members], but there is confusion in South Africa between social responsibility and business responsibility. [SA Metals does] a tremendous number of things that in any other country in the world would be considered as [a societal responsibility], things that should be provided by the government, not by businesses."[22]

ACC managers stressed the company's commitment to community development in rural India, but at the same time expressed concern that functions such as building roads, providing education, and ensuring access to safe drinking water needed contributions from government in the long run, not just private companies. Nand Kumar, head of corporate communications and CSR, said: "In some cases, people expect you to be an overall benefactor and provider; in other cases, they may think you step in and do the role of the government in providing all services, etc. Sometimes even the local administration thinks that way. If there is a road to be done, they sometimes forget that they are perhaps selected and appointed there to make the road themselves."[23]

In short, the companies featured in this book made clear: the private sector has an important role to play in ensuring decent working conditions and better economic outcomes for those at the bottom of the ladder, but it cannot replace government action. Ultimately, sustained long-term competitiveness will require government contributions.

Creating an Environment That Will Support Business Growth That Benefits All

Visionary corporate leaders transformed the companies described here, including publicly traded and privately owned firms. However, as we examined companies around the world looking for leaders in the field, it was impossible not to notice that privately owned firms were responsible for a far greater percentage of the innovations that markedly increased the value and efficiency of production by investing in low-level employees. Moreover, as CFO Richard Galanti at Costco commented, Wall Street had gotten in the habit of rewarding public firms that cut wages, jobs, and investments in employees and punishing those that made such investments. The financial crisis that began in 2008 has revealed numerous weaknesses in the systems by which Wall Street firms estimated the value of investments. As practices on Wall Street and in firms are being rethought, along with the role of the public sector in shaping private investments and rendering the investment process transparent, one of the areas needing a new approach is the evaluation of investments in employees.

Corporate leaders' support in making the long-term investments that are essential to firms' financial strength and to the strength of the overall economy is dramatically affected by the boards they report to, the role of large shareholders, and the response of financial firms estimating their value. Companies' ability to profit together with their employees is also markedly influenced by public sector investments. When countries invest in infrastructure and companies can rely on quality public health care, education, and training systems that are accessible and affordable to all their employees, firms don't need to bear the costs of building roads, clinics, and basic education facilities. While it makes economic sense for companies to invest in these areas when public provision is lacking, and while companies can play an important role in building communities as well as benefiting employees, it should come as no surprise that corporate leaders have ranked countries that have made these investments as the world's most competitive nations.[24]

The need to find ways for companies to profit together with their lowest-level employees has viscerally been brought home by the economic crisis that began in 2008, which has undermined both corporate earnings and confidence in companies' ability to benefit their employees. The practices of the firms featured in this book benefited these companies' bottom lines as well as their employees both in periods of economic growth and in downturns. Jenkins Brick was able to produce and sell more bricks during periods of growth due to its employees' response to the incentive structure. Costco was able to successfully keep pace with dramatic corporate expansion due to the career tracks it had put in place, which led to both strong performance on the warehouse floor and to strong warehouse management as it expanded from 206 warehouses and $16 billion in annual sales in 1993 to 550 warehouses and over $70 billion in sales by 2008. Dancing Deer was able to attract talented bakers, which was essential since the company justified its higher prices by marketing its goods at the top end of the quality spectrum. At the same time, the employee commitment and cross-training that stemmed from Autoliv Australia's flexibility policies enabled the company to adapt to the downturn in car manufacturing in high-income countries. Great Little Box Company's open-book management approach enhanced employees' productivity during the 2008–2009 recession, which hit companies providing packaging to other retailers particularly hard. Managers' openness also enabled them to elicit ideas from the factory floor about the best ways to increase efficiency, and it enabled them to continue to grow by purchasing other companies during the downturn.

These corporate leaders provide not only the foundations of a blueprint for other companies, to build on, but also the beginnings of a blueprint for whole economies to learn from. While there is still a great deal to be discovered about the most effective ways for companies, countries, and employees on every rung of the ladder to profit together, these leaders have laid out a vision and demonstrated the practicality of bringing economic success to companies by supporting—rather than eroding—the success of men and women at the bottom of the ladder.

Notes

Introduction

1. For more information on findings from global studies, see:

S. J. Heymann, *Forgotten Families: Ending the Growing Crisis Confronting Children and Working Parents in the Global Economy* (New York: Oxford University Press, 2006); S. J. Heymann, "Work and Family Health in a Global Context," in *Handbook of Families and Work: Interdisciplinary Perspectives*, eds. D. R. Crane and E. J. Hill (Lanham, MD: University Press of America, 2009); S. J. Heymann, "Meeting the Needs of Children in Working Poor Families Around the World," in *Children and Poverty: Challenges and Solutions* (Montreal: Decision Media Health Collection, 2007); S. J. Heymann, S. Simmons, and A. Earle, "Global Transformations," in *Work, Family, Health and Well-Being*, eds. S. Bianchi, L. Casper, and R. B. King (Mahwah, NJ: Lawrence Erlbaum Associates, 2005); S. J. Heymann, A. Earle, and A. Hanchate, "Bringing a Global Perspective to Community, Work and Family: An Examination of Extended Work Hours in Families in Four Countries," *Community, Work and Family* 7, no. 2 (2004): 247–272; S. J. Heymann, *How Are Workers with Family Responsibilities Faring in the Workplace?* (Geneva: International Labour Organization, 2004).

On Latin America, Africa and Asia, see:

S. J. Heymann, F. Flores-Macias, J. Hayes, M. Kennedy, A. Earle, and C. Lahaie, "The Impact of Migration on the Well-Being of Transnational Families: New Data from Sending Communities in Mexico," *Community, Work and Family* 12, no. 1 (2009): 91–103; M. Ruiz-Casares and S. J. Heymann, "Children Home Alone Unsupervised: Modeling Parental Decisions and Associated Factors in Botswana, Mexico, and Vietnam," *Child Abuse and Neglect* 33, no. 5 (2009): 312–323; D. Rajaraman, A. Earle, and S. J. Heymann, "Working HIV Caregivers in Botswana: Spill-Over Effects on Work and Family Well-Being," *Community, Work and Family* 11, no. 1 (2008): 1–17; S. J. Heymann, A. Earle, D. Rajaraman, C. Miller, and K. Bogen, "Extended Family Caring for Children Orphaned by AIDS: Impacts on Child Well-Being and Economic Survival," *AIDS Care Journal* 19, no. 3 (2007): 337–345.; P. H. Vo, K. Penrose, and S. J. Heymann, "Working to Exit Poverty While Caring for Children's Health and Development in Vietnam," *Community, Work and Family* 10, no. 2 (2007): 197–199; D. Rajaraman, S. Russell, and S. J. Heymann, "HIV/AIDS, Income Loss and Economic Survival in Botswana," *AIDS Care* 18, no. 7 (2006): 656–662; C. A.

Bergstrom and S. J. Heymann, "Impact of Gender Disparities in Family Carework on Women's Life Chances in Chiapas, Mexico," *Journal of Comparative Family Studies* 36, no. 2 (2005): 267–288.

    On North America and Europe, see:

    S. J. Heymann, "Inequalities at Work and at Home: Social Class and Gender Divides," in *Unfinished Work: Building Equality and Democracy in an Era of Working Families*, eds. S. J. Heymann and C. Beem (New York: New Press, 2004); A. Earle and S. J. Heymann, "Work, Family, and Social Class," in *How Healthy Are We? A National Study of Well-Being at Midlife*, eds. O. G. Brimm, C. Ryff, and R. Kessler (Chicago: University of Chicago Press, 2004); S. J. Heymann, A. Fischer, and M. Engelman, "Labor Conditions and the Health of Children, Elderly and Disabled Family Members," in *Global Inequalities at Work: Work's Impact on the Health of Individuals, Families, and Societies*, ed. S. J. Heymann (New York: Oxford University Press, 2003); S. J. Heymann, "Low-Income Parents and the Time Famine," in *Taking Parenting Public: The Case for a New Social Movement*, eds. S. Hewlett, N. Rankin, and C. West (Lanham, MD: Rowman & Littlefield, 2002); A. Earle and S. J. Heymann, "What Causes Job Loss Among Former Welfare Recipients? The Role of Family Health Problems," *Journal of the American Medical Women's Association* 57 (2002): 5–10; S. J. Heymann, P. H. Vo, and C. A. Bergstrom, "Child Care Providers' Experiences Caring for Sick Children: Implications for Public Policy," *Early Child Development and Care* 172, no. 1 (2002): 1–8 ; S. J. Heymann and A. Earle, "The Impact of Parental Working Conditions on School-Age Children: The Case of Evening Work," *Community, Work and Family* 4, no. 3 (2001): 305–325; S. J. Heymann and A. Earle, "Low-Income Parents: How Do Working Conditions Affect Their Opportunity to Help School-Age Children at Risk?" *American Educational Research Journal* 37, no. 2 (2000): 833–848; S. J. Heymann, "What Happens During and After School: Conditions Faced by Working Parents Living in Poverty and Their School-Age Children," *Journal of Children and Poverty* 6, no. 1 (2000): 5–20; S. J. Heymann and A. Earle, "The Impact of Welfare Reform on Parents' Ability to Care for Their Children's Health," *American Journal of Public Health* 89, no. 4 (1999): 502–505; S. J. Heymann and A. Earle, "The Work-Family Balance: What Hurdles Are Parents Leaving Welfare Likely to Confront?" *Journal of Policy Analysis and Management* 17, no. 2 (1998): 312–321; S. J. Heymann, A. Earle, and B. Egleston, "Parental Availability for the Care of Sick Children," *Pediatrics* 98, no. 2, part 1 (1996): 226–230.

    2. For more information on studies on comparative policies, see:

    S. J. Heymann and A. Earle, *Raising the Global Floor: Dismantling the Myth That We Can't Afford Good Working Conditions for Everyone* (Palo Alto, CA: Stanford University Press, 2010); M. Chaussard, M. Gerecke, and S. J. Heymann, "L'Indice Travail et Équité Canada: Comment se Porte le Québec par Rapport au Reste du Monde?" *Quebec Travail* 6, no.1 (2009): 30–35; M. Chaussard, M. Gerecke, and S. J. Heymann, *The Work Equity Canada Index: Where the Provinces and Territories Stand* (Montreal: McGill University, Institute for Health and Social Policy, 2008); A. Earle and S. J. Heymann, "A Comparative Analysis of Paid Leave for the Health Needs of Workers and Their Families Around the World," *Journal of Comparative Policy Analysis* 8, no. 3 (2006): 241–257; S. J. Heymann, K. Penrose, and A. Earle, "Meeting Children's Needs: How Does the U.S. Measure Up?" *Merrill-Palmer Quarterly* 52, no. 2 (2006): 189–216; S. J. Heymann, A. Earle, S. Simmons, S. M. Breslow, and A. Kuehnhoff, *Work, Family, and Equity Index: Where Does the United States Stand Globally?* (Boston: Harvard School of Public Health, Project on Global Working Families, June 2004).

    On sick leave policies, see:

    S. J. Heymann, H. J. Rho, J. Schmitt, and A. Earle, "Ensuring a Healthy and Productive Workforce: Comparing the Generosity of Paid Sick Day and Leave Policies in 22 Countries," *International Journal of Health Services* 40, no.1 (2010): 1–22; S. J. Heymann, H. J. Rho, J. Schmitt, and A. Earle, *Contagion Nation: A Comparison of Paid Sick Day Policies in 22 Countries* (Washington, DC: Center for Economic and Policy Research, 2009); J. Schmitt, H. J. Rho, A. Earle, and S. J. Heymann, *Paid Sick Days Don't Cause Unemployment*, issue brief

(Washington, DC: Center for Economic and Policy Research, 2009); H. J. Rho, J. Schmitt, A. Earle, and S. J. Heymann, *A Review of Sickness-Related Leave in High Human Development Index Countries* (Washington, DC: Center for Economic and Policy Research, 2009); S. J. Heymann, "The Healthy Families Act: The Importance to Americans' Livelihoods, Families, and Health," written testimony submitted to the U.S. Senate Committee on Health, Education, Labor, and Pensions, 2007; S. J. Heymann, S. Toomey, and F. Furstenberg, "Working Parents: What Factors Are Involved in Their Ability to Take Time Off from Work When Their Children Are Sick?" *Archives of Pediatrics & Adolescent Medicine* 153, no. 8 (1999): 870–874.

On family leave policies, see:

S. J. Heymann and M. Kramer, "Public Policy and Breastfeeding: A Straightforward and Significant Solution," *Canadian Journal of Public Health* 100, no.5 (2009): 381–383; S. J. Heymann, "Roundtable on the Family and Medical Leave Act: A Dozen Years of Experience," written testimony for the U.S. Senate Committee on Health, Education, Labor, and Pensions, 2005.

On education policies, see:

S. J. Heymann, "The Role of Early Childhood Care and Education in Ensuring Equal Opportunity," *UNESCO Policy Brief on Early Childhood*, November–December 2003; S. J. Heymann, "The Impact of AIDS on Early Childhood Care and Education," *UNESCO Policy Brief on Early Childhood*, June 2003; S. J. Heymann, "School Children in Families with Young Children: Educational Opportunities at Risk," *UNESCO Policy Brief on Early Childhood*, February 2003; S. J. Heymann, "Social Transformations and Their Implications for the Global Demand for ECCE," *UNESCO Policy Brief on Early Childhood*, November–December 2002.

On policies addressing poverty, see:

S. J. Heymann and M. Barrera, "Addressing Poverty in a Globalised Economy," in *A Progressive Agenda for Global Action*, collection of papers submitted to the Progressive Governance Conference and Summit in London, April 2008 (London: *Policy Network*, 2009); S. J. Heymann, M. Barrera, and A. Earle, "The Working Poor: Canada and the World," *Policy Options* (September 2008); S. J. Heymann, "Poverty, Work and Education: The Key to Addressing the Social Determinants of Canadians' Health," written testimony submitted to the Subcommittee on Population Health of the Canadian Senate Committee on Social Affairs, Science and Technology, 2007.

On HIV/AIDS and disability policies, see:

C. G. Mandic and S. J. Heymann, "Supported Employment in a Lower Income Context: The Case of Banco de Crédito del Perú and Centro Ann Sullivan del Perú," *International Journal of Disability, Community & Rehabilitation* 8, no. 1 (2009) http://www.ijdcr.ca/VOL08_01/articles/mandic.shtml; E. Petrow, S. Simmons, and S. J. Heymann, "AIDS and Work: The Need for Both Public and Private Sector Responses," *McGill International Journal of Sustainable Development Law and Policy* 3, no. 1 (2007): 103–118; R. Kidman, E. Petrow, and S. J. Heymann, "Africa's Orphan Crisis: Two Community-Based Models of Care," *AIDS Care Journal* 19, no. 3 (2007): 326–329.

Chapter 1

1. Organization for Economic Cooperation and Development, Directorate for Employment, Labour and Social Affairs, *OECD Employment Outlook 2004*, vol. 2004, no. 8.

2. Organization for Economic Cooperation and Development, Directorate for Employment, Labour and Social Affairs, *OECD Employment Outlook 2007*, "How Does the United States Compare?" 2007. http://www.oecd.org/dataoecd/27/4/38796234.pdf.

3. Senior managers are referred to by their real names since they are identifiable through their positions at each company. Middle managers and low-level employees were assured confidentiality and are therefore referred to by pseudonyms.

4. Interview conducted with Marty Bailey, vice president for operations and president of manufacturing, American Apparel, April 2007.

5. Interview, Marty Bailey, April 2005.

6. Interview conducted with factory worker, American Apparel, April 2007.

7. Interview conducted with factory worker, American Apparel, April 2007.

8. Interview, Marty Bailey, April 2005.

9. J. K. Liker and J. M. Morgan, "The Toyota Way in Services: The Case of Lean Product Development," *Academy of Management Perspectives* 20, no. 2 (May 2006): 5–20.

10. M. Yavuz and E. Akçali, "Production Smoothing in Just-in-Time Manufacturing Systems: A Review of the Models and Solution Approaches," *International Journal of Production Research* 45, no. 16 (August 2007): 3579–3597.

11. Interview, Marty Bailey, April 2007.

12. Interview, Marty Bailey, April 2005.

13. Interview, Marty Bailey, April 2007.

14. Interview conducted with factory worker, American Apparel, April 2007.

15. Interview, Marty Bailey, April 2007.

16. The Grameen Bank began by providing financial services to the rural poor in Bangladesh, then spread worldwide. Central to its method is the mutual responsibility that groups of poor individuals take for ensuring that each other's loans are repaid.

17. Interview conducted with factory worker, American Apparel, April 2007.

18. Interview, Marty Bailey, April 2005.

19. Interview conducted with Matthew Swansen, marketing, American Apparel, April 2007.

20. American Apparel, Inc. "American Apparel Reports Fourth Quarter and Full Year 2007 Financial Results," March 17, 2008, http://investors.americanapparel.net/releasedetail.cfm?ReleaseID=300055.

21. While most press has been focused on American Apparel's bringing high compensation manufacturing jobs to the United States, in 2009, the company was criticized by the government for hiring improperly documented workers. While questions were raised about the immigration status of some of the employees, American Apparel was not found to have purposefully hired illegal immigrants. Moreover, it was clear they never paid employees who were immigrants less—as other companies in the industry did. Rather they paid salaries far above the minimum wage. See "Broken in U.S.A," editorial, *New York Times*, October 1, 2009; N. Casey, "American Apparel Bares All—Dov Charney's Newly Public Company Makes a Wild Debut," *Wall Street Journal*, April 12, 2008.

22. Interview conducted with Gary Smith, director of personnel and safety, Jenkins Brick, March 2005.

23. Interview conducted with Tommy Andreades, CFO, Jenkins Brick, May 2006.

24. Written communication, Gary Smith, June 2007.

25. Interview, Tommy Andreades, March 2005.

26. Interview conducted with Mike Jenkins, CEO, Jenkins Brick, March 2005.

27. U.S. Department of Labor, Bureau of Labor Statistics, *Occupational Outlook Handbook*, 2008–09 Edition, Occupational Employment and Wages, May 2007, 41-2011 Cashiers, http://www.bls.gov/oes/current/oes412011.htm; 51-3022 Meat, Poultry, and Fish Cutters and Trimmers, http://www.bls.gov/oes/current/oes513022.htm; 53-3033 Truck Drivers, Light or Delivery Services, http://www.bls.gov/oes/current/oes533033.htm.

28. U.S. Department of Labor, Bureau of Labor Statistics, *Occupational Outlook Handbook*, 2008–09 Edition, 41-2011 Cashiers.

29. S. Greenhouse, "How Costco Became the Anti–Wal-Mart," *New York Times*, July 17, 2005.

30. Interview conducted with Vito Romano, director of employee development, Costco, March 2006.

31. Interview conducted with Jim Sinegal, CEO, Costco, March 2006.

32. Interview conducted with Richard Galanti, CFO, Costco, July 2007.

33. Interview, Vito Romano, March 2006.

34. Costco, Annual Report, 2007, 5, http://media.corporate-ir.net/media_files/irol/83/83830/Annual_Report_2007.pdf.

35. Interview, Vito Romano, March 2006.

36. D. DesJardins, "Betting on Benefits: Generosity Strategy Pays Off," *DSN Retailing Today*, December 19, 2005.

37. A. Zimmerman, "Costco's Dilemma: Be Kind to Its Workers, or Wall Street?" *Wall Street Journal*, March 26, 2004.

38. Interview conducted with deli manager at Costco, March 2006.

39. Interview, Richard Galanti, July 2007.

40. Interview, Vito Romano, March 2006.

41. Greenhouse, "How Costco Became the Anti-Wal-Mart."

42. Interview, Richard Galanti, March 2006.

43. S. Holmes and W. Zellner, "The Costco Way," *BusinessWeek*, April 12, 2004.

44. Interview, Jim Sinegal, March 2006.

45. Interview conducted with Jay Tihinen, associate vice president, human resources and disability, Costco, March 2006.

46. Interview, Jim Sinegal, July 2007.

47. Interview, Jim Sinegal, March 2006.

48. Interview, Richard Galanti, March 2006.

49. "The Costco Way."

50. Interview, Richard Galanti, March 2006.

51. Interview, Jim Sinegal, March 2006.

52. Interview, Richard Galanti, March 2006.

53. Interview, Jay Tihinen, March 2006.

Chapter 2

1. Congressional Research Service Report for Congress, *Leave Benefits in the United States*, updated May 7, 2008, Table 1: Percent of Workers with Paid Leave Benefits by Employee and Employer Characteristics.

2. U.S. Department of Labor, Bureau of Labor Statistics, *Employee Benefits Survey*, Databases and Tables: Percent of Blue-Collar Workers with Access to Paid Sick Leave and Percent of White-Collar Workers with Access to Paid Sick Leave; 2008, U. S. Census Bureau, *Statistical Abstract of the United States*, 2008, Section 12, Table 634: Percent of Workers in Private Industry with Access to Selected Employee Benefits 2006, http://www.census.gov/prod/2007pubs/08statab/labor.pdf; T. M. McMenamin, "A Time to Work: Recent Trends in Shift Work and Flexible Schedules," *Monthly Labor Review* 130, no. 12 (December 2007): 3–15.

3. Statistics Canada, *The Canadian Labor Market at a Glance 2005*, http://www.statcan.ca/english/freepub/71-222-XIE/71-222-XIE2006001.pdf.

4. Autoliv Annual Report 2004; Autoliv Annual Report 2007; Workplace Excellence Awards: Autoliv Australia. Industrial Relations Victoria. May 2004.

5. Australian Bureau of Statistics, *Average Weekly Earnings*, Australia, February 2008.

6. Senior managers are referred to by their real names since they are identifiable through their positions at each company. Middle managers and low-level employees were ensured confidentiality and are therefore referred to by pseudonyms.

7. Interview conducted with Bob Franklin, general manager, Autoliv Australia, May 2005.

8. Ibid.

9. The fact that Autoliv Australia was run very independently from the corporate headquarters gave Franklin the latitude he needed to implement policies he believed in such as leave and flexibility. His eventually leaving Australia to take charge of Autoliv operations in the ASEAN countries raised the possibility of implementing a similar approach in other parts of the world, but also raised questions as to whether policies at Autoliv Australia would continue under the new leadership.

10. Ibid.

11. Ibid.

12. Interview conducted with team leader, Autoliv Australia, May 2005.

13. Interview conducted with line worker, Autoliv Australia, May 2005.

14. Interview conducted with maintenance worker, Autoliv Australia, May 2005.

15. Interview, Cheryl Woollard, May 2005.

16. Interview conducted with line worker, Autoliv Australia, November 2006.

17. Ibid.

18. Interview conducted with Seamus Power, general manager for manufacturing, Autoliv Australia, May 2005.

19. Interview conducted with middle manager, Autoliv Australia, May 2005.

20. Interview conducted with Leny Plonsker, employee relations manager, Autoliv Australia, May 2005.

21. Interview, Bob Franklin, May 2005.

22. Employee Surveys. Autoliv Australia. 2004

23. Interview, Bob Franklin, November 2006.

24. Ibid.

25. Interview conducted with team leader, Autoliv Australia, May 2005.

26. Interview, Bob Franklin, May 2005.

27. Interview, Bob Franklin, November 2006.

28. Interview, Bob Franklin, May 2005.

29. Interview, Bob Franklin, November 2006.

30. Interview, Bob Franklin, May 2005.

31. Interview, Cheryl Woollard, May 2005.

32. See Chapter 12 of the Working Environment Act, Act no.62, June 17, 2005; last amended February 23, 2007.

33. Interviews conducted with Terje Uteng, plant manager, Isola, May–June 2006.

34. Interviews conducted with team leader, Isola, May–June 2006.

35. Interviews conducted with truck driver, Isola, May–June 2006.

36. Interviews conducted with mechanic, Isola, May–June 2006.

37. Interviews conducted with Erik Withbro, managing director, Isola, May–June, 2006.

38. Interviews, Erik Withbro, August 2007.

39. D. B. Gilleskie, "A Dynamic Stochastic Model of Medical Care Use and Work Absence," *Econometrica* 66, no. 1(1998): 1–45; A. Grinyer and V. Singleton, "Sickness Absence as Risk-Taking Behaviour: A Study of Organisational and Cultural Factors in the Public Sector," *Health Risk & Society* 2, no. 1 (2000): 7–21; G. Johansson, "Work-Life Balance: The Case of Sweden in the 1990s," *Social Science Information* 41, no. 2 (2002): 303–317; G. Aronsson, K. Gustafsson, and M. Dallner, "Sick but Yet at Work: An Empirical Study of Sickness Presenteeism," *Journal of Epidemiology and Community Health* 54, no. 7 (2000): 502–509; Y. C. Ng, P. Jacobs, and J. A. Johnson, "Productivity Losses Associated with Diabetes in the U.S.," *Diabetes Care* 24, no. 2 (2001): 257–261; J. Crystal-Peters, W. H. Crown, R. Z. Goetzel, and D. C. Schutt, "The Cost of Productivity Losses Associated with Allergic Rhinitis," *American Journal of Managed Care* 6, no. 3 (2000): 373–378; T. D. Szucs, "Influenza: The Role of Burden-of-Illness Research," *Pharmacoeconomics* 16, Suppl. 1 (1999): 27–32; X. H. Hu, L. E. Markson, R. B. Lipton, W. F. Stewart, and M. L. Berger, "Burden of Migraine in the United States: Disability and Economic Costs," *Archives of Internal Medicine* 159, no. 8

(1999): 813–818; J. L. Severens, R. J. Laheij, J. B. Jansen, E. H. Van der Lisdonk, and A. L. Verbeek, "Estimating the Cost of Lost Productivity in Dyspepsia," *Alimentary Pharmacology Therapeutics* 12, no. 9 (1998): 919–923; J. P. Leigh, W. Seavey, and B. Leistikow, "Estimating the Costs of Job Related Arthritis," *Journal of Rheumatology* 28, no. 7 (2001): 1647–1654.

40. The Global Competitiveness Report rankings are based on a combination of publicly available data and an annual survey of business leaders around the world. The report is compiled and published by the World Economic Forum. For the 2007 rankings, over 11,000 business leaders in 131 countries participated. The 2007 report defines competitiveness as "the set of institutions, policies, and factors that determine the level of productivity of a country" (http://www.weforum.org/en/initiatives/gcp/Global%20Competitiveness%20Report/index.htm).

41. Organization for Economic Cooperation and Development, *Country Statistical Profiles 2006: Norway*, Standardised Unemployment Rates: Total, http://stats.oecd.org/WBOS/ViewHTML.aspx?QueryName=194&QueryType=View&Lang=en; and Statistics Norway. Focus on Labor, http://www.ssb.no/arbeid_en/.

42. United Nations Development Programme, *Human Development Report 2007*, http://hdr.undp.org/en/media/hdr_20072008_en_complete.pdf.

43. Ibid.

44. S. J. Heymann, *The Widening Gap: Why Working Families Are in Jeopardy and What Can Be Done About It* (New York: Basic Books, 2000); S. J. Heymann, *Forgotten Families: Ending the Growing Crisis Confronting Children and Working Parents in the Global Economy* (New York: Oxford University Press, 2006).

45. R. Riley, H. Metcalf, and J. Forth, *The Business Case For Equal Opportunities: An Econometric Investigation*, Department for Work and Pensions Research Report No. 483 (London: HMSO, 2008), http://www.dwp.gov.uk/asd/asd5/rports2007-2008/rrep483.pdf; E. L. Kelly, E. E. Kossek, L. B. Hammer, M. Durham, J. Bray, K. Chermack, L. A. Murphy and D. Kaskubar, "Getting There from Here: Research on the Effects of Work-Family Initiatives on Work-Family Conflict and Business Outcomes," *Academy of Management Annals* 2, no.1 (2008): 305–349.

46. A. Hegeswich, "Flexible Working Policies: A Comparative Review," Institute for Women's Policy Research, Research Report 16, 2009.

47. Department of Business, Enterprise and Regulatory Reform (BERR), "Consultation on Implementation of the Recommendations of Imelda Walsh's Independent Review: Amending and Extending the Right to Request Flexible Working to Parents of Older Children," URN 08/1188 (London: BERR, 2008).

48. S. J. Heymann, "The Healthy Families Act: The Importance to Americans' Livelihoods, Families and Health," testimony before the U.S. Senate Committee on Health, Education, Labor and Pensions, February 13, 2007; A. Earle and S. J. Heymann, "A Comparative Analysis of Paid Leave for the Health Needs of Workers and Their Families Around the World," *Journal of Comparative Policy Analysis* 8, no. 3 (2006): 241–257.

49. J. Waldfogel, Y. Higuchi, and M. Abe, "Family Leave Policies and Women's Retention After Childbirth: Evidence from the United States, Britain, and Japan," *Journal of Population Economics* 12, no.4 (1999): 523–545; S. Macran, P. Dex, and H. Joshi, "Employment After Childbearing: A Survival Analysis," *Work, Employment, and Society* 10, no.2 (1996): 273–296.

50. E. Galinsky and J. T. Bond, *The 1998 Business Work-Life Study: A Sourcebook* (New York: The Families and Work Institute, 1998).

51. National Partnership for Women & Families, "Get Well Soon: Americans Can't Afford to Be Sick," 2004, http://www.nationalpartnership.org /site/DocServer/GetWellSoonReport.pdf?docID=342.

52. D. B. Gilleski, "A Dynamic Stochastic Model of Medical Care Use and Work Absence," *Econometrica* 66 (1998): 1–45; G. Aronsson, K. Gustafsson, and M. Dallner, "Sick but Yet at Work: An Empirical Study of Sickness Presenteeism," *Journal of Epidemiology and*

Community Health 54 (2000): 502–509; A. Grinyer and V. Singleton, "Sickness Absence as Risk-Taking Behaviour: A Study of Organizational and Cultural Factors in the Public Sector," *Health, Risk, & Society* 2 (2000): 7–21; G. Johannsson, "Work-Life Balance: The Case of Sweden in the 1990s," *Social Science Information* 41 (2002): 303–317.

53. R. N. Kumar, S. L. Hass, J. Z. Li, D. J. Nickens, C. L. Daenzer, and L. K. Wathen, "Validation of the Health-Related Productivity Questionnaire Diary (HRPQ-D) on a Sample of Patients with Infectious Mononucleosis: Results from a Phase 1 Multicenter Clinical Trial," *Journal of Occupational and Environmental Medicine* 45, vol. 8 (2003): 899–907; Y. C. Ng, P. Jacobs, and J. A. Johnson, "Productivity Losses Associated with Diabetes in the U.S.," *Diabetes Care* 24, no. 2 (2001):257–261, cited in Kumar et al., "Validation of the Health-Related Productivity Questionnaire Diary (HRPQ-D) on a Sample of Patients with Infectious Mononucleosis"; J. Crystal-Peters, W. H. Crown, R. Z. Goetzel, and D. C. Schutt, "The Cost of Productivity Losses Associated with Allergic Rhinitis," *American Journal of Managed Care* 6, no. 3 (2000): 373–378, cited in Kumar et al., "Validation of the Health-Related Productivity Questionnaire Diary (HRPQ-D) on a Sample of Patients with Infectious Mononucleosis"; T. D. Szucs, "Influenza: 1999. The Role of Burden-of-Illness Research," *PharmacoEconomics* 16 (Supplement 1): 27–32, cited in Kumar et al., "Validation of the Health-Related Productivity Questionnaire Diary (HRPQ-D) on a Sample of Patients with Infectious Mononucleosis; X. H. Hu, L. E. Markson, R. B. Lipton, W. F. Stewart, and M. L. Berger, "Burden of Migraine in the United States: Disability and Economic Costs," *Archives of Internal Medicine* 159, no. 8 (1999): 813-818, Kumar et al., "Validation of the Health-Related Productivity Questionnaire Diary (HRPQ-D) on a Sample of Patients with Infectious Mononucleosis; J. L. Severens, R. J. Laheij, J. B. Jansen, E. H. Van der Lisdonk, and A. L. Verbeek, "Estimating the Cost of Lost Productivity in Dyspepsia," Alimentary Pharmacology & Therapeutics 12, no. 9 (1998): 919–923, cited in Kumar et al., "Validation of the Health-Related Productivity Questionnaire Diary (HRPQ-D) on a Sample of Patients with Infectious Mononucleosis"; J. P. Leigh, W. Seavey, and B. Leistikow, "Estimating the Costs of Job Related Arthritis," *Journal of Rheumatology* 28, no. 7 (2001): 1647–1654, cited in Kumar et al., "Validation of the Health-Related Productivity Questionnaire Diary (HRPQ-D) on a Sample of Patients with Infectious Mononucleosis"; W. F. Stewart, J. A. Ricci, E. Chee, S. R. Hahn, and D. Morganstein, "Cost of Lost Productive Work Time Among U.S.Workers with Depression," *Journal of the American Medical Association* 289, no.23 (2003): 3135–3144.

54. R. Z. Goetzel et al., "Health, Absence, Disability, and Presenteeism Cost Estimates of Certain Physical and Mental Health Conditions Affecting U.S. Employers," *Journal of Occupational and Environmental Medicine* 46, no.4 (2004): 398–412.

55. H. R. Thomas and K. A. Raynar, "Scheduled Overtime and Labor Productivity: Quantitative Analysis," *Journal of Construction Engineering and Management* 123, no. 2 (1997): 181–188; A. S. Hanna and D. G. Heale, "Factors Affecting Construction Productivity: Newfoundland Versus Rest of Canada," *Canadian Journal of Civil Engineering* 21 (1994): 663–673; R. Sonmez, "Impact of Occasional Overtime on Construction Labor Productivity: Quantitative Analysis," *Canadian Journal of Civil Engineering* 34 (2007): 803–808; T. Shimizu, S. Horie, S. Nagata, and E. Marui, "Relationship Between Self-Reported Low Productivity and Overtime Working," *Occupational Medicine* 54 (2004): 52–54; E. Shepard and T. Clifton, "Are Longer Hours Reducing Productivity In Manufacturing?" *International Journal of Manpower* 21 (2000): 540–552.

Chapter 3

1. C. Chu and S. Dwyer, "Employer Role in Integrative Workplace Health Management: A New Model in Progress," *Disease Management and Health Outcomes* 10, no. 3 (2002).

2. S. J. Heymann, ed., *Global Inequalities at Work: Work's Impact on the Health of Individuals, Families, and Societies* (New York: Oxford University Press, 2003); S. J. Heymann, *Forgotten Families: Ending the Growing Crisis Confronting Children and Working Parents in the Global Economy* (New York: Oxford University Press, 2006); S. J. Heymann, C. Hertzman, M. Barer, and R. Evans, eds., *Healthier Societies: From Analysis to Action* (New York: Oxford University Press, 2006); S. J. Heymann, *The Widening Gap: Why Working Families Are in Jeopardy and What Can Be Done About It* (New York: Basic Books, 2000).

3. Senior managers are referred to by their real names since they are identifiable through their positions at each company. Middle managers and low-level employees were ensured confidentiality and are therefore referred to by pseudonyms.

4. Interview conducted with Clifford Barnett, general manager, SA Metal, September 2005.

5. Ibid.

6. Interview conducted with Dr. Harold Amaler, head of the clinic, SA Metal, September 2005.

7. Interview conducted with Renata Opperman, head of human resources, SA Metal, September 2005.

8. Interview conducted with boiler maker, SA Metal, September 2005.

9. Interview conducted with driver, SA Metal, September 2005.

10. Department of Health, Republic of South Africa, *National HIV and Syphilis Antenatal Sero-Prevalence Survey in South Africa 2005* (Pretoria, South Africa: Department of Health, 2006).

11. Interview, Dr. Harold Amaler, September 2005.

12. Interview, Clifford Barnett, June 2006.

13. SA Metal, "SA Metal: Investing in Life," SA Metal Group HIV/AIDS Programme Policy Document, 2006.

14. Interview, Clifford Barnett, September 2005.

15. Interview conducted with factory worker, SA Metal, September 2005.

16. Interview, Clifford Barnett, September 2005.

17. Interview, Renata Opperman, September 2005.

18. Internal restructuring of health care entailed the company directly employing the nursing staff and developing its own operating systems instead of contracting an external service provider.

19. Interview, Clifford Barnett, September 2005.

20. Ibid.

21. U.S. Department of Labor, Bureau of Labor Statistics, *Employee Benefits in the United States*, March 2008, http://www.bls.gov/news.release/pdf/ebs2.pdf.

22. C. DeNavas-Walt, B. Proctor, and J. Smith, *Income, Poverty, and Health Insurance Coverage in the United States: 2008* (Washington, DC: U.S. Census Bureau, September 2009), http://www.census.gov/prod/2009pubs/p60-236.pdf.

23. National Coalition on Health Care, *Facts on Health Insurance Coverage*, 2008, http://www.nchc.org/facts/coverage.shtml.

24. Interview conducted with Kristina Moreno, director of human resources, American Apparel, April 2005.

25. Interview conducted with Lupe Caro, safety coordinator, American Apparel, April 2005.

26. Interview conducted with Kristina Ledesma-Davies, director of human resources, American Apparel, April 2007.

27. International Labour Organisation, *Introductory Report: Decent Work—Safe Work* (Geneva: ILO, 2005).

28. World Health Organization, "Global Strategy on Occupational Health for All: The Way to Health at Work," Recommendations of the Second Meeting of the WHO

Collaborating Centres in Occupational Health, Beijing, China, 11–14 October 1994 (Geneva: WHO, 1995).

29. J. Vahtera, P. Virtanen, M. Kivimäki, and J. Penti, "Workplace as an Origin of Health Inequalities, *Journal of Epidemiology and Community Health* 53 (1999): 399–407; C. T. Schrijvers, H. D. van de Mheen, K. Stronks, and J. P. Mackenbach, "Socioeconomic Inequalities in Health in the Working Population: The Contribution of Working Conditions," *International Journal of Epidemiology* 27 (1998): 1011–1018; G. W. Evans and E. Kantrowitz, "Socioeconomic Status and Health: The Potential Role of Environmental Risk Exposure," *Annual Review of Public Health* 23 (2002): 303–331.

30. Employment Conditions Knowledge Network (EMCONET), Final Report, September 20, 2007.

31. S. Holmes, "Work-Related Stress: A Brief Review," *Journal of the Royal Society for the Promotion of Health* 121, no. 4 (December 2001): 230–235; K. E. Kelloway and A. L. Day, "Building Healthy Workplaces: What We Know So Far," *Canadian Journal of Behavioural Science* 37, no. 4 (2005): 223–235.

32. M. L. Nielsen, R. Rugulies, L. Smith-Hansen, K. B. Christensen, and T. S. Kristensen, "Psychosocial Work Environment and Registered Absence from Work: Estimating Etiologic Fraction," *American Journal of Industrial Medicine* 49 (2006): 187–196; Kelloway and Day, "Building Healthy Workplaces: What We Know So Far"; Holmes, "Work-Related Stress: A Brief Review."

33. R. G. Feachem and M. A. Koblinsky, "Interventions for the Control of Diarrhoeal Diseases Among Young Children: Promotion of Breast-Feeding," *Bulletin of the World Health Organization* 62, no. 2 (1984): 271–291; J. P. Habicht, J. DaVanzo, and W. P. Butz, "Does Breastfeeding Really Save Lives, or Are Apparent Benefits Due to Biases?" *American Journal of Epidemiology* 123, no. 2 (1986): 279–290; J. N. Hobcraft, J. W. McDonald, and S. O. Rutstein, "Demographic Determinants of Infant and Early Child Mortality: A Comparative Analysis," *Population Studies* 39, no. 3 (1985): 363–385; J. M. Jason, P. Nieburg, and J. S. Marks, "Mortality and Infectious Disease Associated with Infant-Feeding Practices in Developing Countries," *Pediatrics* 74, no. 4, part 2 (1984): 702–727.

34. Feachem and Koblinsky, "Interventions for the Control of Diarrhoeal Diseases Among Young Children: Promotion of Breast-Feeding"; A. S. Cunningham, D. B. Jelliffe, and E. F. Jelliffe, "Breast-Feeding and Health in the 1980s: A Global Epidemiologic Review," *Journal of Pediatrics* 118, no. 5 (1991): 659–666; K. G. Dewey, M. J. Heinig, and L. A. Nommsen-Rivers, "Differences in Morbidity Between Breast-Fed and Formula-Fed Infants," *Journal of Pediatrics* 126, no. 5, Part 1 (1995): 696–702; P. W. Howie, J. S. Forsyth, S. A. Ogston, A. Clark, and C. D. Florey, "Protective Effect of Breast Feeding Against Infection," *British Medical Journal* 300, no. 6716 (1990): 11–16; P. Lepage, C. Munyakazi, and P. Hennart, "Breastfeeding and Hospital Mortality in Children in Rwanda," *Lancet* 1, no. 8268 (1982): 403; M. C. Cerqueiro, P. Murtagh, A. Halac, M. Avila, and M. Weissenbacher, "Epidemiologic Risk Factors for Children with Acute Lower Respiratory Tract Infection in Buenos Aires, Argentina: A Matched Case-Control Study," *Reviews of Infectious Diseases* 12, no. 8 (1990): 1021–1028; C. J. Watkins, S. R. Leeder, and R. T. Corkhill, "The Relationship Between Breast and Bottle Feeding and Respiratory Illness in the First Year of Life," *Journal of Epidemiology and Community Health* 33, no. 3 (1979): 180–182; A. L. Wright, C. J. Holberg, F. D. Martinez, W. J. Morgan, and L. M. Taussig, "Breast Feeding and Lower Respiratory Tract Illness in the First Year of Life: Group Health Medical Associates," *British Medical Journal* 299, no. 6705 (1989): 946–949; G. Aniansson, B. Alm, B. Andersson, A. Hakansson, P. Larsson, O. Nylen, H. Peterson, P. Rigner, M. Svanborg, H. Sabharwal, et al., "A Prospective Cohort Study on Breast-Feeding and Otitis Media in Swedish Infants," *Pediatric Infectious Disease Journal* 13, no. 3 (1994): 183–188; B. Duncan, J. Ey, C. J. Holberg, A. L. Wright, F. D. Martinez, and L. M. Taussig, "Exclusive Breast-Feeding for at Least 4 Months Protects Against Otitis Media," *Pediatrics* 91, no. 5 (1993): 867–872; C. Arnold, S. Makintube, and G. R. Istre, "Day Care Attendance and Other Risk

Factors for Invasive Haemophilus Influenzae Type B Disease," *American Journal of Epidemiology* 138, no. 5 (1993): 333–340.

35. J. E. Fielding, W. G. Cumberland, and L. Pettitt, "Immunization Status of Children of Employees in a Large Corporation," *Journal of the American Medical Association* 271, no. 7 (1994): 525–530; J. Coreil, A. Augustin, N. A. Halsey, and E. Holt, "Social and Psychological Costs of Preventive Child Health Services in Haiti," *Social Science and Medicine* 38, no. 2 (1994): 231–238; K. Streatfield, and M. Singarimbun, "Social Factors Affecting Use of Immunization in Indonesia," *Social Science and Medicine* 27, no. 11 (1988): 1237–1245; L. K. McCormick, L. K. Bartholomew, M. J. Lewis, M. W. Brown, and I. C. Hanson, "Parental Perceptions of Barriers to Childhood Immunization: Results of Focus Groups Conducted in an Urban Population," *Health Education Research* 12, no. 3 (1997): 355–362; C. Lannon, V. Brack, J. Stuart, M. Caplow, A. McNeill, W. C. Bordley, and P. Margolis, "What Mothers Say About Why Poor Children Fall Behind on Immunizations. A Summary of Focus Groups in North Carolina," *Archives of Pediatrics & Adolescent Medicine* 149, no. 10 (1995): 1070–1075.

36. P. R. Mahaffy Jr., "The Effects of Hospitalization on Children Admitted for Tonsillectomy and Adenoidectomy," *Nursing Research* 14 (1965): 12–19; G. van der Schyff, "The Role of Parents During Their Child's Hospitalisation," *Australian Nurses' Journal* 8, no. 11 (1979): 57–58, 61; S. J. Palmer, "Care of Sick Children by Parents: A Meaningful Role," *Journal of Advanced Nursing* 18, no. 2 (1993): 185–191; J. Bowlby, M. D. S. Ainsworth, and M. Fry, *Child Care and the Growth of Love*, 2nd ed. (Baltimore: Penguin Books, 1965); J. Robertson, *Young Children in Hospital*, 2nd ed. (London: Tavistock Publications, 1970).

37. S. J. Heymann, S. Toomey, and F. Furstenberg, "Working Parents: What Factors Are Involved in Their Ability to Take Time Off from Work When Their Children Are Sick?" *Archives of Pediatrics & Adolescent Medicine* 153, no. 8 (1999): 870–874.

38. R. Bertera, "The Effects of Workplace Health Promotion on Absenteeism and Employment Costs in a Large Industrial Population," *American Journal of Public Health*, September 1990, 1101–1105.

39. S. Pronk, "Population Health Improvement—The Next Era of the Health Care Management Evolution," *Benefits Quarterly* 3 (2005): 12–15.

40. K. Pelletier, "A Review and Analysis of the Health and Cost-Effective Outcome Studies of Comprehensive Health Promotion and Disease Prevention Programs at the Worksite 1991–1993," *American Journal of Health Promotion*, September/October 1993, 50–62.

41. L. Makrides, "The Case for Workplace Health Promotion," Canadian Association of Cardiac Rehabilitation, *Newsbeat* 12, no. 1 (2004): 1–4.

Chapter 4

1. M. Y. Khan, "Disparities in Global Assets," *Business Line*, June 7, 2007, http://www.businessline.in/cgi-bin/print.pl?file=2007060700420800.htm&date=2007/06/07/&prd=bl&; J. B. Davies, S. Sandström, A. Shorrocks, and E. N. Wolff, "The World Distribution of Household Wealth," United Nations University World Institute for Development Economics Research, discussion paper 2008/03, February 2008, http://www.wider.unu.edu/publications/working-papers/discussion-papers/2008/en_GB/dp2008-03/_files/78918010772127840/default/dp2008-03.pdf.

2. E. Wolff, "Changes in Household Wealth in the 1980s and 1990s in the United States," in E. Wolff, ed., *International Perspectives on Household Wealth* (Cheltenham, U.K.: Edward Elgar Publishing Ltd., 2006), 107–150.

3. Davies et al., "The World Distribution of Household Wealth."

4. S. Estrin, V. Perotin, A. Robinson, and N. Wilson, "Profit-Sharing in OECD Countries: A Review and Some Evidence," *Business Strategy Review* 8, no. 4 (1997): 27–32.

5. A. M. Robinson and N. Wilson, "Employee Financial Participation and Productivity: An Empirical Reappraisal," *British Journal of Industrial Relations* 44, no. 1 (2006): 31–50.

6. Y. Ohkusa and F. Ohtake, "The Productivity Effects of Information Sharing, Profit Sharing, and ESOPs," *Journal of the Japanese and International Economies* 11, no. 3 (1997): 385–402.

7. D. L. Kruse, "Does Profit Sharing Affect Productivity?" working paper 4542, National Bureau of Economic Research, November 1993.

8. M. Magnan and S. St-Onge, "The Impact of Profit Sharing on the Performance of Financial Services Firms," *Journal of Management Studies* 42, no. 4 (2005): 761–791.

9. E. M. Shepard, "Profit-Sharing and Productivity—Further Evidence from the Chemicals Industry," *Industrial Relations* 33, no. 4 (1994): 452–466.

10. S. Kim, "Does Profit Sharing Increase Firms' Profits?" *Journal of Labor Research* 19, no. 2 (1998): 351–370.

11. O. Azfar and S. Danninger, "Profit Sharing, Employment Stability, and Wage Growth," *Industrial & Labor Relations Review* 54, no. 3 (2001): 619–630.

12. N. Cahill, "Profit Sharing, Employee Share Ownership and Gainsharing: What Can they Achieve?" National Economic and Social Council, Research Series no. 4, May 2000.

13. J. Luffman, "Taking Stock of Equity Compensation," Statistics Canada *Perspectives*, March 2003, http://www.statcan.ca/english/studies/75-001/archive/2003/2003-03-03.pdf.

14. Senior managers are referred to by their real names since they are identifiable through their positions at each company. Middle managers and low-level employees were ensured confidentiality and are therefore referred to by pseudonyms.

15. Interview conducted with Mike Jenkins IV, CEO, Jenkins Brick, March 2005.

16. Ibid.

17. Ibid.

18. Interview conducted with Wyatt Shorter, member of the board of directors, Jenkins Brick, March 2005.

19. Interview conducted with Tommy Andreades, executive vice president and CFO, Jenkins Brick, March 2005.

20. Interview, Mike Jenkins IV, March 2005.

21. Ibid.

22. Interview conducted with Anita Barrera, controller, Jenkins Brick, March 2005.

23. The experience of Jenkins Brick has been shared by other companies. Research has demonstrated that incentives for manufacturing sector workers lead to marked increases in performance. J. C. Sesil, "Sharing Decision-Making and Group Incentives: The Impact on Performance," *Economic and Industrial Democracy* 27, no. 4 (2006).

24. Interview, Wyatt Shorter, March 2005.

25. Interview, Mike Jenkins IV, March 2005.

26. D. Cusick "How One Energy-Hungry Company Learned to Love Landfill Gas," *Greenwire*, October 2007.

27. Interview, Tommy Andreades, March 2005.

28. Interview conducted with Trish Karter, CEO, Dancing Deer, March 2005.

29. Ibid.

30. Ibid.

31. U.S. Department of Labor, Bureau of Labor Statistics, *Employee Benefits Survey*, Statistics Data, generated tables. 2007.

32. Interview, Trish Karter, July 2007.

33. Interview conducted with Keith Rousseau, controller, Dancing Deer, July 2007.

34. Dancing Deer Employee Handbook, Employee Stock Option Plan, October 31, 2005.

35. Interview, Keith Rousseau, February 2005.

36. Interview, Trish Karter, March 2005.

37. Interview, Keith Rousseau, February 2005.

38. Interview, Keith Rousseau, July 2007.

39. Interview conducted with packer, Dancing Deer, July 2007.

40. Interview, Keith Rousseau, February 2005.

41. Interview conducted with Lissa McBurney, production manager, Dancing Deer, February 2005.

42. Interview, Keith Rousseau, July 2007.

43. Interview, Trish Karter, March 2005.

44. Interview, Lissa McBurney, February 2005.

45. Dancing Deer has received the Smaller Business Association of New England's New Englander Award for Innovation (2000), Awards for Excellence from the Greater Boston Chamber of Commerce (2001 and 2004), and a Small Business Leadership Award for Innovation from FleetBoston Financial Corporation (2002). The company was included in *Inc.* magazine and the Initiative for a Competitive Inner City's Inner City 100 list for four years (2001, 2002, 2003, 2008).

46. "Female Ownership Matters," *BusinessWeek*, October 15, 2007.

Chapter 5

1. A. P. Bartel, "Productivity Gains from the Implementation of Employee Training Programs," working paper 3893, National Bureau of Economic Research 1991; L. M. Lynch and S. E. Black, "Beyond the Incidence of Training: Evidence from a National Employers Survey," working paper 5231, National Bureau of Economic Research, 1995.

2. R. Euwals and R. Winkelman, "Why Do Firms Train? Empirical Evidence on the Firms' Labour Market Outcomes of Graduated Apprentices," discussion paper 319, Institute for the Study of Labor (IZA), Bonn, 2001.

3. V. Peters, "Working and Training: First Results of the 2003 Adult Education and Training Survey," Statistics Canada, 2004

4. "Encouraging More Low-Skilled People to Take Part in Training," *Industrial and Commercial Training* 36, no. 4 (2004): 182–183.

5. U.S. Department of Labor, Bureau of Labor Statistics, *Survey of Employer-Provided Training*, Table 3: Percent of Employees Who Received Training by Selected Demographic Characteristics, 1996, http://www.bls.gov/news.release/sept.t03.htm.

6. Senior managers are referred to by their real names since they are identifiable through their positions at each company. Middle managers and low-level employees were ensured confidentiality and are therefore referred to by pseudonyms.

7. Interview conducted with factory worker, Isola, August 2007.

8. Interview conducted with Erik Withbro, managing director, Isola, August 2007.

9. Interview conducted with machine operator, Isola, May and June 2006.

10. Interview conducted with sales employee, Isola, May and June 2006.

11. Interview conducted with Lissa McBurney, production manager, Dancing Deer, February 2005.

12. A. Sum, I. Kirsch, and K. Yamamoto, *A Human Capital Concern: The Literacy Proficiency of U.S. Immigrants* (Princeton, NJ: Educational Testing Service, 2004).

13. Interview conducted with Trish Karter, CEO, Dancing Deer, March 2005.

14. Ibid.

15. Novo Nordisk Annual Report 2008 http://annualreport2008.novonordisk.com/images/downloads/Novo_Nordisk_UK_AR2008.pdf.

16. Interview conducted with Christian Larsen, senior manager of economy and logistics, Novo Nordisk Tianjin, August 2006.

17. Interview conducted with line worker, Novo Nordisk Tianjin, July 2006.

18. Interview conducted with machine operator, Novo Nordisk Tianjin, July 2006.

19. Interview conducted with line worker, Novo Nordisk Tianjin, July 2006.

20. Interview conducted with machine operator, Novo Nordisk Tianjin, July 2006.

21. Interview conducted with line worker, Novo Nordisk Tianjin, July 2006.

22. A. Elwan, "Poverty and Disability: A Survey of the Literature," social protection discussion paper 9932, World Bank, December 1999.

23. S. Stoddard, L. Jans, J. Ripple, and L. Kraus, *Chartbook on Work and Disability in the United States, 1998*, An InfoUse Report (Washington, DC: U.S. National Institute on Disability and Rehabilitation Research, 1998), http://www.infouse.com/disabilitydata/workdisability/intro.php.

24. This is how Liliana Mayo, founder and director of CASP, described the fundamental principle on which they developed their program. Interview conducted with Liliana Mayo, November 2005.

25. Interview conducted with Maria Teresa Merino, director of selection and training, Banco de Crédito del Peru, November 2005.

26. Interview conducted with Enrique Burgos, director of supported employment, Ann Sullivan Center, October 2005.

27. Examples of the more than twenty media articles include "80 chicos especiales de Peru son reinsertados al campo laboral," *El Comercio Ecuador*, September 26, 2006; W. A. Agustin "Viva la Diferencia," *Revista Somos, El Comercio Peru* January 19, 2004; E. Vega, "Empleo con Apoyo," *Generaccion* 43 (June 2006).

28. Interview conducted with Raimundo Morales, CEO, Banco de Crédito del Peru, November 2005.

29. Ibid.

30. Interview conducted with human resources manager, Banco de Crédito del Peru, November 2005.

Chapter 6

1. Search conducted on the Web of Science, a comprehensive computerized database providing access to information from thousands of journals in the sciences, social sciences, arts, and humanities. Searching for career, advancement, or promotion resulted in over 99,000 articles; searching for career, advancement, or promotion for low-skilled or lower-income workers resulted in 610 articles.

2. S. Hillmer, B. Hillmer, and G. McRoberts, "The Real Costs of Turnover: Lessons from a Call Center," *Human Resource Planning* 27, no. 3 (2004): 34–41.

3. Senior managers are referred to by their real names since they are identifiable through their positions at each company. Middle managers and low-level employees were ensured confidentiality and are therefore referred to by pseudonyms.

4. Interview conducted with acting team leader, Xerox Europe, January 2006.

5. Xerox Corp., Annual Report, 2006.

6. Interview conducted with technical agent, Xerox Europe, July 2006.

7. Interview conducted with Lorlene Duggan, Xerox Office Services manager, Xerox Europe, January 2006.

8. Interview conducted with team leader, Xerox Europe, January 2006.

9. Interview, technical agent, January 2006.

10. Interview, team leader, January 2006.

11. Interview, Lorlene Duggan, January 2006.

12. Interview conducted with Bob Horastead, general manager, Xerox Europe Service Centre, July 2006.

13. Interview conducted with Xerox Office Services employee, Xerox Europe Service Centre, July 2006.

14. Interview, Bob Horastead, July 2006.

15. Ibid.

16. Interview, Xerox Office Services employee, July 2006.

17. Interview, Bob Horastead, January 2006.

18. Interview conducted with Richard Dunphy, controller, Xerox Europe, January 2006.

19. Interview conducted with food court manager, Costco, March 2006.

20. Interview conducted with assistant manager, Costco, March 2006.

21. Interview conducted with warehouse manager, Costco, July 2007.

22. Interview conducted with Dave Haruff, vice president of regional operations, Costco, March 2006.

23. Interview conducted with Mark Stalwich, director of personnel, Costco, March 2006.

24. Interview conducted with Vito Romano, director of employee development, Costco, March 2006.

25. Interview, Mark Stalwich, March 2006.

26. Interview conducted with Jim Sinegal, CEO, Costco, March 2006.

27. Interview, Mark Stalwich, March 2006.

28. Interview, Jim Sinegal, March 2006.

29. Interview conducted with John McKay, vice president for regional operations northwest, Costco, March 2006.

30. S. Greenhouse and M. Barbaro, "Costco Bias Suit Is Given Class-Action Status," *New York Times*, January 12, 2007; "Costco Class Website," http://genderclassactionagainstcostco.com/costco94.pl.

31. Interview conducted with a warehouse marketing employee, Costco, March 2006.

32. Interview conducted with cashier, Costco, March 2006.

33. Interview conducted with membership department employee, Costco, March 2006.

34. Interview, Dave Haruff, March 2006.

35. Interview conducted with marketing employee, Costco, March 2006.

36. S. Holmes and W. Zellner "The Costco Way," *BusinessWeek*, April 12, 2004.

37. Interview conducted with utility player, Costco, March 2006.

38. Interview conducted with greeter, Costco, March 2006.

39. Interview conducted with marketing employee, Costco, March 2006.

40. M. Boyle, "Why Costco Is So Addictive," *Fortune*, October 2006.

41. Interview conducted with Richard Galanti, CFO, Costco, July 2007.

42. Ibid.

43. Interview, Jim Sinegal, July 2007.

44. Interview, Jim Sinegal, March 2006.

45. Costco Code of Ethics. http://media.corporate-ir.net/media_files/NSD/cost/reports/our_mission.pdf.

46. Interview, Dave Haruff, March 2006.

47. Ibid.

48. Interview, John McKay, March 2006.

49. Interview, Jim Sinegal, March 2006.

50. Interview, Richard Galanti, March 2006.

Chapter 7

1. HR.com, The Human Resources Portal, *Engaged Employees Help Boost the Bottom Line*, June 29, 2006.

2. Towers Perrin, *Employee Engagement Underpins Business Transformation*, Towers Perrin International Survey Research, September 2009, 2, http://www.towersperrin.com/tp/getwebcachedoc?country=global&webc=GBR/2008/200807/TP_ISR_July08.pdf.

3. Towers Perrin, *Employee Engagement Improves the Bottom Line*, Towers Perrin International Survey Research, September 2009, 3, http://www.towersperrin.com/tp/

getwebcachedoc?country=global&webc=HRS/GBR/2008/200805/ENGAGEMENT_IM
PROVES_BOTTOM_LINE.pdf.

4. G. M. Endres, and L. Mancheno-Smoak, "The Human Resource Craze: Human Performance Improvement and Employee Engagement," *Organization Development Journal* 26, no. 1 (2008): 69–78. This article draws on data from a Gallup survey known as the Gallup Q12, the Gallup Workplace Audit, the Gallup Engagement Index, and the Employee Engagement Index, which had been administered in 114 countries by 2006.

5. U.S. Department of Labor, *High Performance Work Practices and Firm Performance* (Washington, DC: U.S. Department of Labor, 1993).

6. J. P. MacDuffie, "Human Resource Bundles and Manufacturing Performance: Organizational Logic and Flexible Production Systems in the World Auto Industry," *Industrial and Labour Relations Review* 48, no. 2 (1995): 197–221.

7. C. Ichniowski, T. A. Kochan, D. Levine, C. Olson, and G. Strauss, "What Works at Work: Overview and Assessment," *Industrial Relations* 35, no. 3 (1996): 299–333.

8. U.S. Department of Labor, *High Performance Work Practices and Firm Performance*.

9. CIPD, *Annual Survey Report 2006: How Engaged Are British Employees?* (London: Chartered Institute of Personnel and Development, 2006), 11, http://www.cipd.co.uk/NR/rdonlyres/E6871F47-558A-466E-9A74-4DFB1E71304C/0/howengbritempssr.pdf.

10. Towers Perrin, *Key Findings: An Interview with Julie Gebauer on Towers Perrin's Just Released Global Workforce Study, Part 2*, Towers Perrin International Survey Research, 2007, http://www.towersperrin.com/tp/showhtml.jsp?url=global/publications/gws/key-findings_2.htm&country=global.

11. BlessingWhite, *The State of Employee Engagement 2008: Highlights for U.K. and Ireland*, 2008, 3.

12. BlessingWhite, *The State of Employee Engagement 2008: Asia-Pacific Overview*, 2008, 1.

13. BlessingWhite, *The State of Employee Engagement 2008: North American Overview*, 2008, 11.

14. Chiumento UK, *Get Engaged*, 2004, 4, http://www.chiumento.co.uk/attachments/Get%20engaged_2004%20report.pdf.

15. Ibid., 5.

16. C. Romano, "Innovation for Motivation," *Management Review* 85, no. 3 (March 1996): 6.

17. L. Barbaro, "An Open Book," *Wall Street Journal*, February 23, 2009.

18. J. Carrick Dalton, "Between the Lines," *CFO*, March 1999, 58–64.

19. J. Nocera, "Want to Rally the Troops? Try Candor," *New York Times*, February 11, 2006.

20. Great Little Box Company Employee Handbook, p.10.

21. Interview conducted with Robert Meggy, CEO, Great Little Box Company, March 2009.

22. Ibid.

23. Interview conducted with Margaret Meggy, CFO, Great Little Box Company, March 2009.

24. Interview conducted with plant worker, Great Little Box Company, March 2009.

25. Interview conducted with machine operator, Great Little Box Company, March 2009.

26. Interview, Robert Meggy, March 2009.

27. Interview conducted with plant worker, Great Little Box Company, March 2009.

28. Interview, plant worker, June 2007.

29. Interview, Robert Meggy, March 2009.

30. Interview conducted with Nick Reiach, VP of manufacturing, Great Little Box Company, March 2009.

31. Interview, Margaret Meggy, March 2009.

32. Interview, Robert Meggy, March 2009.

33. Interview, plant worker, March 2009.

34. Ibid.

35. Interview, Robert Meggy, March 2009.

36. Interview conducted with Miguel Hernandez-Mondaca, quality and safety manager, Great Little Box Company, March 2009.

37. Interview, plant worker, March 2009.

38. Interview, Nick Reiach, March 2009.

39. Interview, Robert Meggy, March 2009.

40. Interview, machine operator, March 2009.

41. Interview, Nick Reiach, March 2009.

42. Interview, Margaret Meggy, March 2009.

43. Ibid.

44. Interviews conducted with Erik Withbro, managing director, Isola, May–June , 2006.

45. Ibid.

46. Isola, "Work Conditions Analysis," October/November 2004.

47. Interview conducted with team leader, Isola, August 2007.

48. Interview conducted with Trish Karter, CEO, Dancing Deer, February 2005.

49. Interview conducted with Lissa McBurney, production manager, Dancing Deer, February 2005.

50. Interview conducted with Keith Rousseau, controller, Dancing Deer, February 2005.

51. Ibid.

52. Interview, Trish Karter, February 2005.

53. Ibid.

Chapter 8

1. The fact that Nand Kumar was both ACC's head of corporate social responsibility and head of corporate communications reflected ACC's vision that their commitment to CSR is the public face of the company.

2. Senior managers are referred to by their real names since they are identifiable through their positions at each company. Middle managers and low-level employees were ensured confidentiality and are therefore referred to by pseudonyms.

3. Interview conducted with Nand Kumar, head of corporate social responsibility and head of corporate communications, ACC India, July 2007.

4. Ibid.

5. Ibid.

6. A. Chaturvedi and A. Chaturvedi, *ACC: A Corporate Saga* (Mumbai: Associated Cement Companies Limited, 1997).

7. Interview conducted with Paramjit Pabby, head of human resources, ACC India, July 2007.

8. It is a common practice in some parts of India for people to refer to themselves by first initials and not by a full first name.

9. Interview conducted with K. Anjeneyan, company secretary, ACC India, July 2007.

10. Ibid.

11. Interview conducted with painter, ACC India, February 2007.

12. Interview conducted with machine operator, ACC India, February 2007.

13. "10 plus 2" refers to an educational system used in India, in which there is a standardized set of board exams after ten years of schooling that decides the students' streams or specializations for the final two years of school.

14. Interview, Paramjit Pabby, July 2007.

15. Interview conducted with N. Shembavnekar, senior manager of human resources, ACC India, July 2007.

16. Interview, Paramjit Pabby, July 2007.

17. Interview conducted with Behram Sherdiwala, head of organization management, ACC India, February 2007.

18. Interview, Nand Kumar, July 2007.

19. Interview conducted with Sumit Bannerjee, managing director, ACC India, July 2007.

20. ACC changed its fiscal year in 2005 to follow the calendar instead of the April–March fiscal year. This means the 2005 results reflect a shorter nine-month year.

21. B. Sabharwal, "India's Cement Makers Shine—Building Spree, Rise in Demand and Share Price Likely Will Go On," *Wall Street Journal*, May 3, 2006.

22. Interview, Sumit Bannerjee, July 2007.

23. W. R. Stanley, "Socioeconomic Impact of Oil in Nigeria," *GeoJournal* 2, no. 1 (1990): 67–79; J. E. Okeagu et al., "The Environmental and Social Impact of Petroleum and Natural Gas Exploitation in Nigeria,." *Journal of Third World Studies*, Spring 2006; V. T. Jike, "Environmental Degradation, Social Disequilibrium, and the Dilemma of Sustainable Development in the Niger-Delta of Nigeria," *Journal of Black Studies* 34, no. 5 (2004): 686–701.

24. S. Swartz, "Nigeria Oil Violence Continues as Militants Threaten Offshore," *Dow Jones International News*, September 17, 2008; W. Connors, "New Attacks on Pipelines in Delta of Nigeria," *New York Times*, September 18, 2008.

25. E. Worrell, L. Price, N. Martin, C. Hendriks, and L. Ozawa Meida. "Carbon Dioxide Emissions from the Global Cement Industry," *Annual Review of Energy and the Environment* 26 (November 2001): 303–329, http://arjournals. annualreviews.org/doi/abs/10.1146/annurev.energy.26.1.303; D. Huntzinger and T. D. Eatmon, "A Life-Cycle Assessment of Portland Cement Manufacturing: Comparing the Traditional Process with Alternative Technologies," *Journal of Cleaner Production* 17, no. 7 (May 2009): 668–675.

26. Interview, Sumit Bannerjee, July 2007.

27. "Gauging the Wal-Mart Effect," *Wall Street Journal*, December 3, 2005.

28. Interview conducted with Jim Sinegal, CEO, Costco, March 2006.

29. U.S. Department of Labor, Bureau of Labor Statistics, *History of Federal Minimum Wage Rates Under the Fair Labor Standards Act, 1938–2007*, http://www.dol.gov/esa/minwage/chart.pdf; U.S. Department of Labor, Bureau of Labor Statistics, *Occupational Outlook Handbook*, 2008–09 Edition, Occupational Employment and Wages, May 2007, 41-2011 Cashiers, http://www.bls.gov/oes/current/oes412011.htm and 53-3033 Truck Drivers, Light or Delivery Services, http://www.bls.gov/oes/current/oes533033.htm.

30. U.S. Department of Labor, Bureau of Labor Statistics, *Occupational Outlook Handbook*, 2008–09 Edition, 41-2011 Cashiers.

31. Interview conducted with Sheri Flies, senior manager, legal department, Costco, March 2006.

32. N. Wu, "Reception to Wal-Mart, Target Like Night and Day," March 31, 2007, http://starbulletin.com/2007/03/31/business/story01.html; P. Krugman, "Big Box Balderdash," *New York Times* op-ed column, December 12, 2005, A. Linn, "Target Thrives in Wal-Mart's Shadows," *MSNBC*, June 20, 2007.

33. Datamonitor International, *Wal-Mart Company Profile 2007*, 27.

34. R. Abelson, "States Are Battling Against Wal-Mart Over Health Care," *New York Times*, November 1, 2004.

35. M. Barbaro, "Maryland Sets a Health Cost for Wal-Mart," *New York Times*, January 16, 2006.

Chapter 9

1. Interview conducted with Lars Nielsen, durable device senior manager, Novo Nordisk Tianjin, August 2006.

2. Ibid.

3. Interview conducted with Christian Larsen, senior manager economy and logistics, Novo Nordisk Tianjin, August 2006.

4. Interview, Lars Nielsen, August 2006.

5. Interview conducted with factory operator, Novo Nordisk Tianjin, July 2006.

6. Interview, Christian Larsen, August 2006.

7. Interview, Lars Nielsen, August 2006.

8. Ibid.

9. Interview conducted with factory operator, Novo Nordisk Tianjin, July 2006.

10. Interview conducted with factory operators, Novo Nordisk Tianjin, August 2006.

11. Data provided by Novo Nordisk from study conducted in China by Hewitt Associates in 2006.

12. Interview, Christian Larsen, August 2006.

13. Interview conducted with factory operators, Novo Nordisk Tianjin, July 2006.

14. Interview, Lars Nielsen, July 2006.

15. Interview, Christian Larsen, July 2006.

16. Interview, Christian Larsen, August 2006.

17. Interview, Christian Larsen, July 2006.

18. Interview conducted with facility manager, Novo Nordisk Tianjin, July 2006.

19. Interview conducted with factory operator, Novo Nordisk Tianjin, July 2006.

20. Interview conducted with middle manager, Novo Nordisk Tianjin, July 2006.

21. Interview, Christian Larsen, August 2006.

22. Interview conducted with facility manager, Novo Nordisk Tianjin, July 2006.

23. Interview, Christian Larsen, August 2006.

24. Interview conducted with Preben Haaning, plant director, Novo Nordisk Tianjin, July 2007.

25. Interview, Christian Larsen, August 2006.

26. L. Kafanov, "Toy Makers to Face House Fury in Next Round of Hearings," *Environment & Energy Daily*, September 17, 2007.

27. "Mattel Posts 1Q Net Loss Due to China Costs," *China Economic Review*, Daily Briefings, April 22, 2008.

28. A. Veiga, "Toy Recalls Could Pose Toughest Challenge Yet for Mattel CEO," Associated Press Newswires, September 7, 2007.

29. "Mattel Posts 1Q Net Loss Due to China Costs"; M. Mehta, "China's Loss, Malaysia's Gain," *Malaysian Business*, October 16, 2007.

30. H. de Quetteville, "Steiff Bears Abandon China," *Daily Telegraph*, July 4, 2008.

31. "Teddy Bear Firm Leaving China," *Calgary Herald*, July 4, 2008; C. Mortished, "Chinese Picnic Is Over as Steiff Bears Toddle Off Home," *Times* (London), July 4, 2008.

32. Quetteville, "Steiff Bears Abandon China."

33. Gap Inc., 2005–2006 Corporate Social Responsibility Report.

34. H. C. Katz, T. A. Kochan, and K. R. Gobeille. "Industrial Relations Performance, Economic Performance, and QWL Programs: An Interplant Analysis," *Industrial and Labour Relations Review* 37, no. 1 (1983): 3–17; H. C. Katz, T. A. Kochan, and M. R. Weber, "Assessing the Effects of Industrial Relations Systems and Efforts to Improve the Quality of Work Life on Organizational Effectiveness," *Academy of Management Journal* 28, no. 3 (1985): 509–526.

35. M. A. Huselid, "The Impact of Human Resource Management Practices on Turnover, Productivity, and Corporate Financial Performance," *Academy of Management Journal* 38, no. 3 (1995): 635–672.

36. G. S. MacMillan and M. P. Joshi , "Sustainable Competitive Advantage and Firm Performance: The Role of Intangible Resources," *Corporate Reputation Review* 1, no. 1 (Summer/Fall 1997).

37. Quoted in I. Zeldenrust and N. Ascoly, *Codes of Conduct for Transnational Corporations: An Overview* (Tilberg, Netherlands: International Restructuring Education Network Europe, 1998).

38. Program on International Policy Attitudes. World Public Opinion.Org, http://www.americans-world.org/digest/global_issues/intertrade/laborstandards.cfm.

39. Program on International Policy Attitudes. World Public Opinion.Org, http://www.americans-world.org/digest/global_issues/intertrade/data_laborstand.htm#1a.

40. World Public Opinion.Org, http://americans-world.org/digest/global_issues/globalization/laborlaw.cfm.

41. S. Roberts, J. Keeble, and D. Brown, *The Business Case for Corporate Citizenship*, Arthur D. Little report, London, 2002.

42. D. B. Turban and D. M. Cable, "Firm Reputation and Applicant Pool Characteristics," *Journal of Organizational Behavior* 24 (2003): 733–751.

43. GlobeScan, 2003 Global Campus Monitor.

44. Quoted in Zeldenrust and Ascoly, *Codes of Conduct for Transnational Corporations*.

45. U.S. Department of Labor, *The Apparel Industry and Codes of Conduct: A Solution to the International Child Labor Problem?* 1996, http://actrav.itcilo.org/actrav-english/telearn/global/ilo/code/apparel3.htm.

46. Insight Investment Management, *Buying Your Way into Trouble? The Challenge of Responsible Supply Chain Management*, 2004.

47. Ibid., p.8; K. Astill and M. Griffith, *Clean Up Your Computer: Working Conditions in the Electronics Sector*, CAFOD report, 2004; Oxfam International, *Trading Away Our Rights—Women Working in Global Supply Chains*, campaign report, February 2004.

48. Interview conducted with Sheri Flies, senior manager, legal department, Costco, March 2006.

49. Interview conducted with Jim Sinegal, CEO, Costco, July 2007.

50. R. B. Freeman, "The Battle Over Labor Standards in the Global Economy," *Integration and Trade Journal* 25 (July–December 2006): 11-51.

51. A. Shea, M. Nakayama, and S. J. Heymann, "Improving Labour Standards in Clothing Factories: Lessons from Stakeholder Views and Monitoring Results in Cambodia," *Journal of Global Social Policy*, forthcoming.

52. Ibid.

53. Marymount University Center for Ethical Concerns, "The Consumer and Sweatshops," November 1999, http://www.marymount.edu/news/garmentstudy/index.html.

54. Program on International Policy Attitudes. WorldPublicOpinion.Org, http://americans-world.org/digest/global_issues/intertrade/laborstandards.cfm.

55. P. Pelsmacker, L. Driesen, and G. Rayp, "Are fair trade labels good business? Ethics and coffee buying intentions," working paper. Ghent University, January 2003.

56. M. Hiscox and N. Smyth, "Is There Consumer Demand for Improved Labour Standards? Evidence from Field Experiments in Social Labeling," working paper, Department of Government, Harvard University, 2006.

57. M. Hiscox, "Consumer Demand for Labor Standards: Experiments with Ethical Labeling of Imported Products," Business and Government Seminar Series, Mossavar-Rahmani Center for Business and Government, February 28, 2008; S. Schorow, "Consumers Want to Do the Right Thing," Harvard University *Gazette Online*, March 6, 2008, http://www.news.harvard.edu/gazette/2008/03.06/09-labor.html.

58. M. Prasad, H. Kimeldorf, R. Meyer, and I. Robinson, "Consumers of the World Unite: A Market-Based Response to Sweatshops," *Labor Studies Journal* 29, no. 3 (2004): 57–80.

59. H. Kimeldorf, R. Meyer, M. Prasad, and I. Robinson, "Consumers with a Conscience: Will They Pay More?" *Contexts* 5, no. 1 (February 2006): 24–29.

Chapter 10

1. Bureau of Economic Analysis; National Economic Accounts; Gross Domestic Product: Percentage Change from Previous Period Table; October 29, 2009.

2. European Commission, Eurostat Statistical Books, Eurostatistics: Data for short-term economic analysis. Issue number 10/2009.

3. The Bank of Korea Research Department. Quarterly Bulletin. September 2009. Hong Kong Economy, The Government of the Government of Hong Kong Special Administrative Region. Hong Kong Economic Reports. Half-Yearly Economic Report 2009. August 2009. http://www.hkeconomy.gov.hk/en/pdf/er_09q2_ch1.pdf.

4. U.S. Courts Bankruptcy Statistics. 2007-2008 Calendar Year Comparisons Table.

5. B. Rochelle, "Bankruptcy Filings by Businesses Increase 78% in First Quarter," *Bankruptcy Statistics*, April 9, 2009, http://www.bankruptcy-statistics.com/index.php?option=com_content&view=article&id=256:bankruptcy-filings-by-businesses-increase-78-in-first-quarter-&catid=81:national&Itemid=198.

6. International Labour Organization, *Global Wage Report 2008/09*, http://www.ilo.org/wcmsp5/groups/public/---dgreports/---dcomm/documents/publication/wcms_100786.pdf.

7. E. Wolff, "Changes in Household Wealth in the 1980s and 1990s in the United States," in Edward Wolff, ed., *International Perspectives on Household Wealth* (Cheltenham, U.K.: Edward Elgar Publishing Ltd., 2006), 107–150.

8. J. B. Davies, S. Sandström, A. Shorrocks, and E. N. Wolff, "The World Distribution of Household Wealth," United Nations University World Institute for Development Economics Research, discussion paper 2008/03, February 2008, http://www.wider.unu.edu/publications/working-papers/discussion-papers/2008/en_GB/dp2008-03/_files/78918010772127840/default/dp2008-03.pdf.

9. "Confidence in Institutions," Gallup poll, June 2009. http://www.gallup.com/poll/1597/Confidence-Institutions.aspx.

10. "Big Business," Gallup poll, March 2009. http://www.gallup.com/poll/5248/Big-Business.aspx.

11. Interview conducted with Tommy Andreades, CFO, Jenkins Brick, March 2005.

12. S. Hillmer, B. Hillmer, and G. McRoberts," The Real Costs of Turnover: Lessons from a Call Center," *Human Resource Planning* 27, no. 3 (2004): 34–41.

13. Interview conducted with Vito Romano, director of employee development, Costco, March 2006.

14. R. Bertera, "The Effects of Workplace Health Promotion on Absenteeism and Employment Costs in a Large Industrial Population," *American Journal of Public Health*, September 1990, 1101–1105.

15. S. Pronk, "Population Health Improvement—The Next Era of the Health Care Management Evolution," *Benefits Quarterly* 3 (2005): 12–15.

16. Employee Surveys, Autoliv Australia, 2004.

17. Data provided by Novo Nordisk from study conducted in China by Hewitt Associates in 2006.

18. Interview conducted with Bob Franklin, general manager, Autoliv Australia, November 2006.

19. Ibid.

20. Interview conducted with Jim Sinegal, CEO, Costco, July 2007.

21. Interview conducted with Paramjit Pabby, head of human resources, ACC India, February 2007.

22. Interview conducted with Clifford Barnett, general manager, SA Metal, September 2005.

23. Interview conducted with Nand Kumar, head of corporate communications and CSR, ACC India, February 2007.

24. World Economic Forum, *Global Competitiveness Report 2008–2009*, http://www.weforum.org/en/initiatives/gcp/Global%20Competitiveness%20Report/index.htm.

Index

About the Authors

Jody Heymann is the Founding Director of the Institute for Health and Social Policy, the WORLD Global Data Centre, and the Project on Global Working Families. An internationally renowned researcher on health and social policy, Dr. Heymann holds a Canada Research Chair in Global Health and Social Policy. She has authored and edited over 150 publications, including *Raising the Global Floor* (Stanford University Press, 2010), *Trade and Health* (McGill Queens University Press, 2007), *Forgotten Families* (Oxford University Press, 2006), *Healthier Societies* (Oxford University Press, 2006), *Unfinished Work* (New Press, 2005), *Global Inequalities at Work* (Oxford University Press, 2003), and *The Widening Gap* (Basic Books, 2000).

Heymann established and leads the first global initiative to examine policy affecting the public and private sector in all 192 UN nations. Deeply committed to translating research into action that will improve population health and economic outcomes, Heymann has worked with leaders in the public and private sectors in North America, Europe, Africa, and Latin America. Heymann's research has been presented to heads of state and senior policymakers around the world and has been widely featured on internationally and nationally syndicated media.

Magda Barrera grew up in Buenos Aires, Argentina. She received her BA in Economics from Williams College and her MA in International Affairs from Carleton University's Norman Paterson School of International Affairs. For the past four years she has been working at McGill University's

Institute for Health and Social Policy, conducting research and writing on working conditions and how to effectively improve social conditions in an economically sustainable way. She has co-led a fellowship program designed to examine policies and programs in countries around the world on topics such as working conditions and sustainable development.